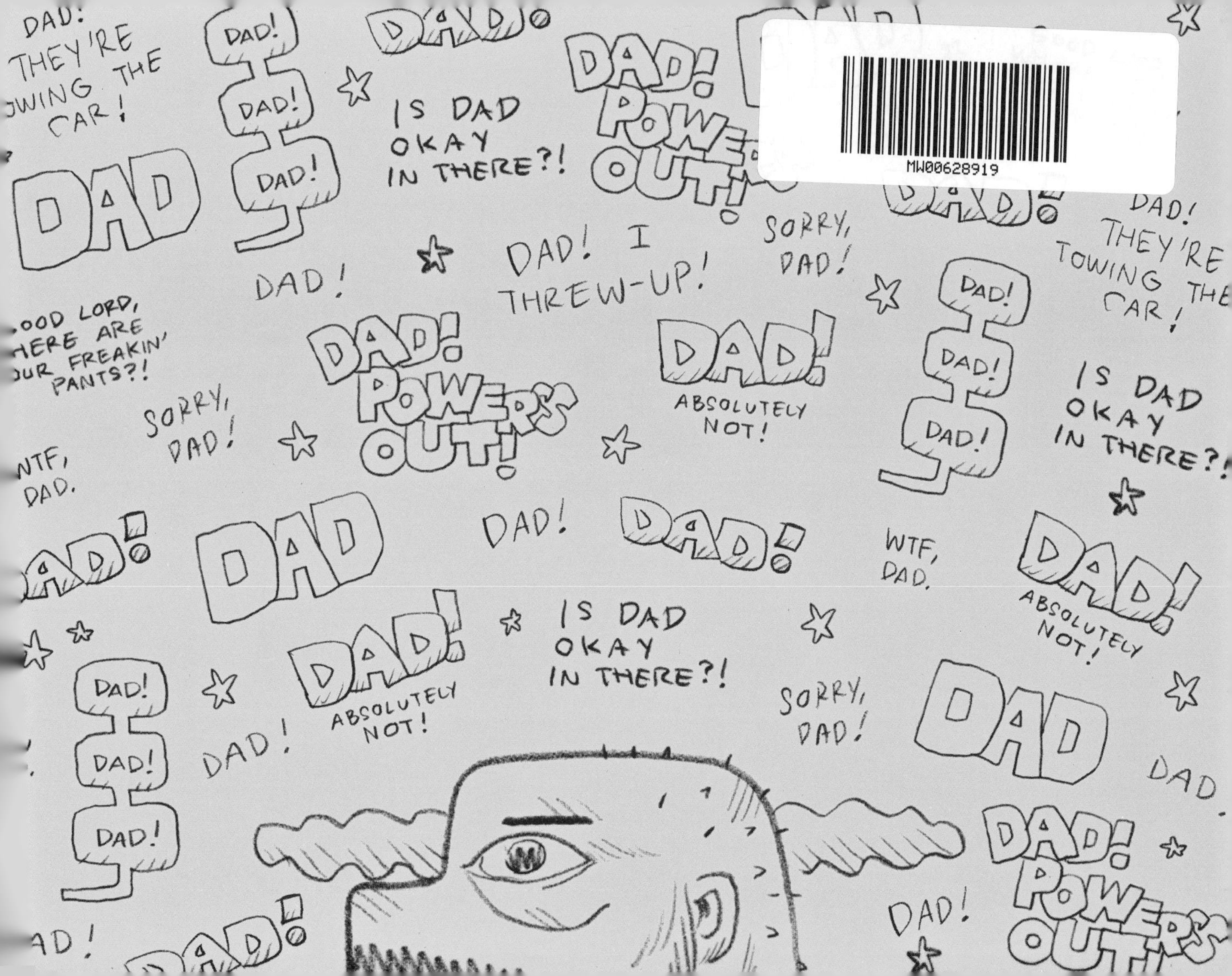
DAD: THEY'RE TOWING THE CAR!
DAD! DAD! DAD!
DAD!
DAD
IS DAD OKAY IN THERE?!
DAD! POWER'S OUT!
DAD!
DAD! I THREW-UP!
SORRY, DAD!
DAD! THEY'RE TOWING THE CAR!
DAD!
GOOD LORD, WHERE ARE YOUR FREAKIN' PANTS?!
DAD! POWER'S OUT!
DAD! ABSOLUTELY NOT!
DAD! DAD! DAD!
IS DAD OKAY IN THERE?!
SORRY, DAD!
WTF, DAD.
DAD!
DAD
DAD!
DAD!
WTF, DAD.
DAD! ABSOLUTELY NOT!
IS DAD OKAY IN THERE?!
DAD! ABSOLUTELY NOT!
DAD! DAD! DAD!
DAD!
SORRY, DAD!
DAD
DAD
DAD! POWER'S OUT!
DAD!
DAD!

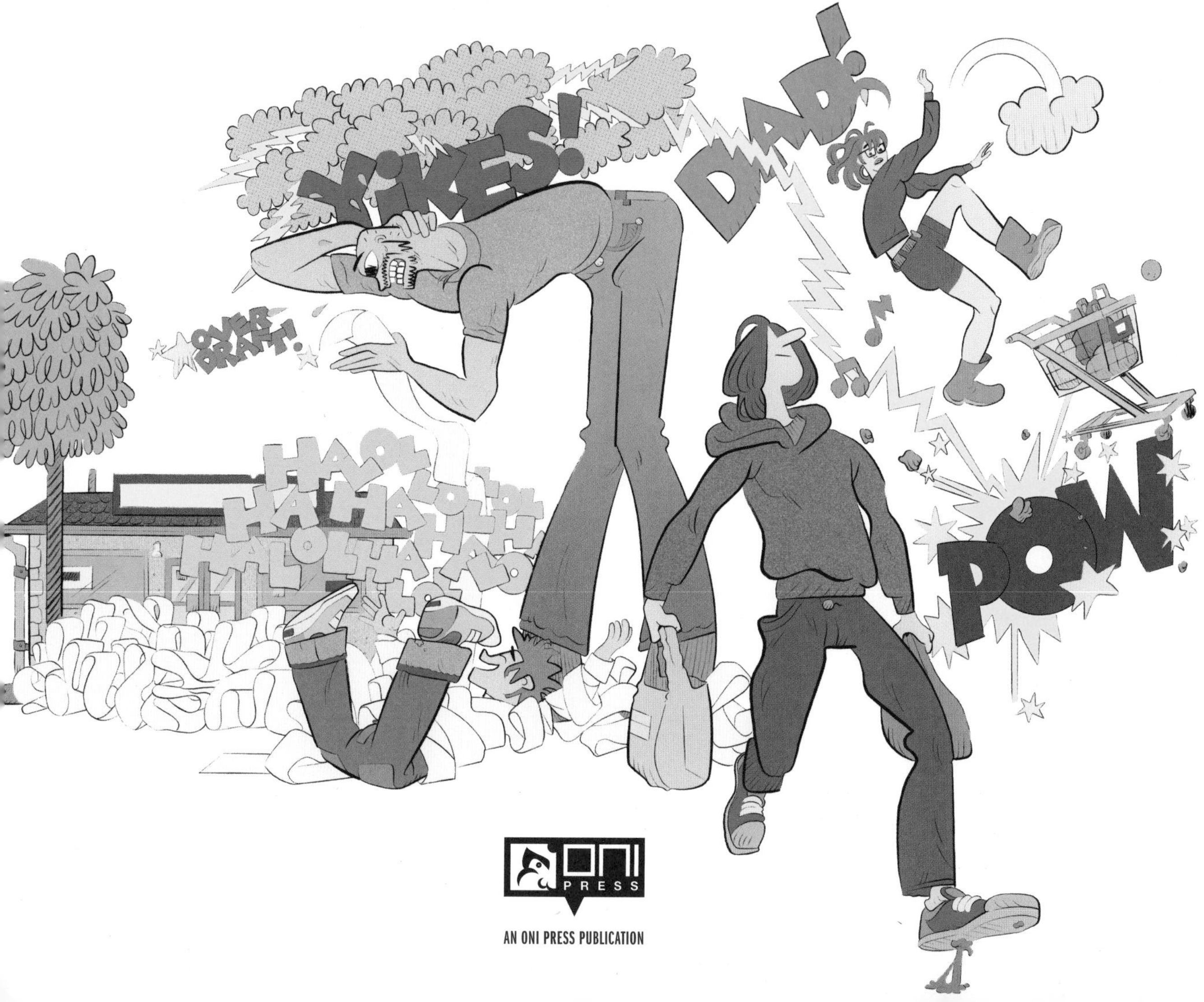

YIKES!
DAD!
OVER DRAFT!
POW

AN ONI PRESS PUBLICATION

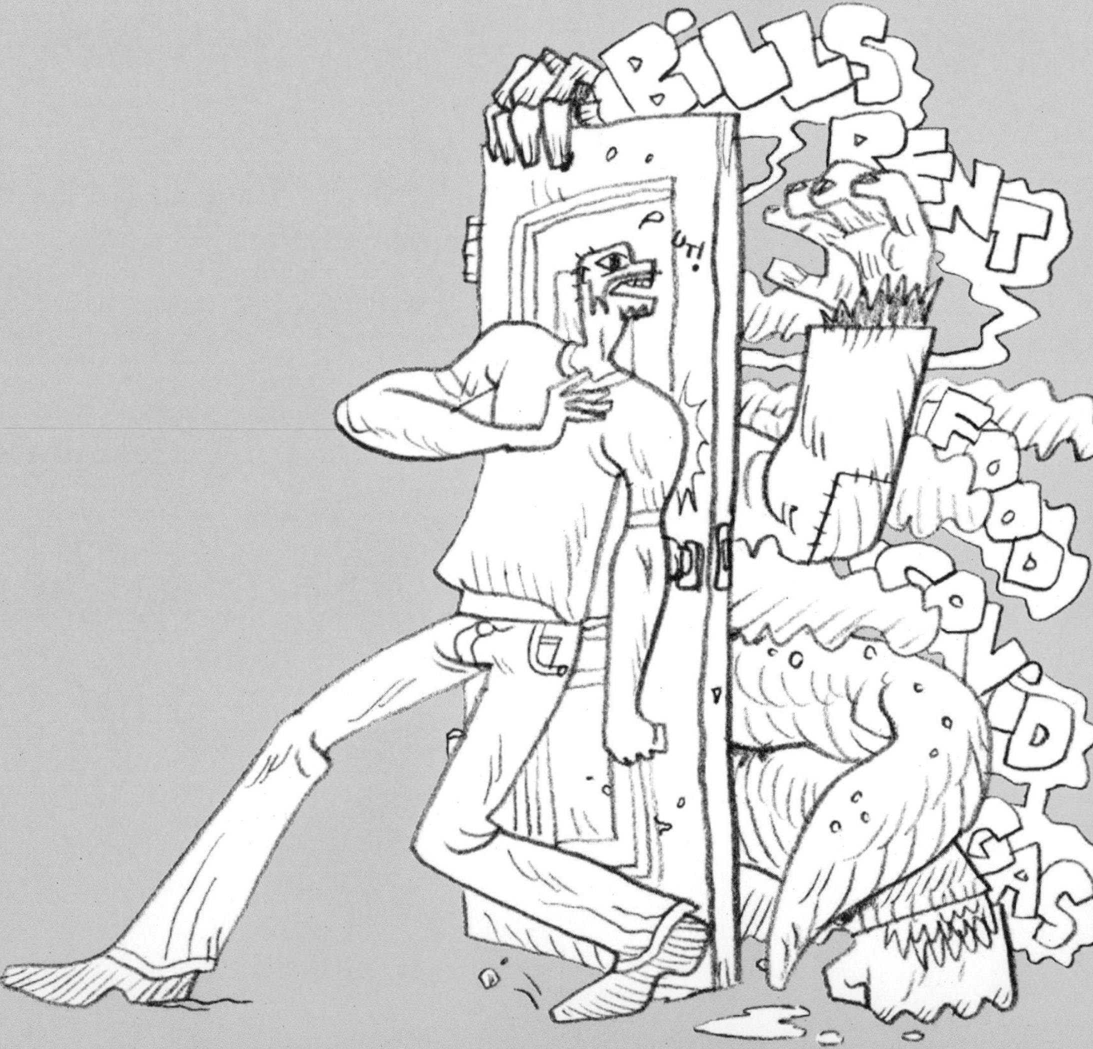
BILLS
RENT
FOOD
COVID
GAS

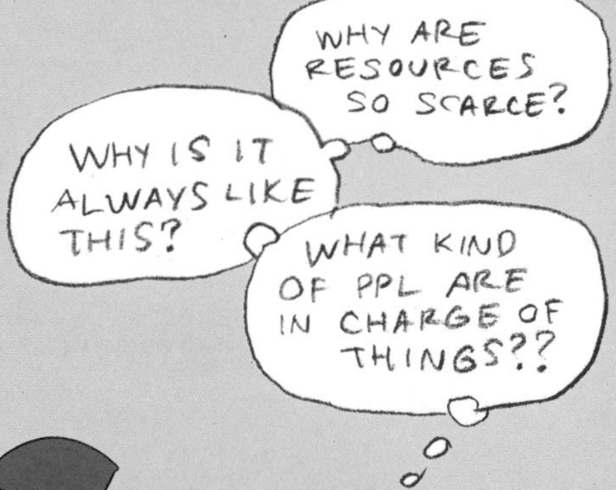
WHY ARE RESOURCES SO SCARCE?
WHY IS IT ALWAYS LIKE THIS?
WHAT KIND OF PPL ARE IN CHARGE OF THINGS??

CARTOONSHOW

By Derek M. Ballard

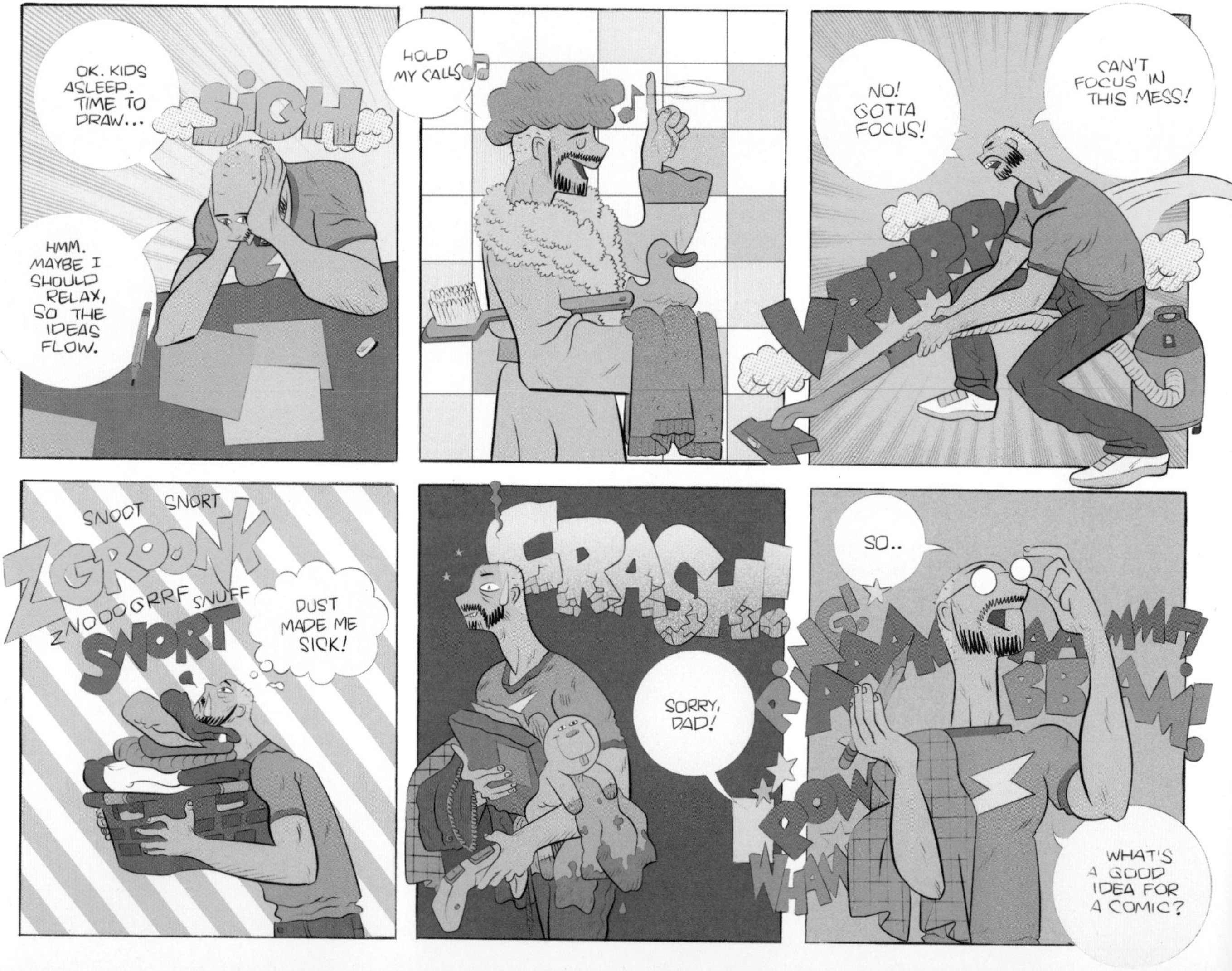
OK. KIDS ASLEEP. TIME TO DRAW...
SIGH
HMM. MAYBE I SHOULD RELAX, SO THE IDEAS FLOW.
HOLD MY CALLS
NO! GOTTA FOCUS!
CAN'T FOCUS IN THIS MESS!
SNOOT SNORT
ZGROONK
ZNOOOGRRF SNUFF
SNORT
DUST MADE ME SICK!
FRASH!
SORRY, DAD!
SO..
RING!
POW
WHAM
WHAT'S A GOOD IDEA FOR A COMIC?

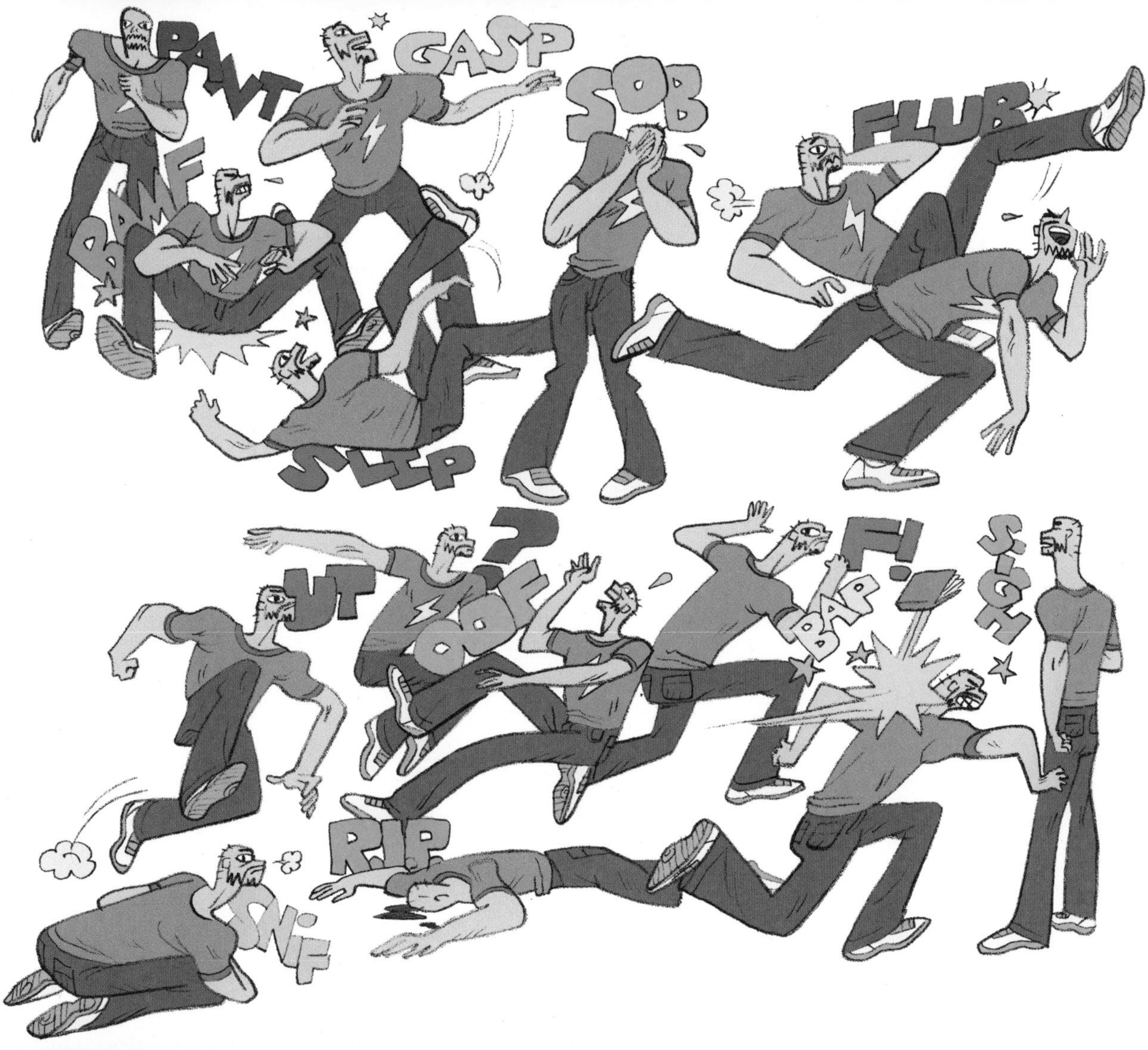
PANT
GASP
SOB
FLUB
BAMF
SLIP
?
UT
OOF
F!
BAP
SIGH
RIP
SNIF

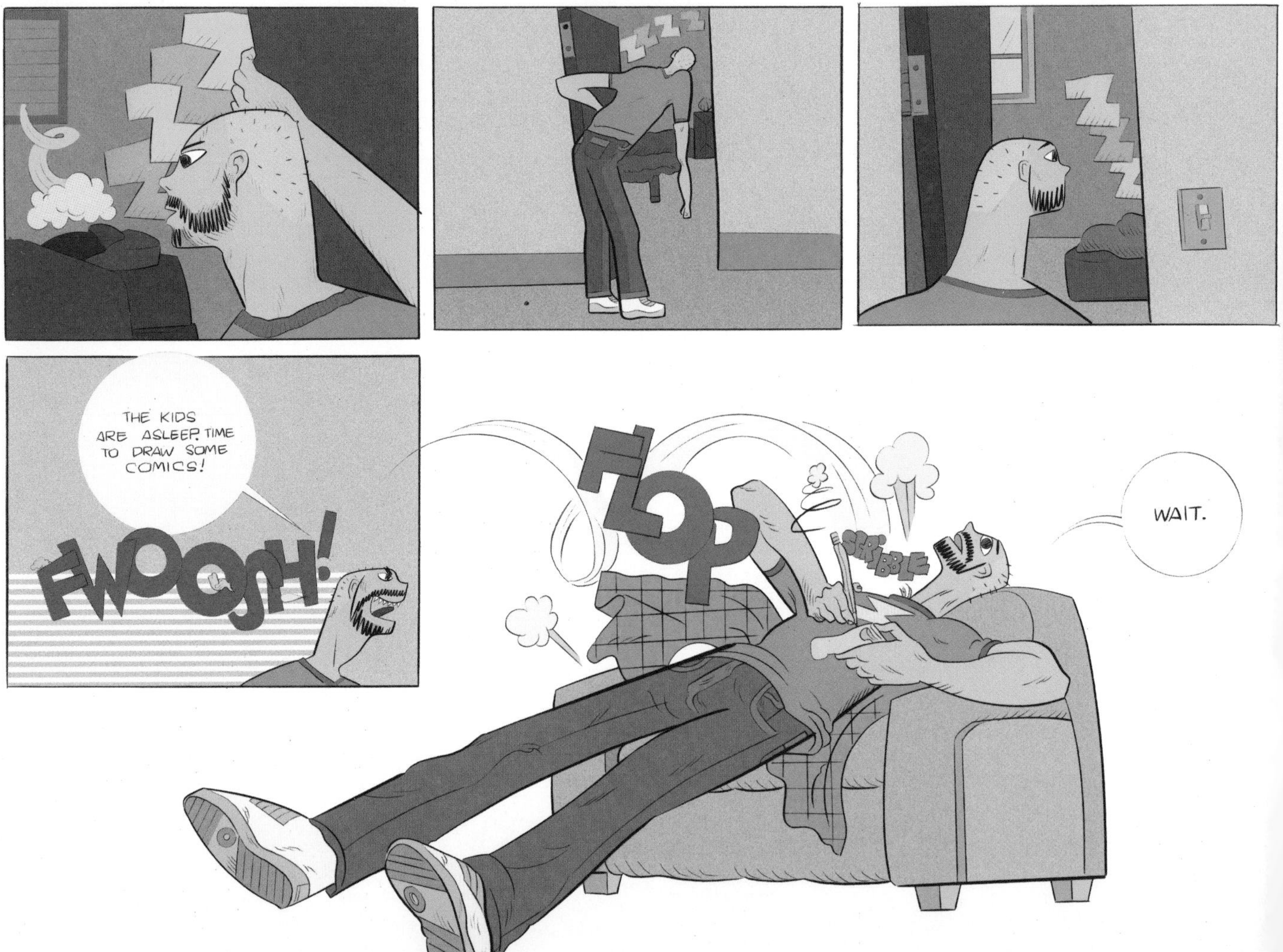
THE KIDS ARE ASLEEP. TIME TO DRAW SOME COMICS!
FWOOSH!
FLOP
SCRIBBLE
WAIT.

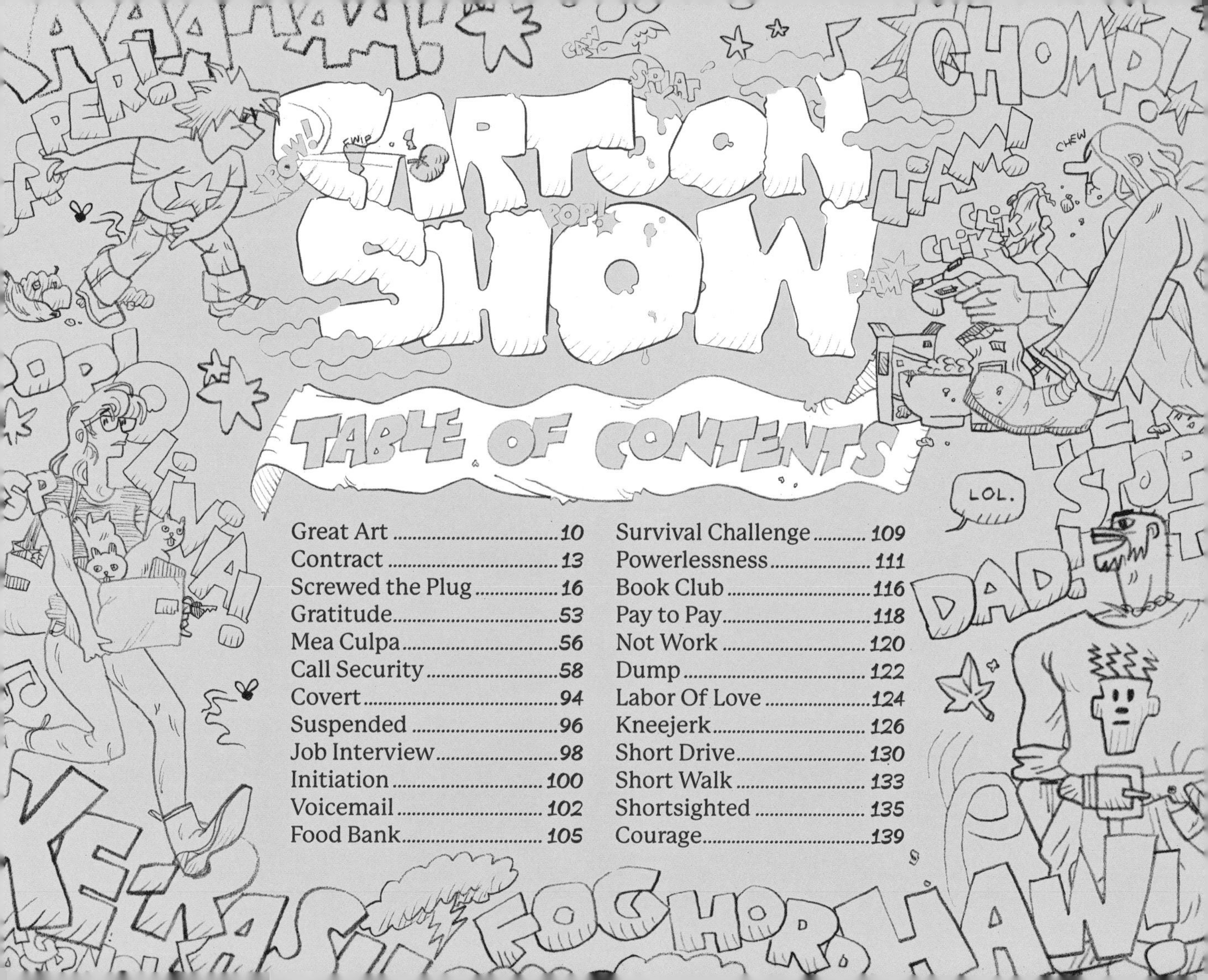
CHOMP!
POW!
FWIP
SPLAT
POP!
CHEW
CLIK
CLIK
BAM
LOL.
DAD!
STOP

CARTOON SHOW

TABLE OF CONTENTS

By Derek M. Ballard
Designed by Carey Soucy & Derek M. Ballard
Edited by Zack Soto

Published by Oni-Lion Forge Publishing Group, LLC.
1319 SE Martin Luther King Jr. Blvd. Suite 240 Portland, OR 97214

Hunter Gorinson, president & publisher * Sierra Hahn, editor in chief * Troy Look, vp of publishing services Katie Sainz, director of marketing * Angie Knowles, director of design & production * Michael Torma, senior sales manager * Desiree Rodriguez, digital marketing manager * Sarah Rockwell, senior graphic designer * Carey Soucy, senior graphic designer * Matt Harding, digital prepress technician * Chris Cerasi, managing editor * Bess Pallares, senior editor * Grace Scheipeter, senior editor * Gabriel Granillo, editor * Zack Soto, editor * Sara Harding, executive assistant * Jung Hu Lee, logistics coordinator & editorial assistant * Kuian Kellum, warehouse assistant Joe Nozemack, publisher emeritus

onipress.com

 facebook.com/onipress twitter.com/onipress instagram.com/onipress
Cartoonshow.bigcartel.com   @derekmballard

FIRST EDITION AUGUST 2023 **ISBN** 978-1-63715-218-8 **eISBN** 978-1-63715-588-2
LIBRARY OF CONGRESS CONTROL NUMBER 2023931965 **PRINTED IN** CHINA
1 2 3 4 5 6 7 8 9 10

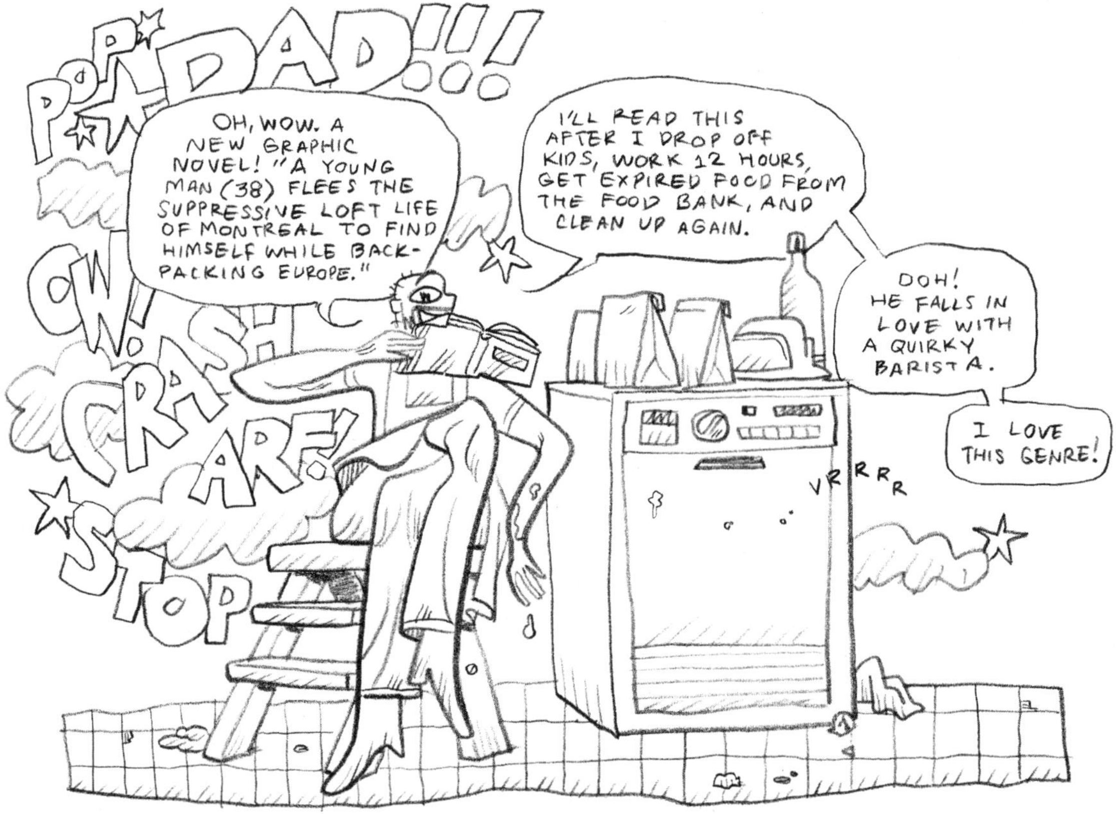
POP
DAD!!!
OW!
CRASH
ARF!
STOP
OH, WOW. A NEW GRAPHIC NOVEL! "A YOUNG MAN (38) FLEES THE SUPPRESSIVE LOFT LIFE OF MONTREAL TO FIND HIMSELF WHILE BACK-PACKING EUROPE."
I'LL READ THIS AFTER I DROP OFF KIDS, WORK 12 HOURS, GET EXPIRED FOOD FROM THE FOOD BANK, AND CLEAN UP AGAIN.
DOH! HE FALLS IN LOVE WITH A QUIRKY BARISTA.
I LOVE THIS GENRE!
VRRRR

THIS WHOLE BOOK IS DEDICATED TO MY THREE KIDS.

OUR CIRCUMSTANCES ARE NOT UNCOMMON. WE ARE A PRETTY AVERAGE AMERICAN FAMILY. I HOPE THAT SHARING OUR STORY CAN HELP Y'ALL FEEL LESS ALONE.

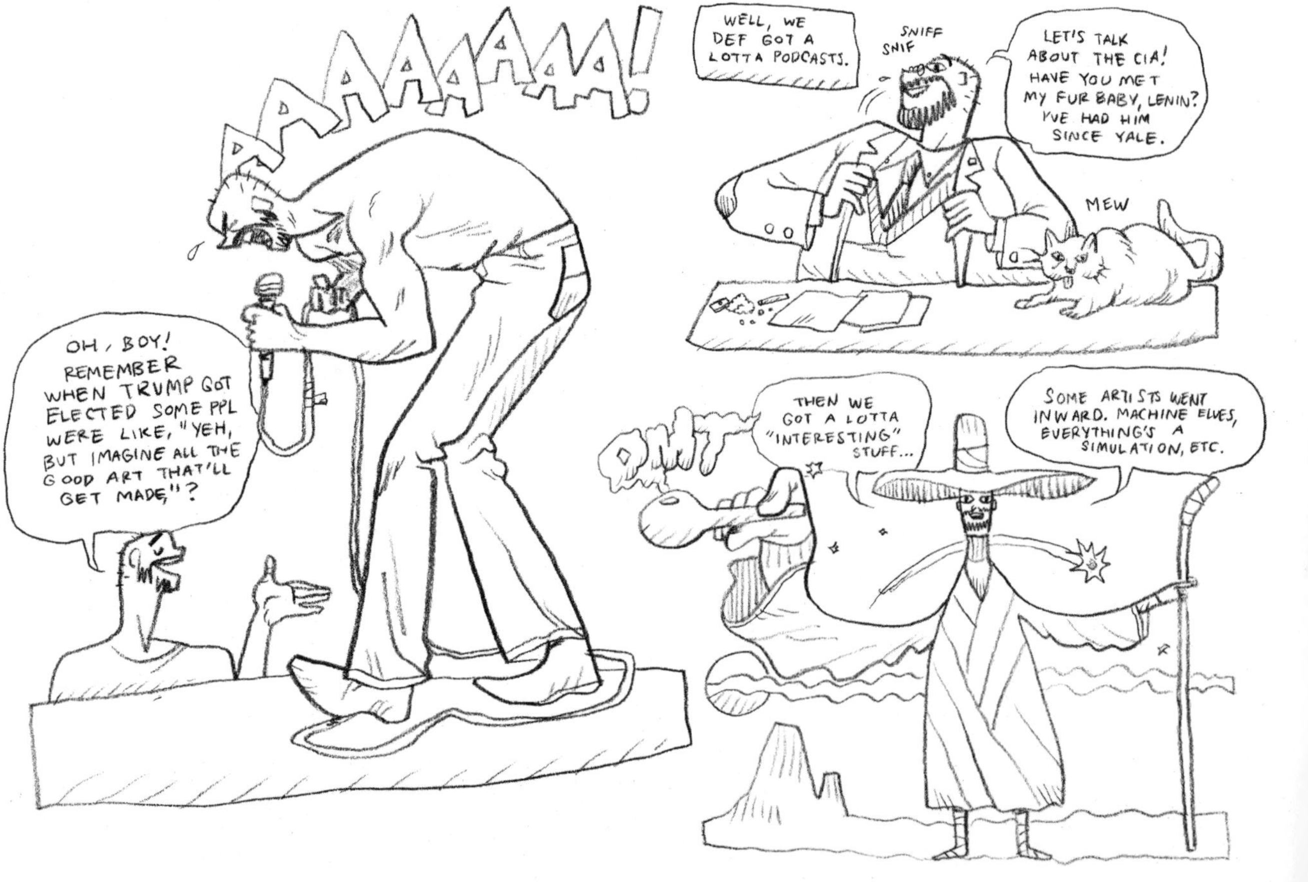
AAAAAAAA!
OH, BOY! REMEMBER WHEN TRUMP GOT ELECTED SOME PPL WERE LIKE, "YEH, BUT IMAGINE ALL THE GOOD ART THAT'LL GET MADE,"?
WELL, WE DEF GOT A LOTTA PODCASTS.
SNIFF SNIF
LET'S TALK ABOUT THE CIA! HAVE YOU MET MY FUR BABY, LENIN? I'VE HAD HIM SINCE YALE.
MEW
THEN WE GOT A LOTTA "INTERESTING" STUFF...
DMT
SOME ARTISTS WENT INWARD. MACHINE ELVES, EVERYTHING'S A SIMULATION, ETC.

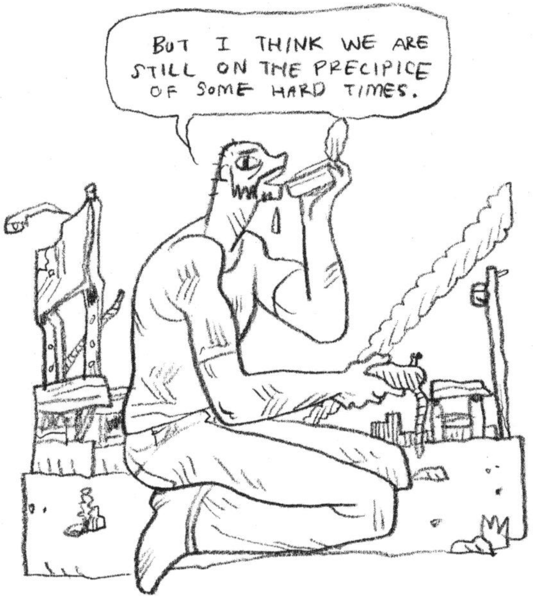
BUT I THINK WE ARE STILL ON THE PRECIPICE OF SOME HARD TIMES.

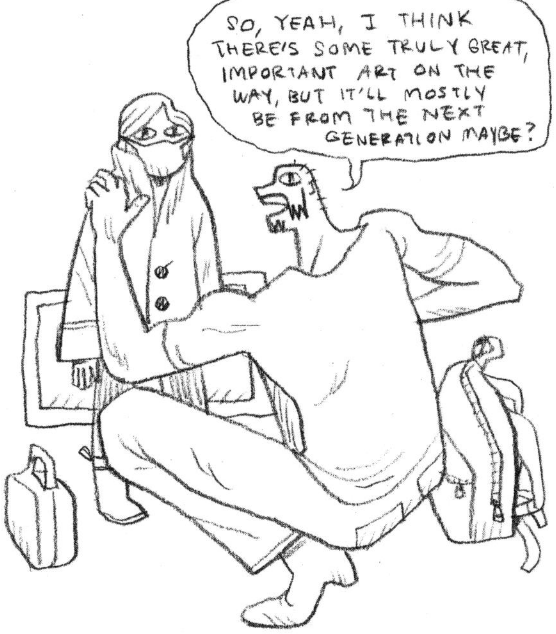
SO, YEAH, I THINK THERE'S SOME TRULY GREAT, IMPORTANT ART ON THE WAY, BUT IT'LL MOSTLY BE FROM THE NEXT GENERATION MAYBE?

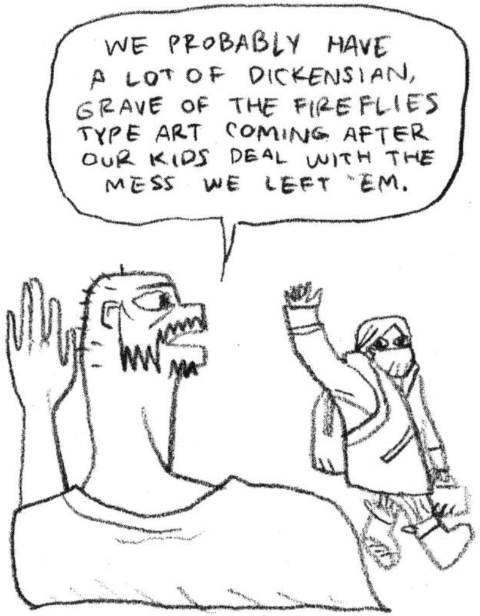
WE PROBABLY HAVE A LOT OF DICKENSIAN, GRAVE OF THE FIREFLIES TYPE ART COMING AFTER OUR KIDS DEAL WITH THE MESS WE LEFT 'EM.

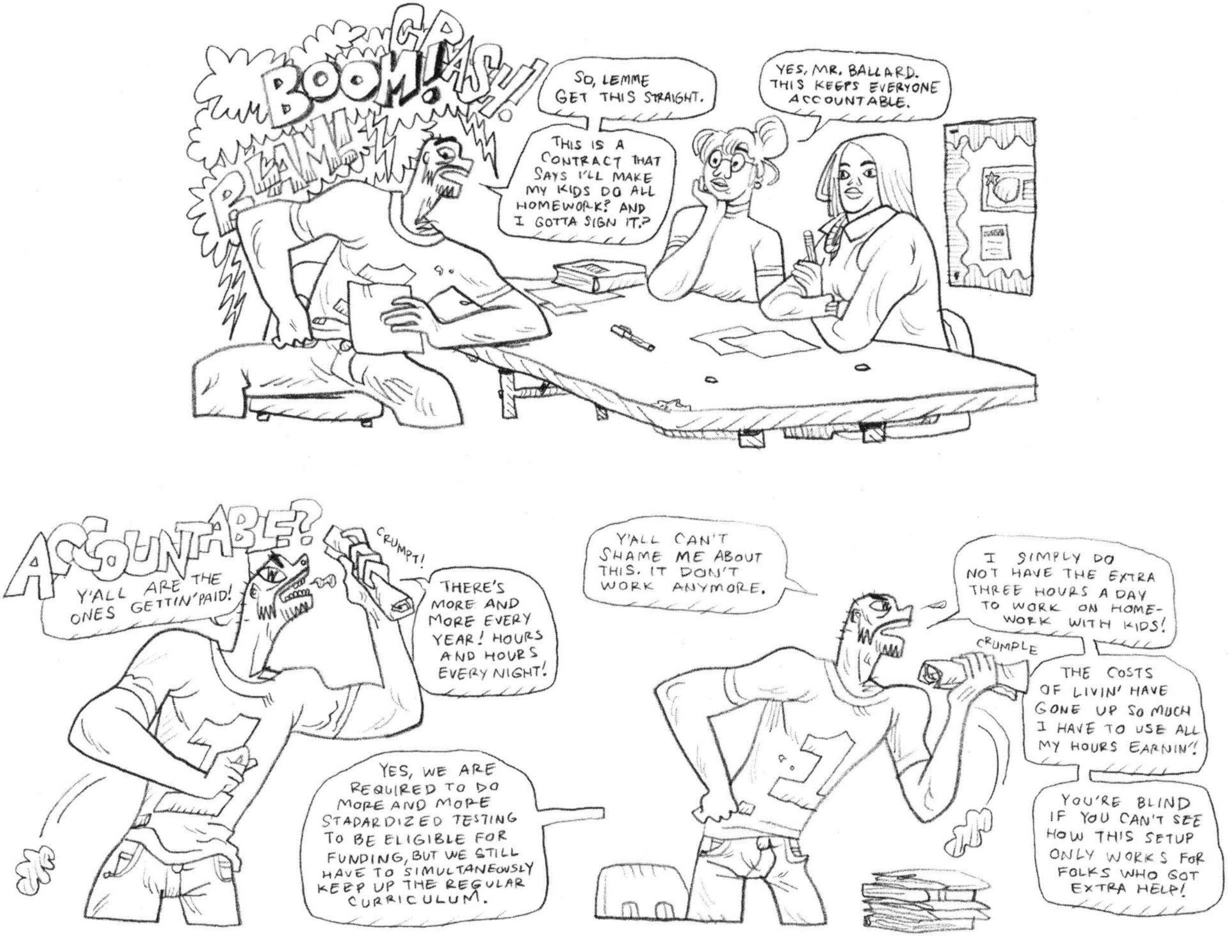
BOOM!
SO, LEMME GET THIS STRAIGHT.
THIS IS A CONTRACT THAT SAYS I'LL MAKE MY KIDS DO ALL HOMEWORK? AND I GOTTA SIGN IT.?
YES, MR. BALLARD. THIS KEEPS EVERYONE ACCOUNTABLE.
ACCOUNTABLE?
Y'ALL ARE THE ONES GETTIN' PAID!
CRUMPT!
THERE'S MORE AND MORE EVERY YEAR! HOURS AND HOURS EVERY NIGHT!
YES, WE ARE REQUIRED TO DO MORE AND MORE STADARDIZED TESTING TO BE ELIGIBLE FOR FUNDING, BUT WE STILL HAVE TO SIMULTANEOUSLY KEEP UP THE REGULAR CURRICULUM.
Y'ALL CAN'T SHAME ME ABOUT THIS. IT DON'T WORK ANYMORE.
I SIMPLY DO NOT HAVE THE EXTRA THREE HOURS A DAY TO WORK ON HOME-WORK WITH KIDS!
CRUMPLE
THE COSTS OF LIVIN' HAVE GONE UP SO MUCH I HAVE TO USE ALL MY HOURS EARNIN'!
YOU'RE BLIND IF YOU CAN'T SEE HOW THIS SETUP ONLY WORKS FOR FOLKS WHO GOT EXTRA HELP!

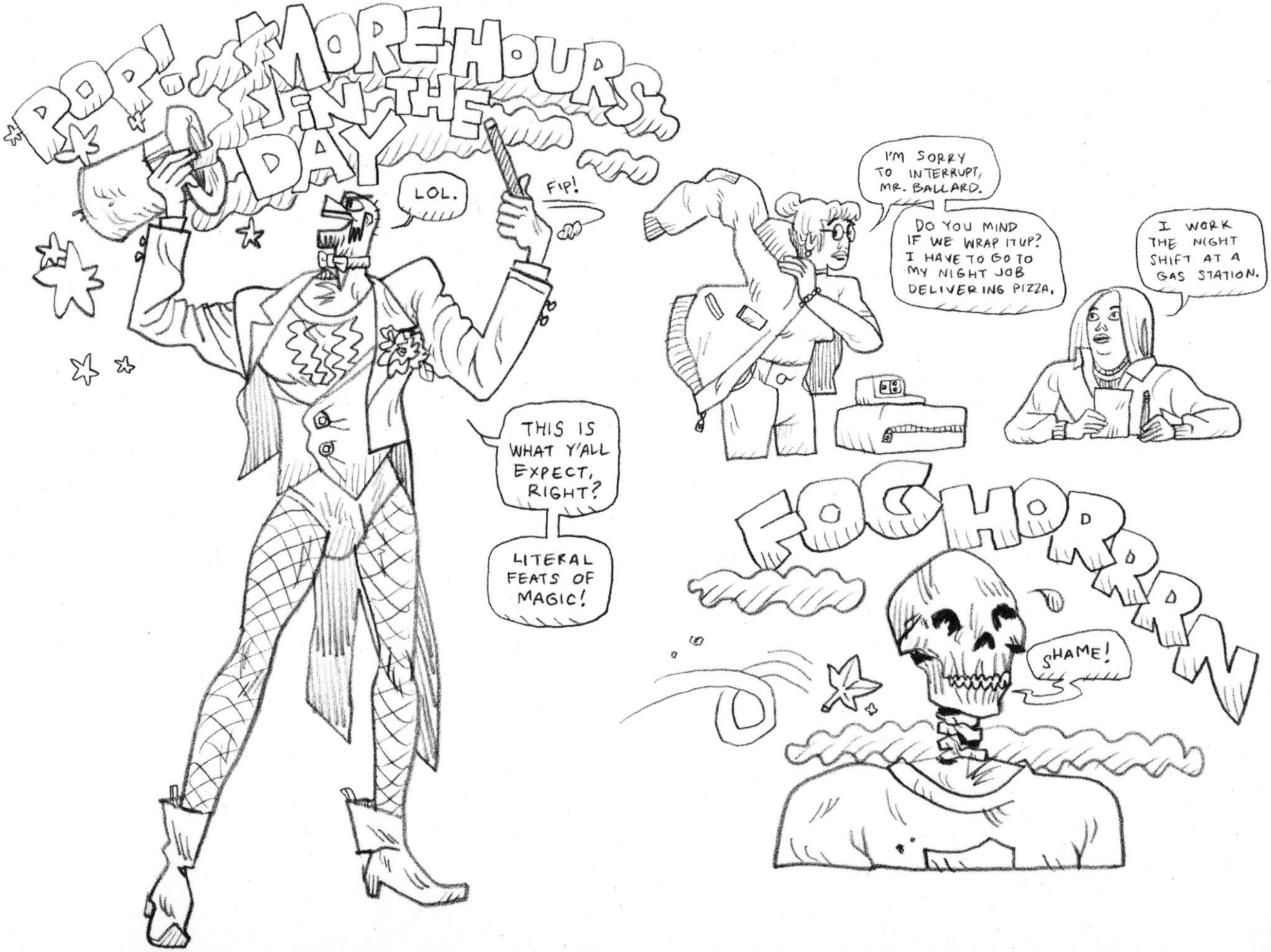
POP!
MORE HOURS IN THE DAY
LOL.
FIP!
THIS IS WHAT Y'ALL EXPECT, RIGHT?
LITERAL FEATS OF MAGIC!
I'M SORRY TO INTERRUPT, MR. BALLARD.
DO YOU MIND IF WE WRAP IT UP? I HAVE TO GO TO MY NIGHT JOB DELIVERING PIZZA.
I WORK THE NIGHT SHIFT AT A GAS STATION.
FOGHORRRRN
SHAME!

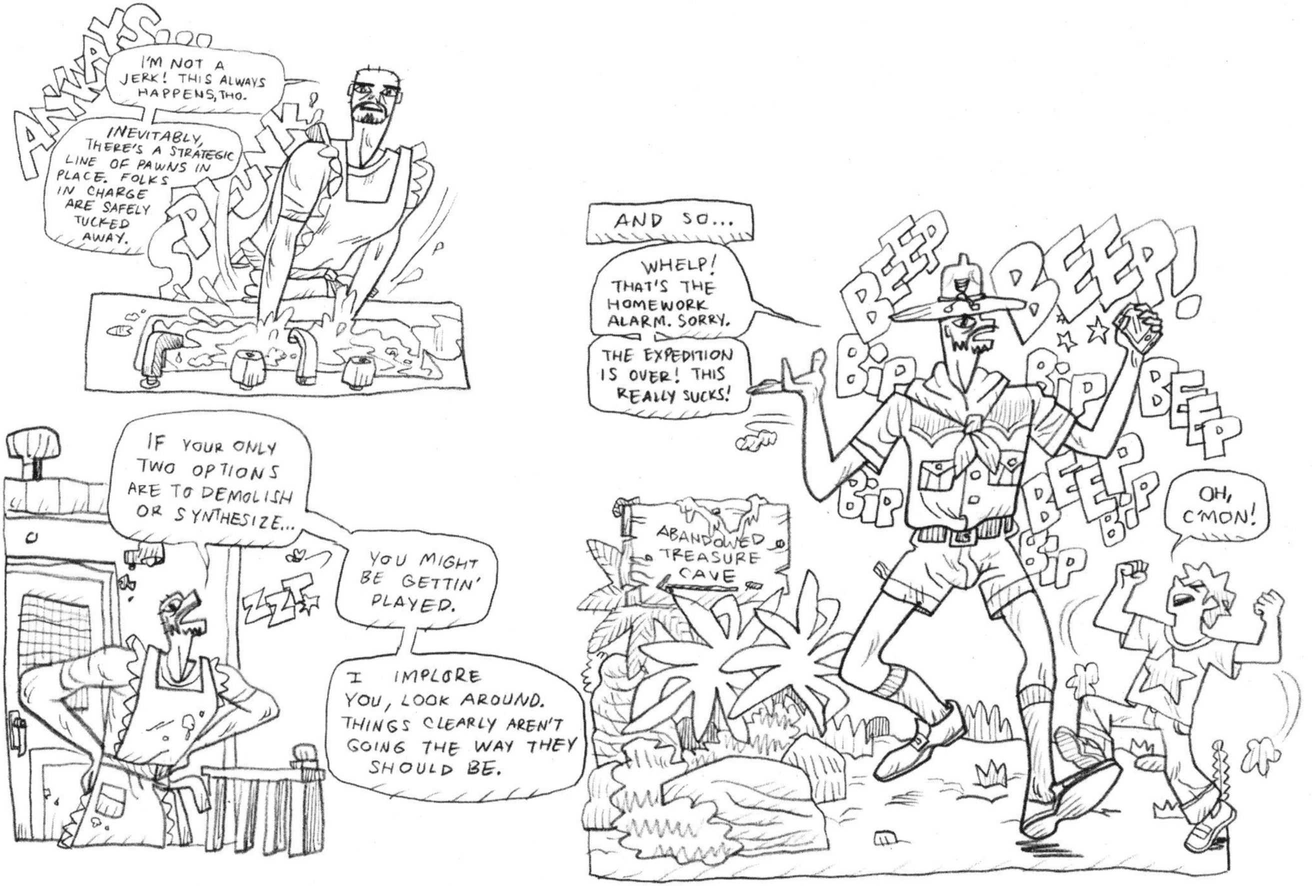
ANYWAYS...
I'M NOT A JERK! THIS ALWAYS HAPPENS, THO.
SPLUNK!
INEVITABLY, THERE'S A STRATEGIC LINE OF PAWNS IN PLACE. FOLKS IN CHARGE ARE SAFELY TUCKED AWAY.
IF YOUR ONLY TWO OPTIONS ARE TO DEMOLISH OR SYNTHESIZE...
ZZT
YOU MIGHT BE GETTIN' PLAYED.
I IMPLORE YOU, LOOK AROUND. THINGS CLEARLY AREN'T GOING THE WAY THEY SHOULD BE.
AND SO...
WHELP! THAT'S THE HOMEWORK ALARM. SORRY.
THE EXPEDITION IS OVER! THIS REALLY SUCKS!
BEEP BEEP! BIP BIP BEEP BEEP BIP BEEP BIP BIP
ABANDONED TREASURE CAVE
OH, C'MON!

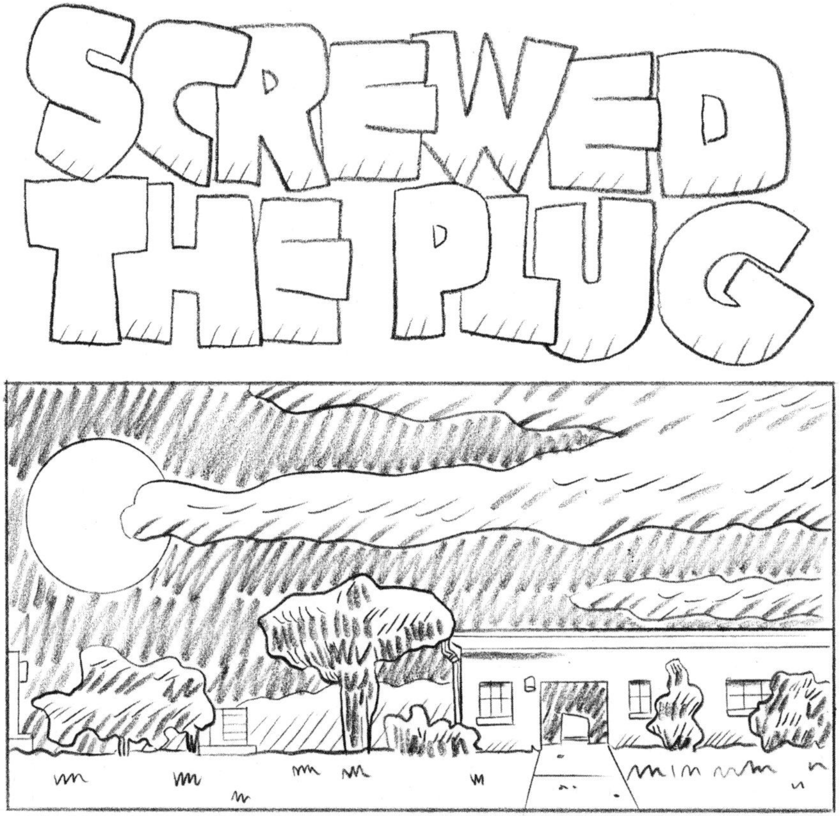
SCREWED
THE PLUG

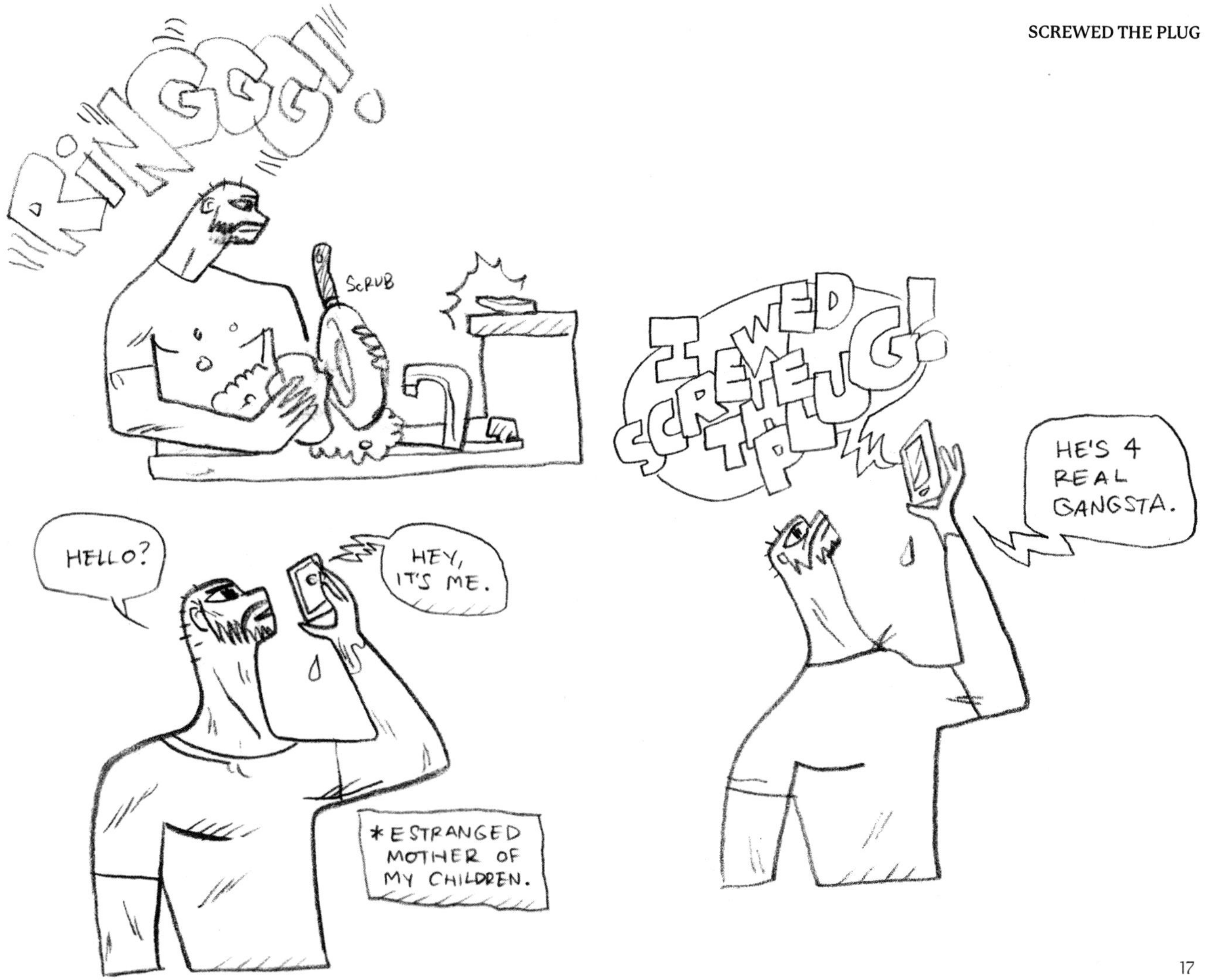
RINGGG!
SCRUB
HELLO?
HEY, IT'S ME.
*ESTRANGED MOTHER OF MY CHILDREN.
I SCREWED THE PLUG!
HE'S 4 REAL GANGSTA.

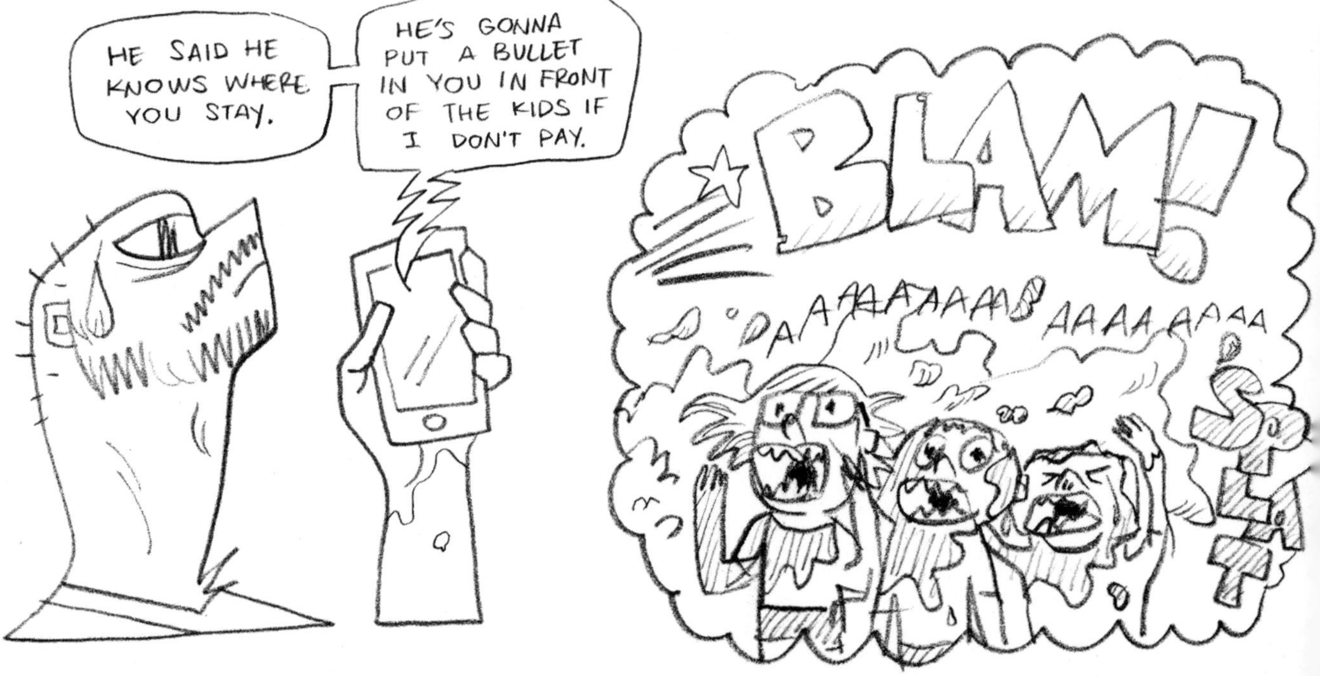
HE SAID HE KNOWS WHERE YOU STAY.
HE'S GONNA PUT A BULLET IN YOU IN FRONT OF THE KIDS IF I DON'T PAY.
BLAM!

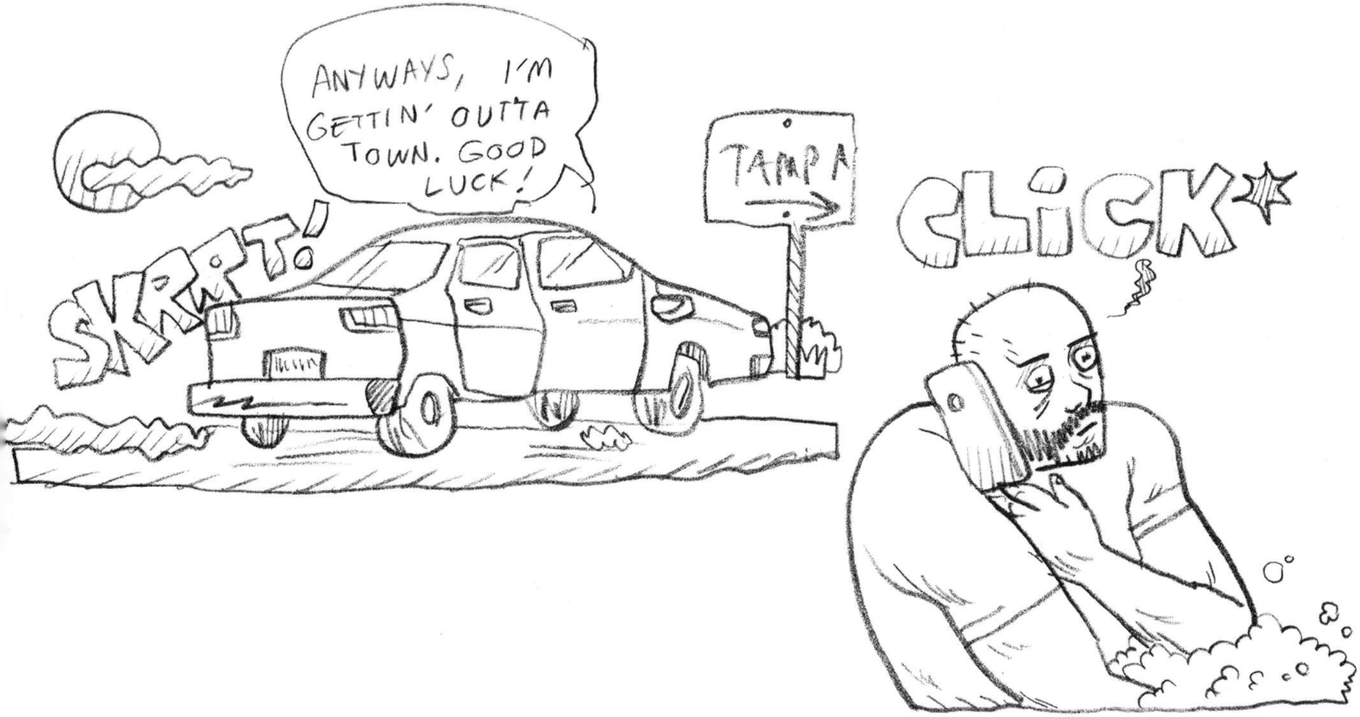
ANYWAYS, I'M GETTIN' OUTTA TOWN. GOOD LUCK!
SKRRRT!
TAMPA
CLICK

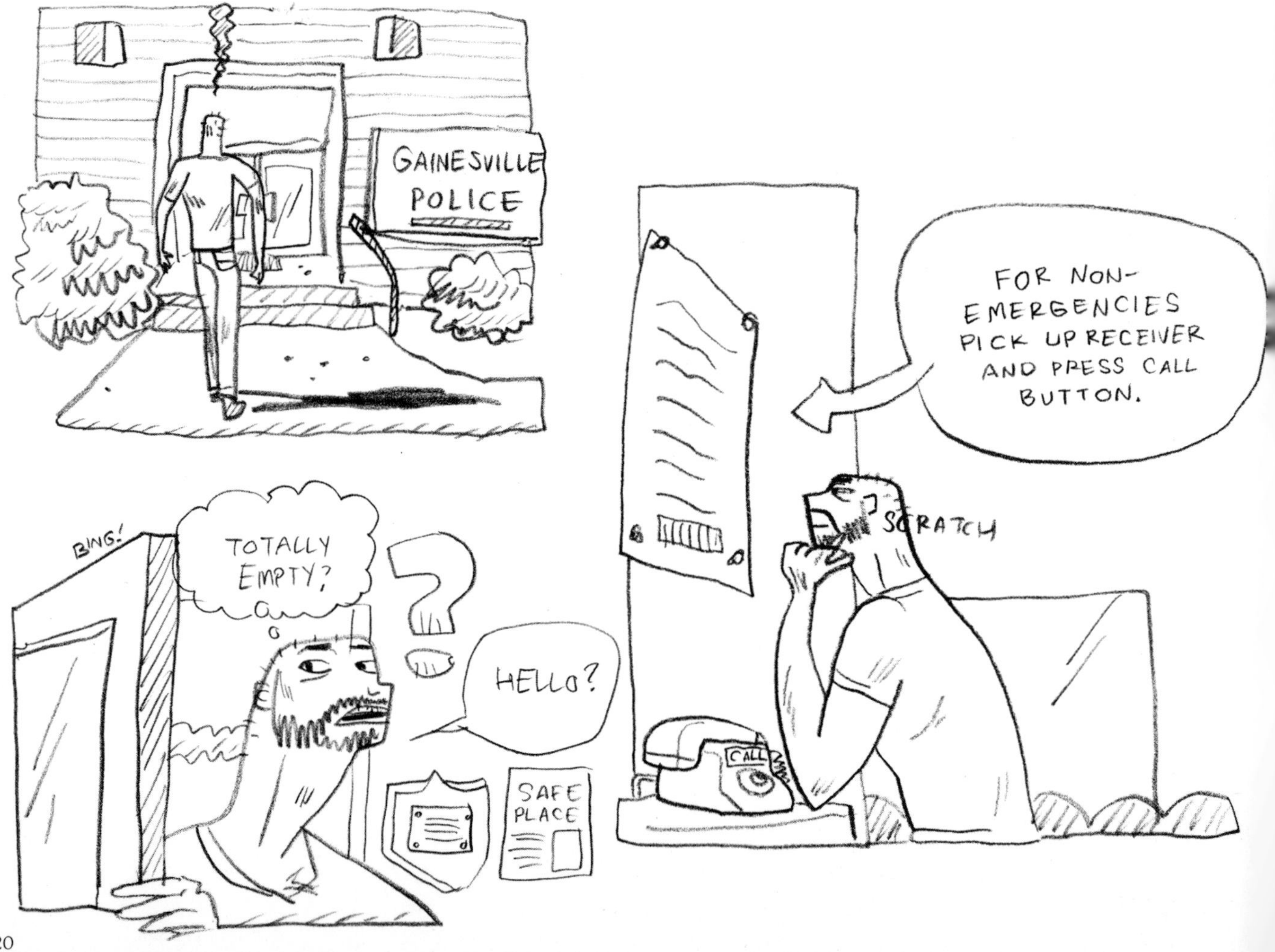
GAINESVILLE POLICE
BING!
TOTALLY EMPTY?
HELLO?
SAFE PLACE
FOR NON-EMERGENCIES PICK UP RECEIVER AND PRESS CALL BUTTON.
SCRATCH
CALL

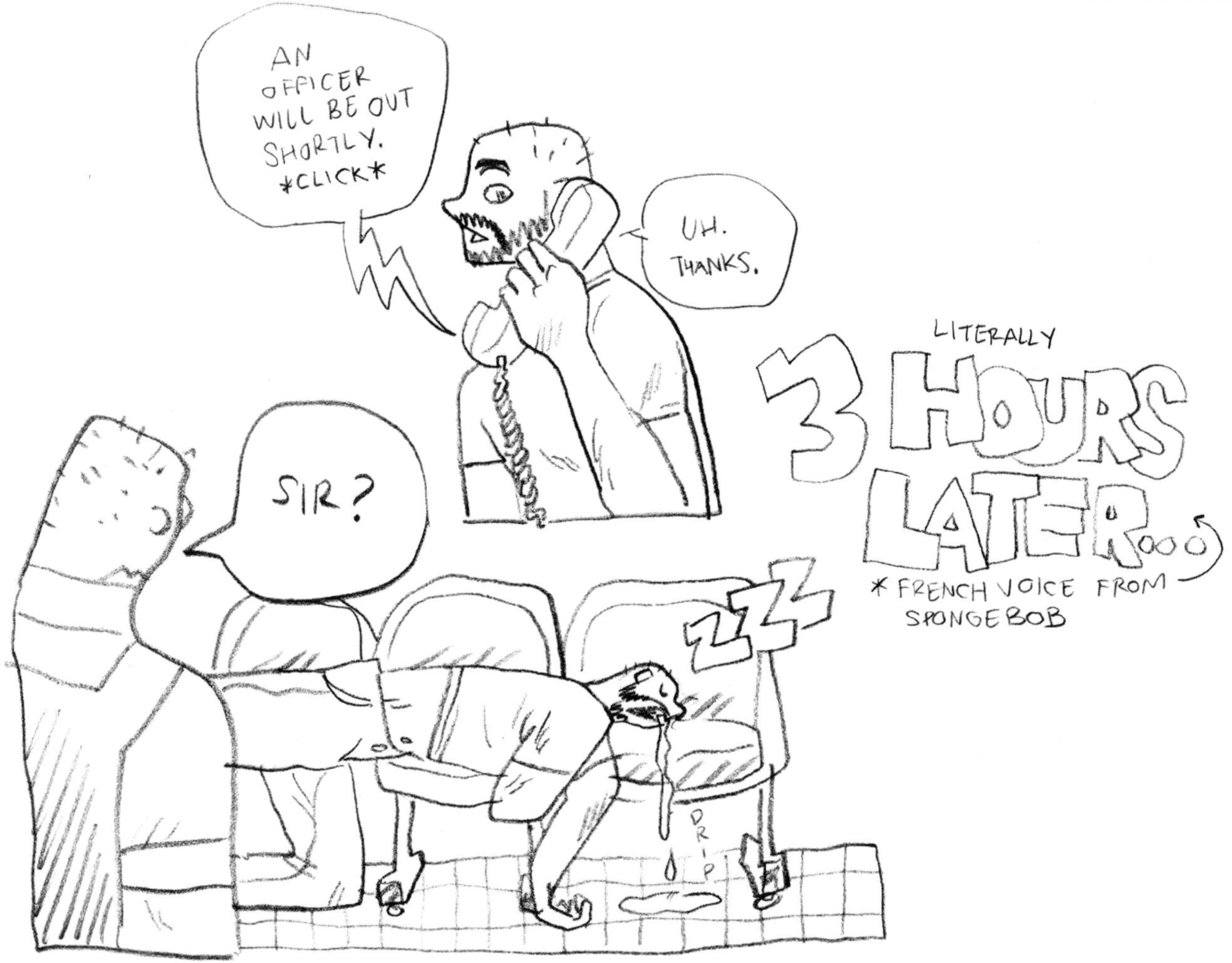
AN OFFICER WILL BE OUT SHORTLY. *CLICK*
UH. THANKS.
LITERALLY 3 HOURS LATER...
* FRENCH VOICE FROM SPONGEBOB
SIR?
ZZZ
DRIP

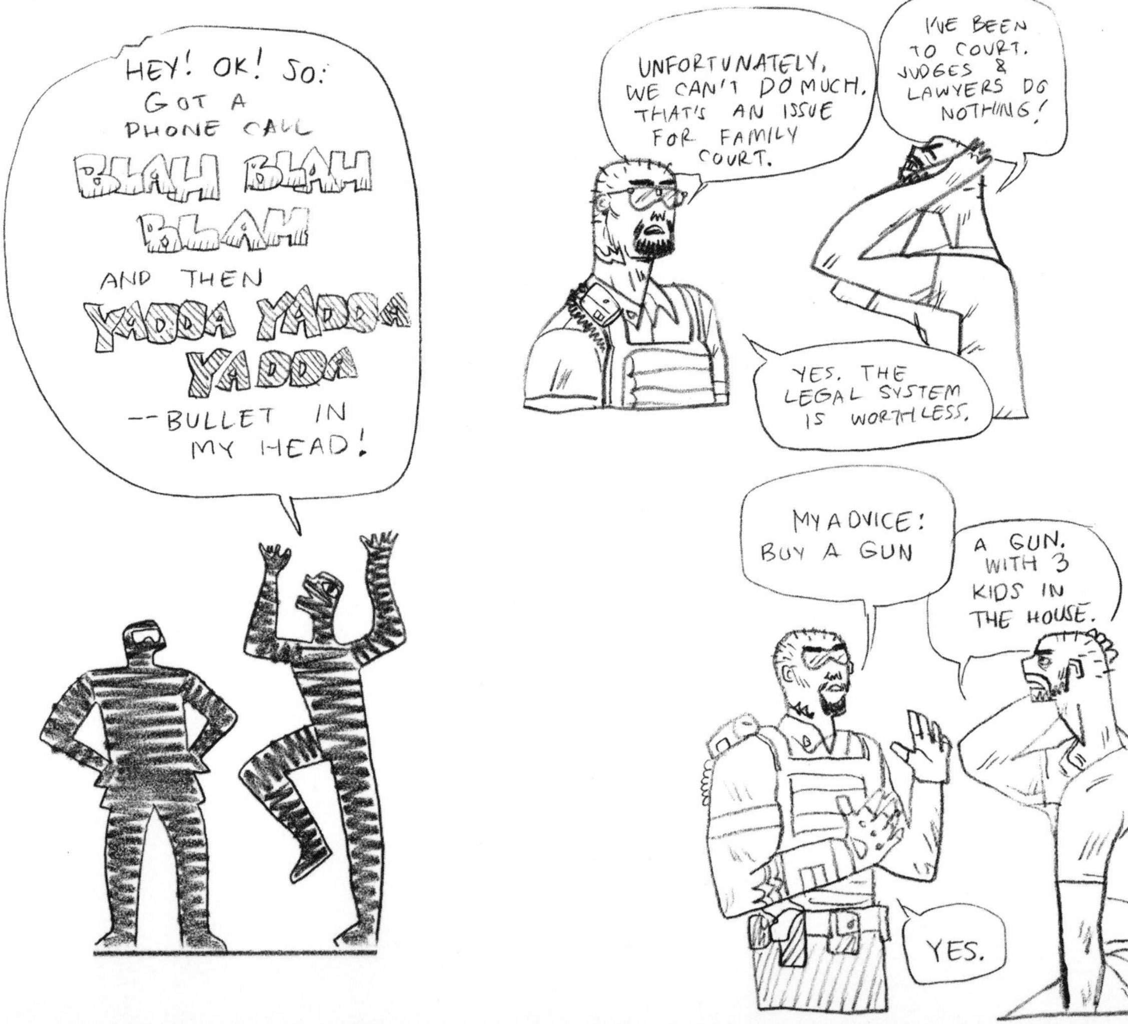
HEY! OK! SO: GOT A PHONE CALL BLAH BLAH BLAH AND THEN YADDA YADDA YADDA --BULLET IN MY HEAD!
UNFORTUNATELY, WE CAN'T DO MUCH. THAT'S AN ISSUE FOR FAMILY COURT.
I'VE BEEN TO COURT. JUDGES & LAWYERS DO NOTHING!
YES. THE LEGAL SYSTEM IS WORTHLESS.
MY ADVICE: BUY A GUN
A GUN. WITH 3 KIDS IN THE HOUSE.
YES.

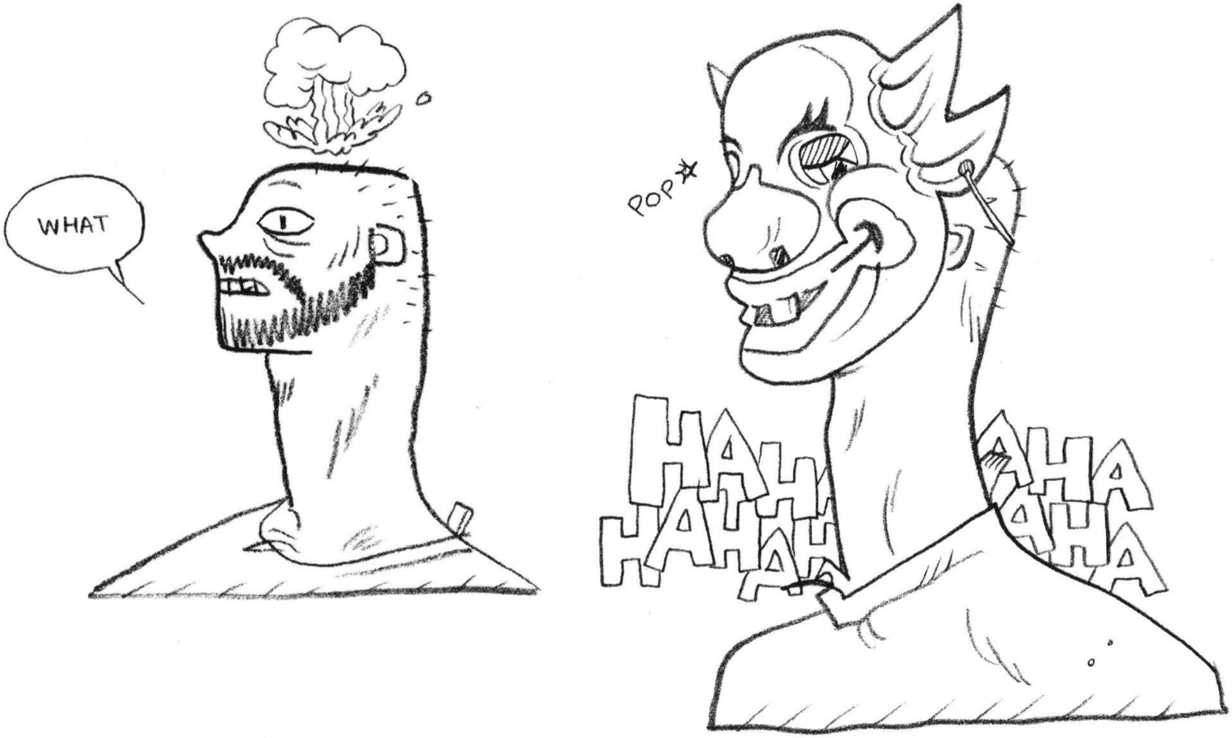
WHAT
POP
HAHA

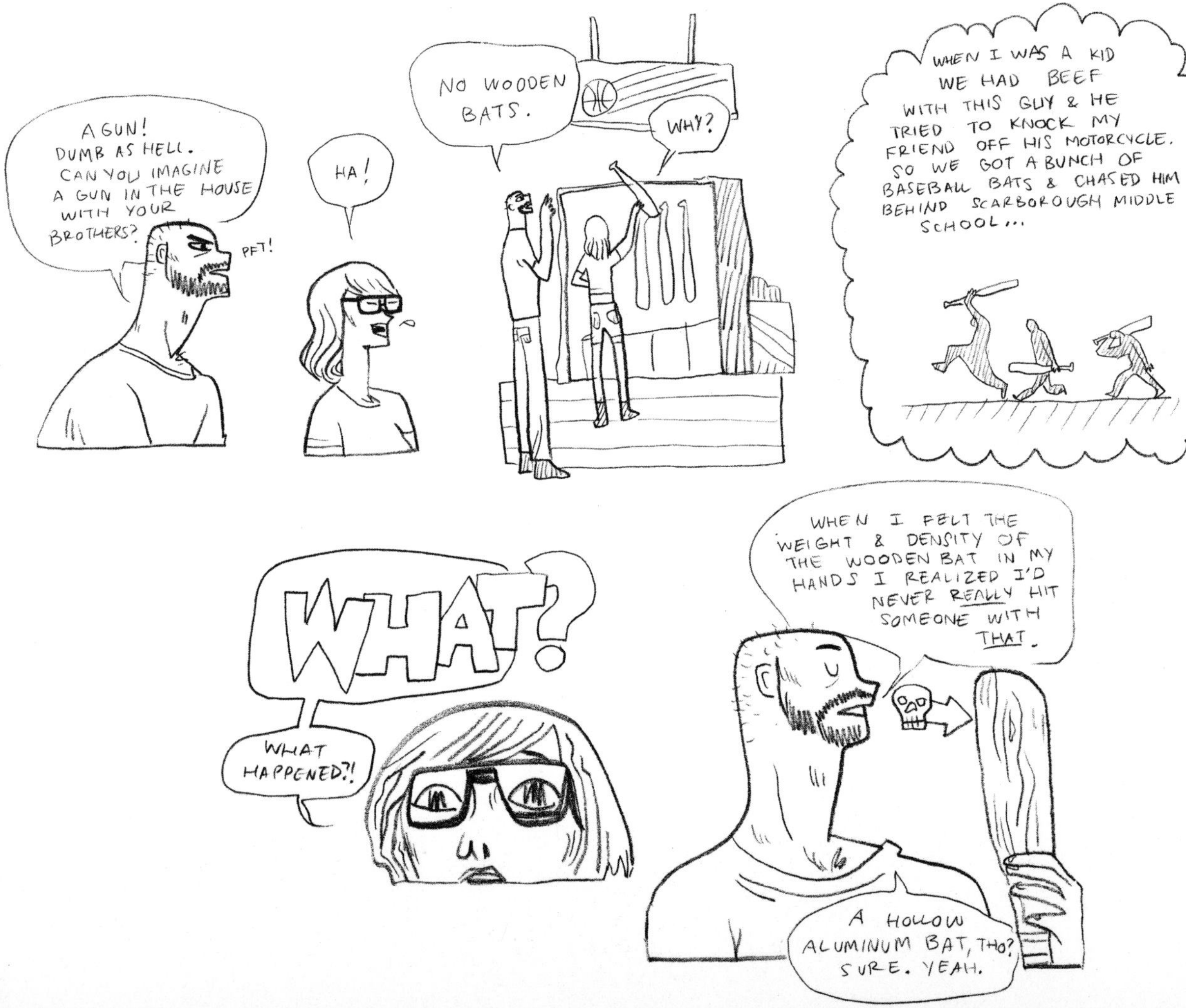
A GUN! DUMB AS HELL. CAN YOU IMAGINE A GUN IN THE HOUSE WITH YOUR BROTHERS?
PFT!
HA!
NO WOODEN BATS.
WHY?
WHEN I WAS A KID WE HAD BEEF WITH THIS GUY & HE TRIED TO KNOCK MY FRIEND OFF HIS MOTORCYCLE. SO WE GOT A BUNCH OF BASEBALL BATS & CHASED HIM BEHIND SCARBOROUGH MIDDLE SCHOOL...
WHAT?
WHAT HAPPENED?!
WHEN I FELT THE WEIGHT & DENSITY OF THE WOODEN BAT IN MY HANDS I REALIZED I'D NEVER REALLY HIT SOMEONE WITH THAT.
A HOLLOW ALUMINUM BAT, THO? SURE. YEAH.

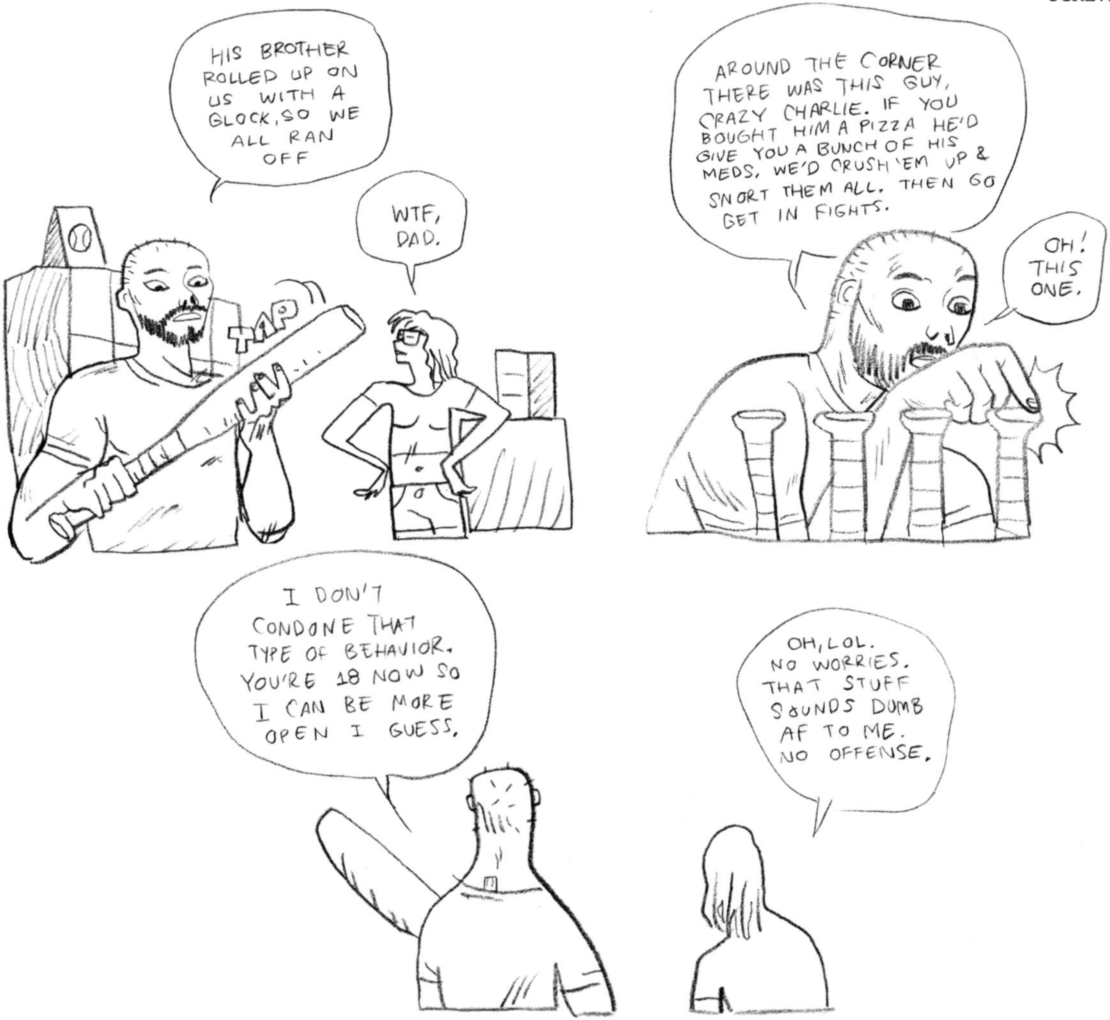
HIS BROTHER ROLLED UP ON US WITH A GLOCK, SO WE ALL RAN OFF
TAP
WTF, DAD.
AROUND THE CORNER THERE WAS THIS GUY, CRAZY CHARLIE. IF YOU BOUGHT HIM A PIZZA HE'D GIVE YOU A BUNCH OF HIS MEDS, WE'D CRUSH 'EM UP & SNORT THEM ALL. THEN GO GET IN FIGHTS.
OH! THIS ONE.
I DON'T CONDONE THAT TYPE OF BEHAVIOR. YOU'RE 18 NOW SO I CAN BE MORE OPEN I GUESS.
OH, LOL. NO WORRIES. THAT STUFF SOUNDS DUMB AF TO ME. NO OFFENSE.

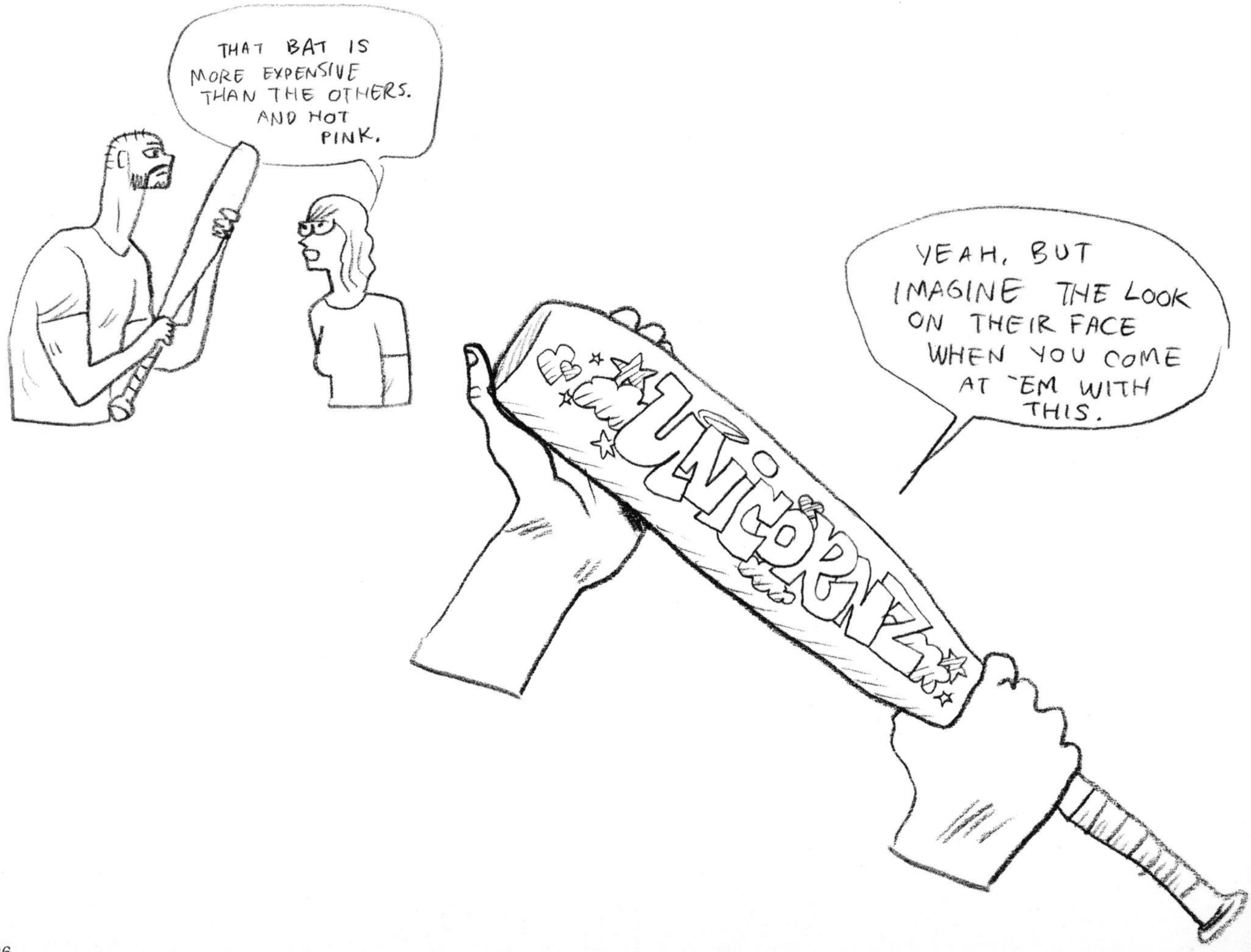
THAT BAT IS MORE EXPENSIVE THAN THE OTHERS. AND HOT PINK.
YEAH, BUT IMAGINE THE LOOK ON THEIR FACE WHEN YOU COME AT 'EM WITH THIS.
UNICORNZ

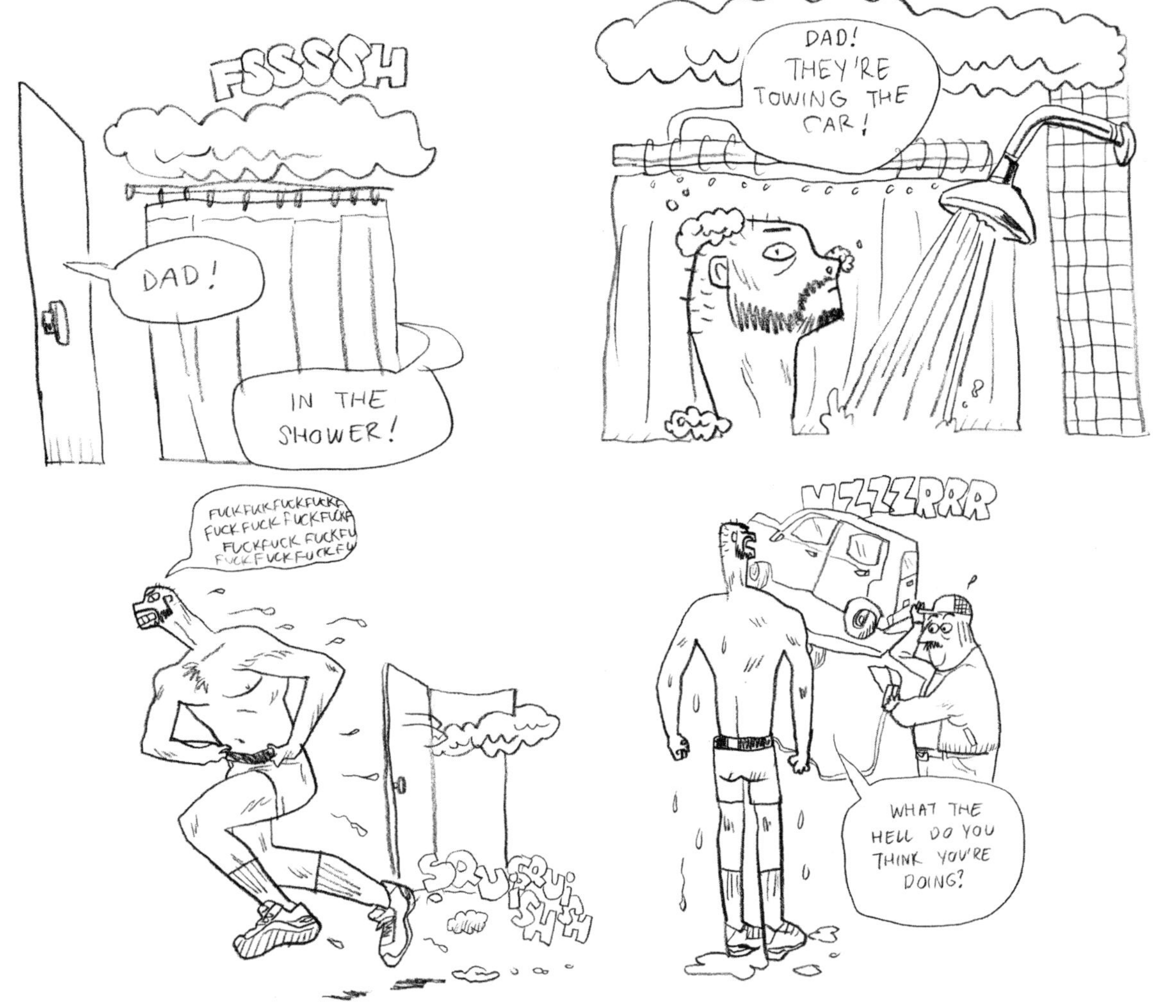
FSSSSH
DAD!
IN THE SHOWER!
DAD! THEY'RE TOWING THE CAR!
FUCKFUCKFUCKFUCKF
FUCKFUCK FUCKFUCKF
FUCKFUCK FUCKFU
FUCKFUCKFUCKFU
WHAT THE HELL DO YOU THINK YOU'RE DOING?

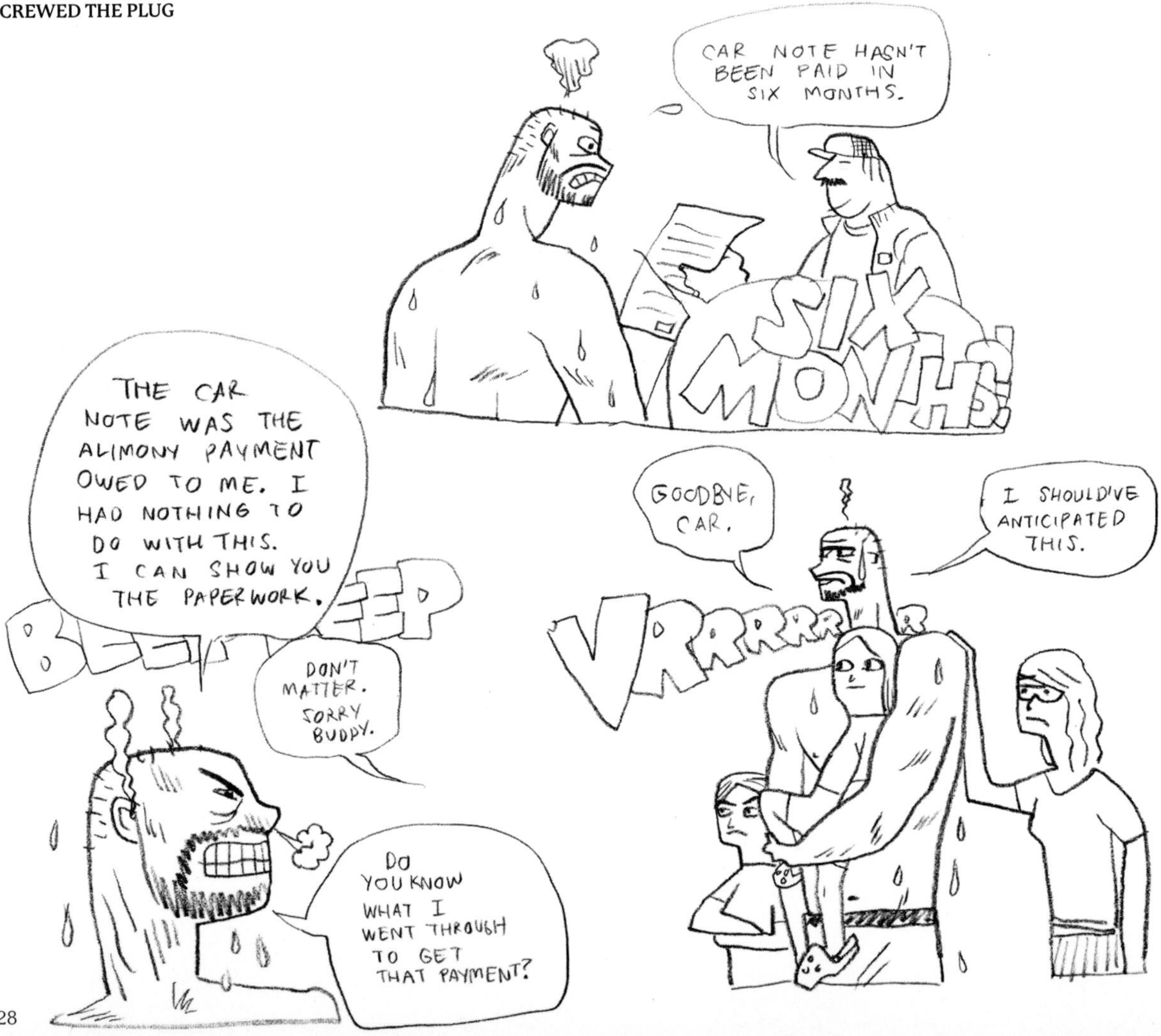
CAR NOTE HASN'T BEEN PAID IN SIX MONTHS.
SIX MONTHS!
THE CAR NOTE WAS THE ALIMONY PAYMENT OWED TO ME. I HAD NOTHING TO DO WITH THIS. I CAN SHOW YOU THE PAPERWORK.
DON'T MATTER. SORRY BUDDY.
DO YOU KNOW WHAT I WENT THROUGH TO GET THAT PAYMENT?
GOODBYE, CAR.
I SHOULD'VE ANTICIPATED THIS.

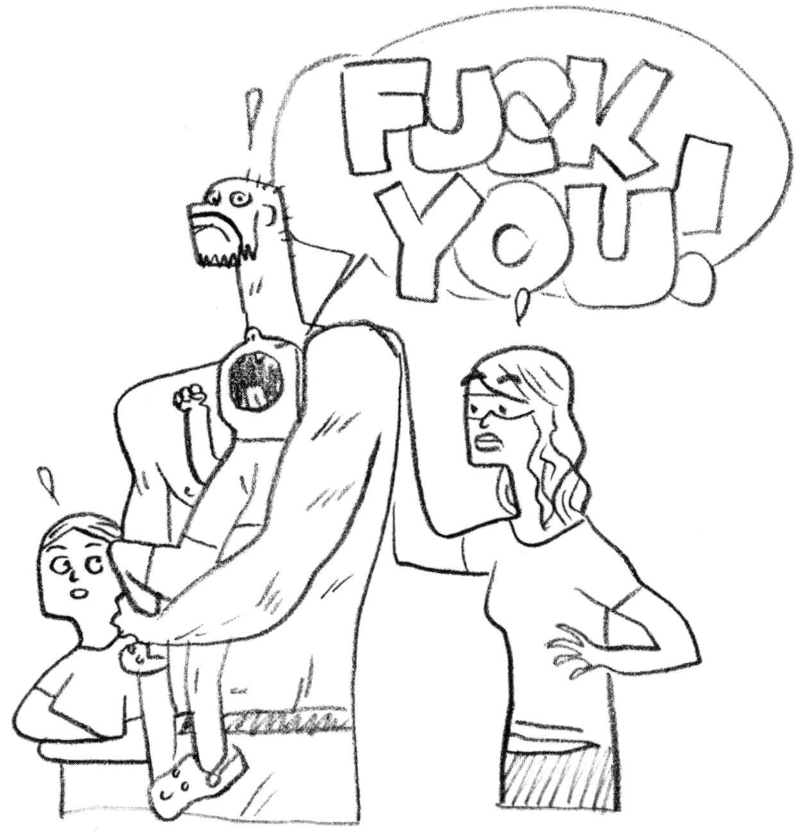
FUCK YOU!

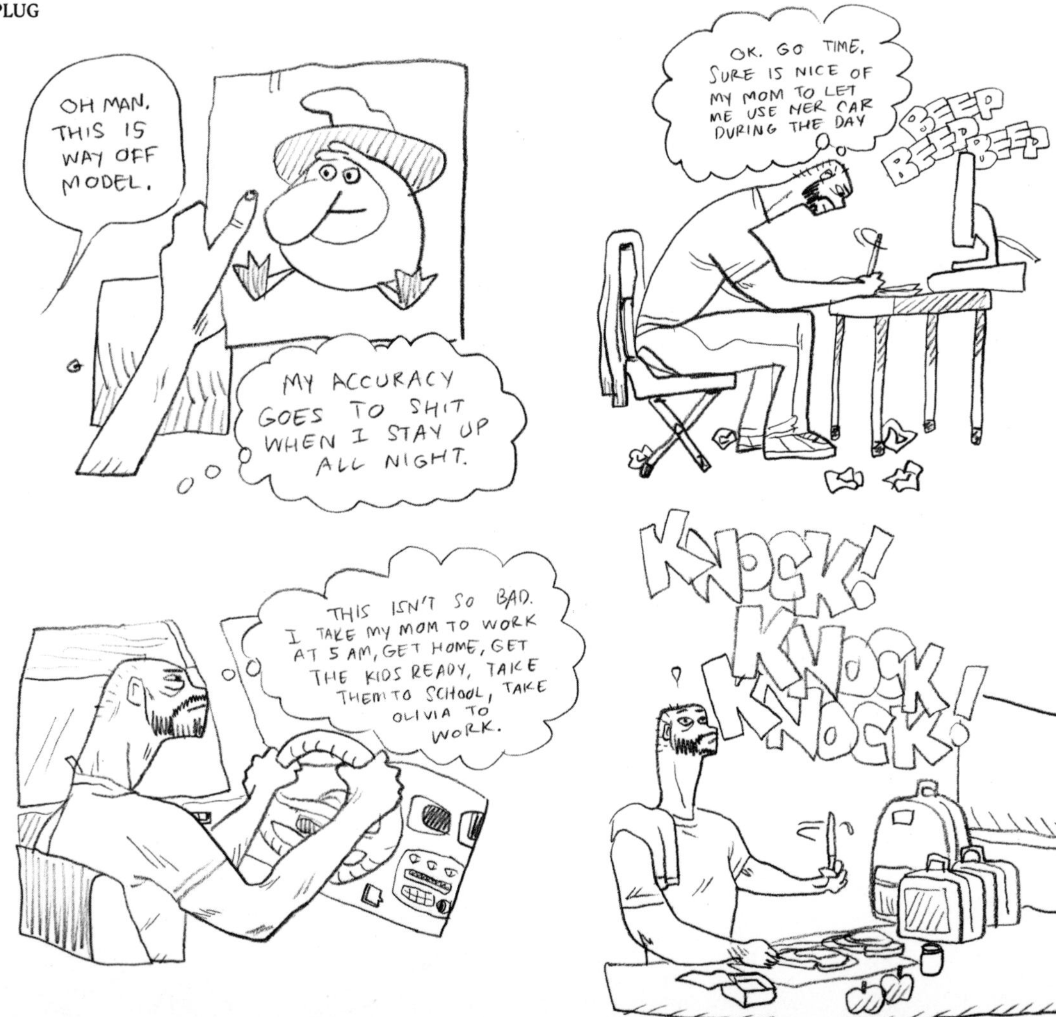
OH MAN. THIS IS WAY OFF MODEL.
MY ACCURACY GOES TO SHIT WHEN I STAY UP ALL NIGHT.
OK. GO TIME. SURE IS NICE OF MY MOM TO LET ME USE HER CAR DURING THE DAY
BEEP BEEP BEEP
THIS ISN'T SO BAD. I TAKE MY MOM TO WORK AT 5 AM, GET HOME, GET THE KIDS READY, TAKE THEM TO SCHOOL, TAKE OLIVIA TO WORK.
KNOCK! KNOCK! KNOCK!

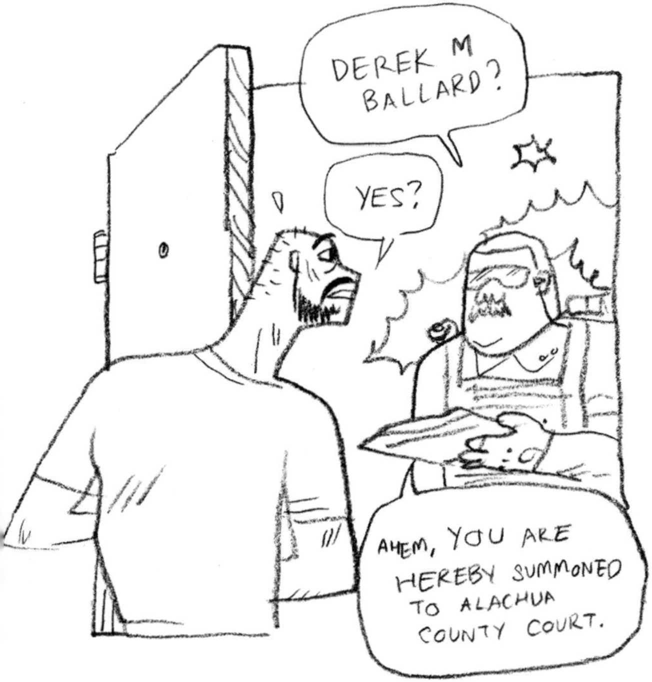
DEREK M BALLARD?
YES?
AHEM, YOU ARE HEREBY SUMMONED TO ALACHUA COUNTY COURT.

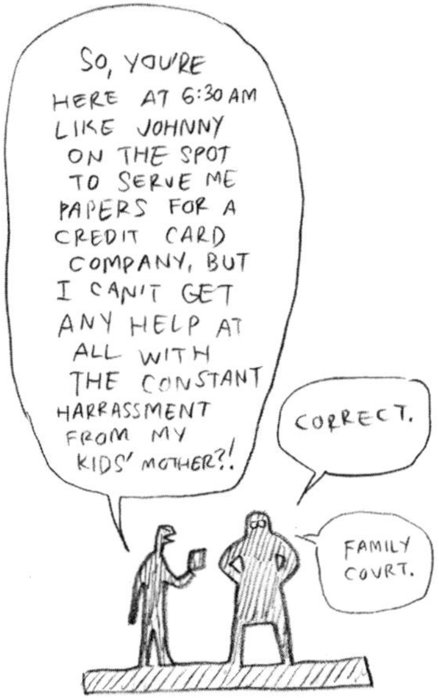
SO, YOU'RE HERE AT 6:30 AM LIKE JOHNNY ON THE SPOT TO SERVE ME PAPERS FOR A CREDIT CARD COMPANY, BUT I CAN'T GET ANY HELP AT ALL WITH THE CONSTANT HARRASSMENT FROM MY KIDS' MOTHER?!
CORRECT.
FAMILY COURT.

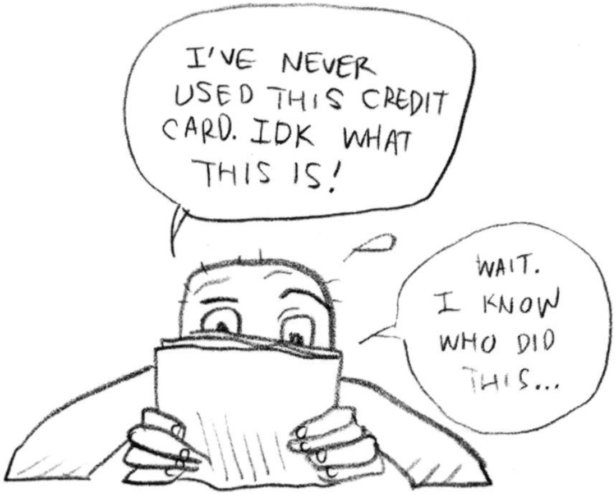
I'VE NEVER USED THIS CREDIT CARD. IDK WHAT THIS IS!
WAIT. I KNOW WHO DID THIS...

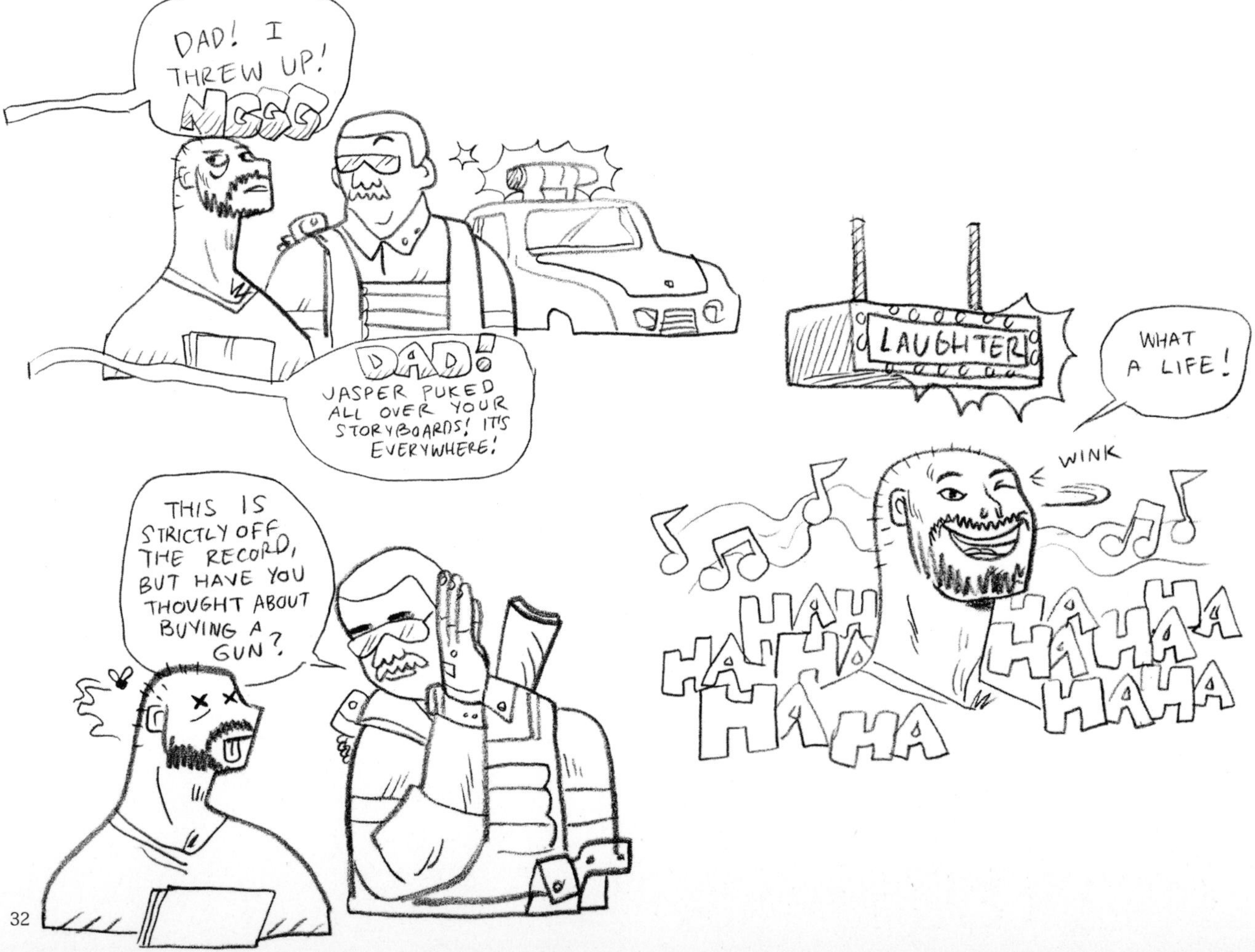
DAD! I THREW UP!
NGGG
DAD!
JASPER PUKED ALL OVER YOUR STORYBOARDS! IT'S EVERYWHERE!
THIS IS STRICTLY OFF THE RECORD, BUT HAVE YOU THOUGHT ABOUT BUYING A GUN?
LAUGHTER
WHAT A LIFE!
WINK
HAHA HAHA HAHA HAHA HA
HAHAHA HAHAHA HAHA

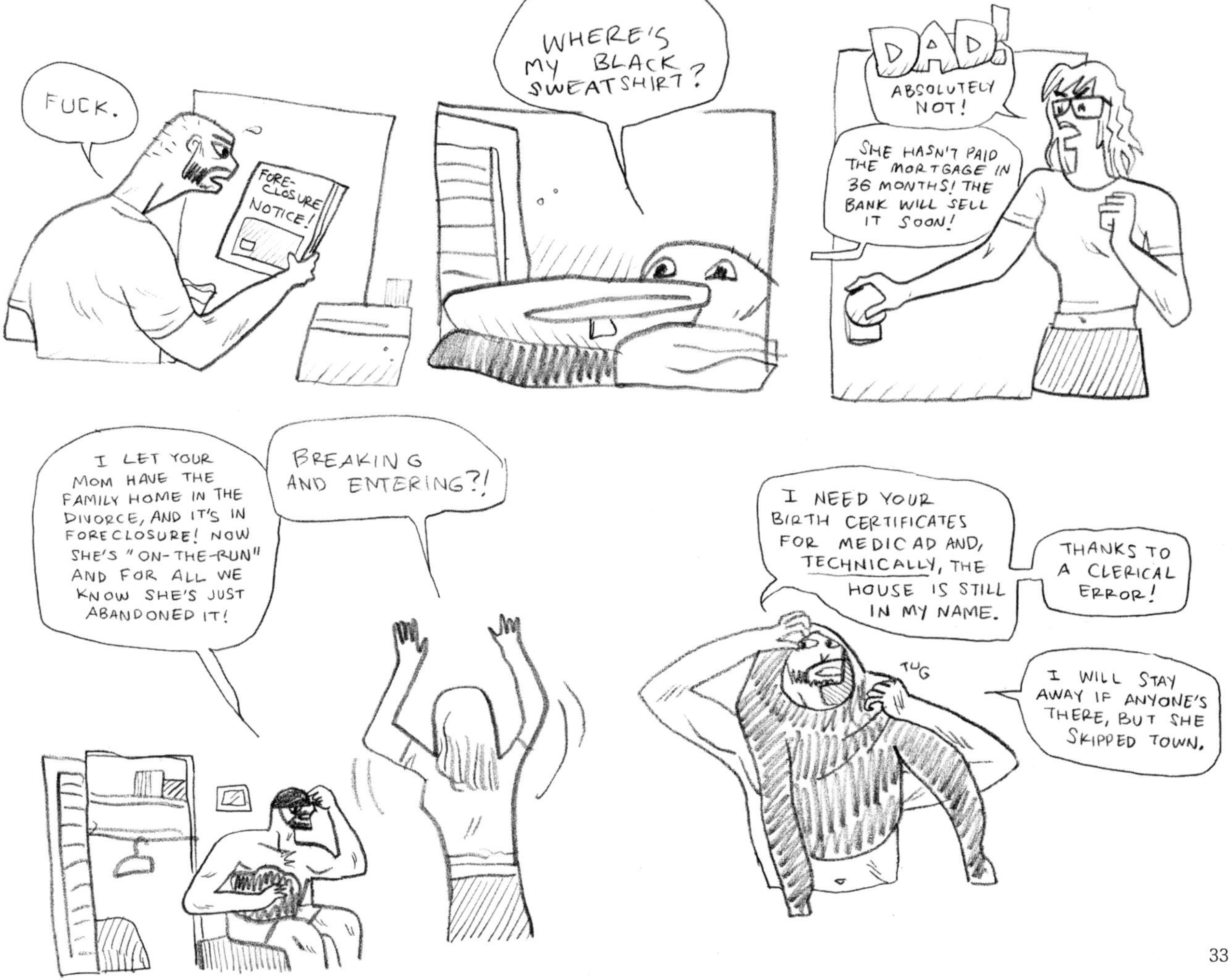
FUCK.
FORE-CLOSURE NOTICE!
WHERE'S MY BLACK SWEATSHIRT?
DAD!
ABSOLUTELY NOT!
SHE HASN'T PAID THE MORTGAGE IN 36 MONTHS! THE BANK WILL SELL IT SOON!
I LET YOUR MOM HAVE THE FAMILY HOME IN THE DIVORCE, AND IT'S IN FORECLOSURE! NOW SHE'S "ON-THE-RUN" AND FOR ALL WE KNOW SHE'S JUST ABANDONED IT!
BREAKING AND ENTERING?!
I NEED YOUR BIRTH CERTIFICATES FOR MEDICAD AND, TECHNICALLY, THE HOUSE IS STILL IN MY NAME.
THANKS TO A CLERICAL ERROR!
TUG
I WILL STAY AWAY IF ANYONE'S THERE, BUT SHE SKIPPED TOWN.

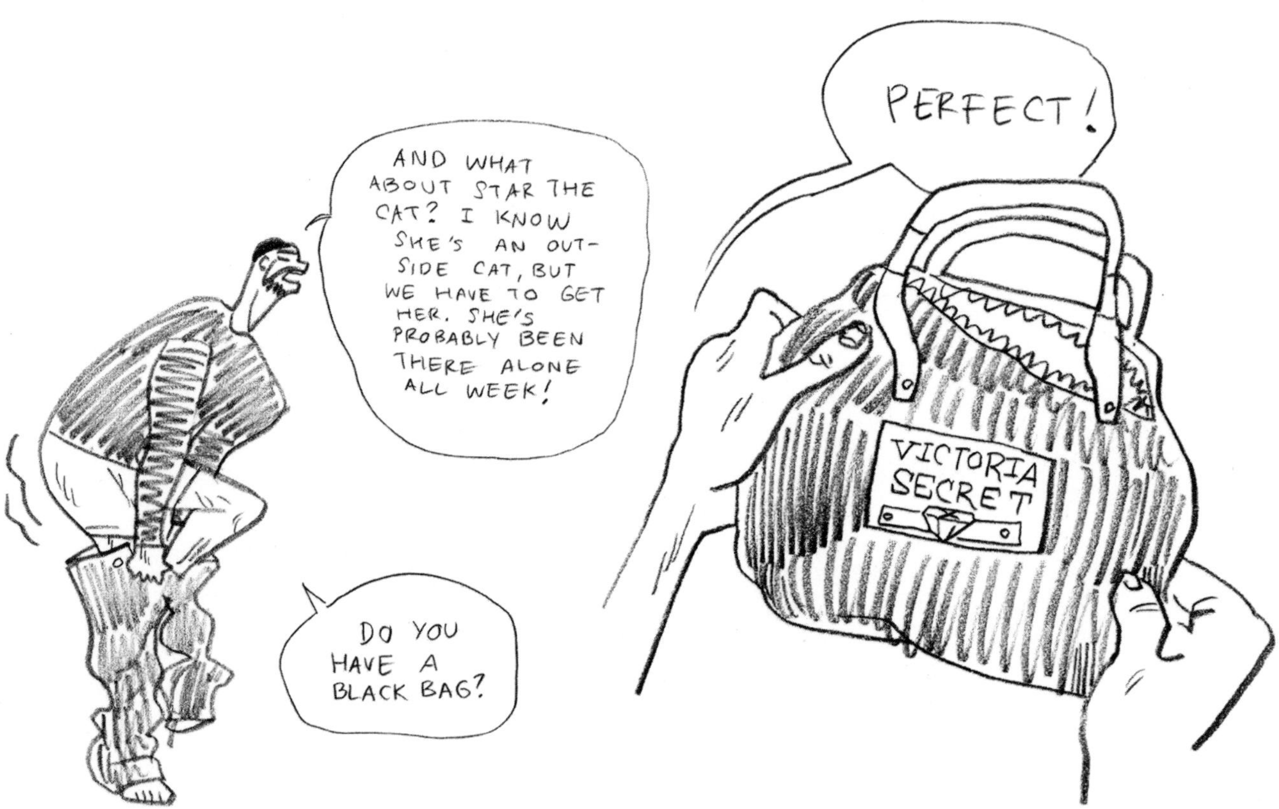
AND WHAT ABOUT STAR THE CAT? I KNOW SHE'S AN OUT-SIDE CAT, BUT WE HAVE TO GET HER. SHE'S PROBABLY BEEN THERE ALONE ALL WEEK!
DO YOU HAVE A BLACK BAG?
PERFECT!
VICTORIA SECRET

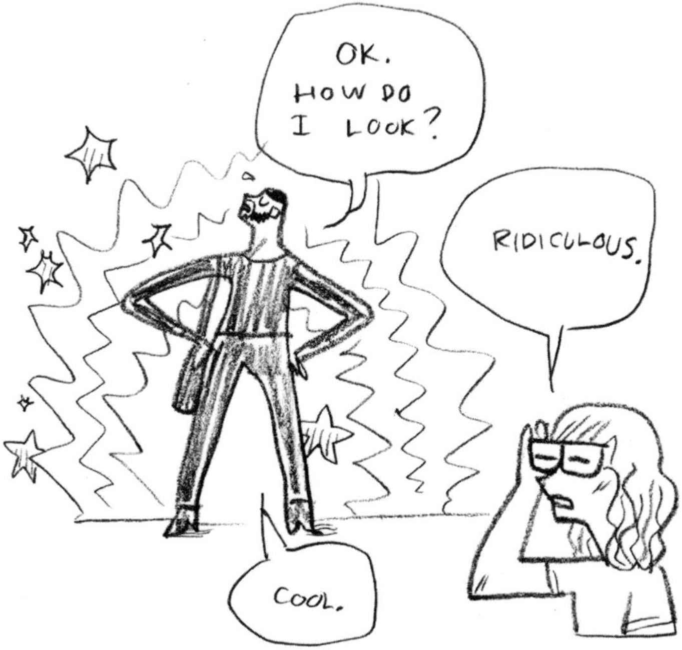
OK. HOW DO I LOOK?
RIDICULOUS.
COOL.

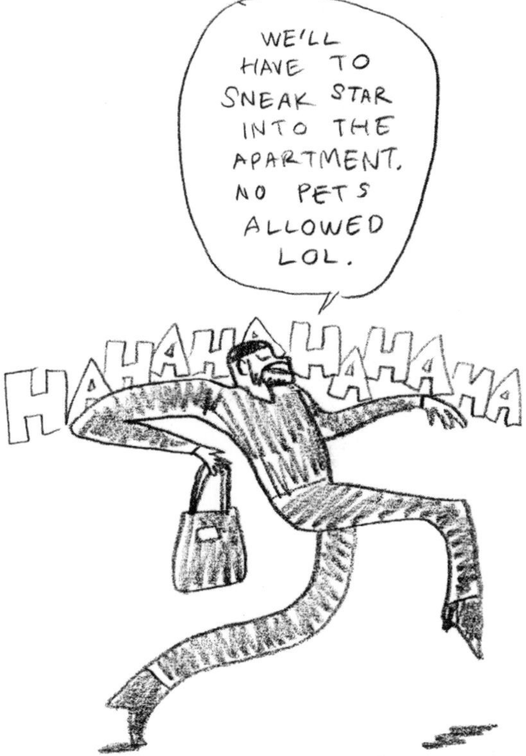
WE'LL HAVE TO SNEAK STAR INTO THE APARTMENT. NO PETS ALLOWED LOL.
HAHAHAHAHAHA

(RUSTLE CRUNCH)

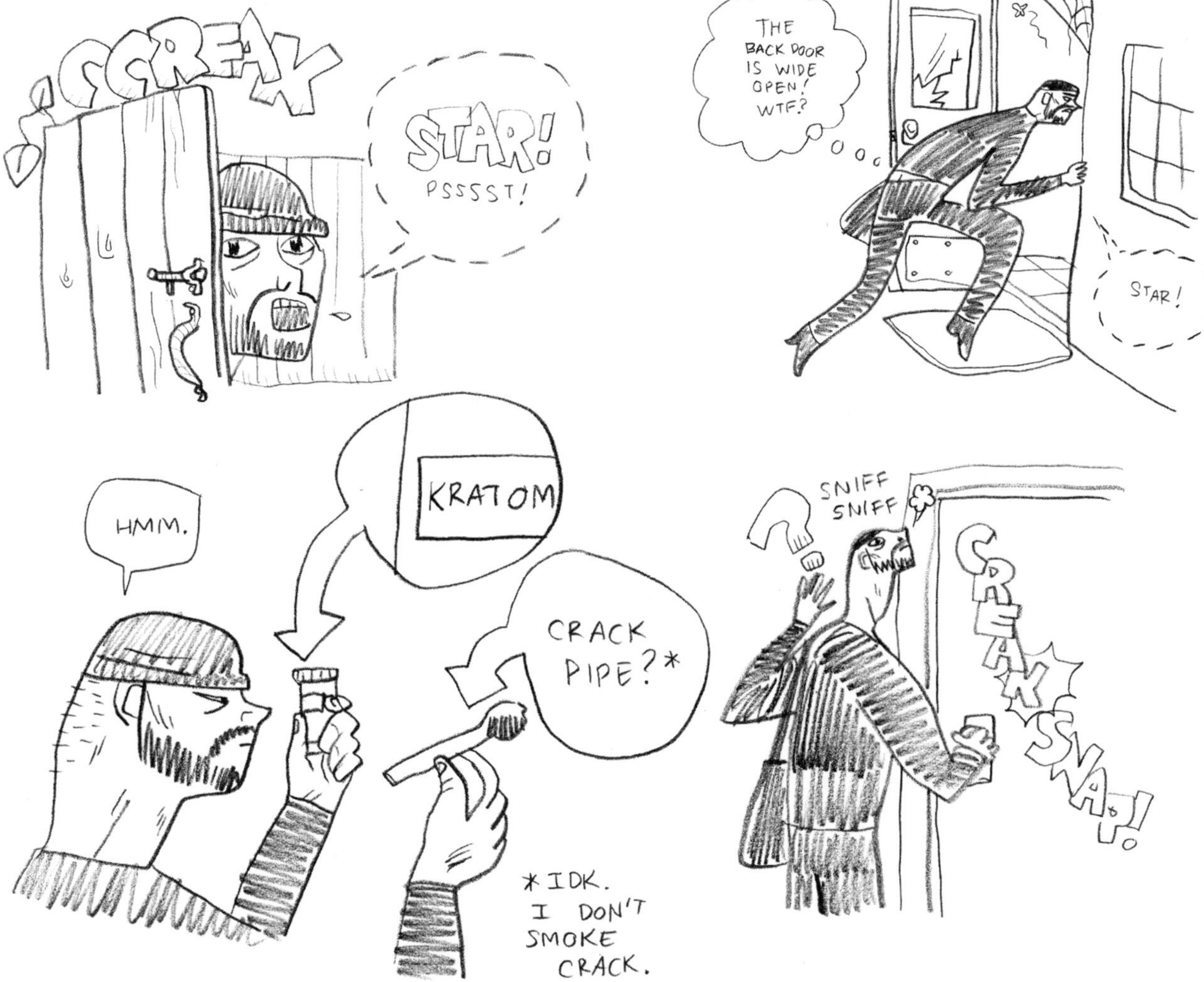
CREAK
STAR!
PSSSST!
THE BACK DOOR IS WIDE OPEN! WTF?
STAR!
HMM.
KRATOM
CRACK PIPE?*
*IDK. I DON'T SMOKE CRACK.
SNIFF SNIFF
?
CREAK
SNAP!

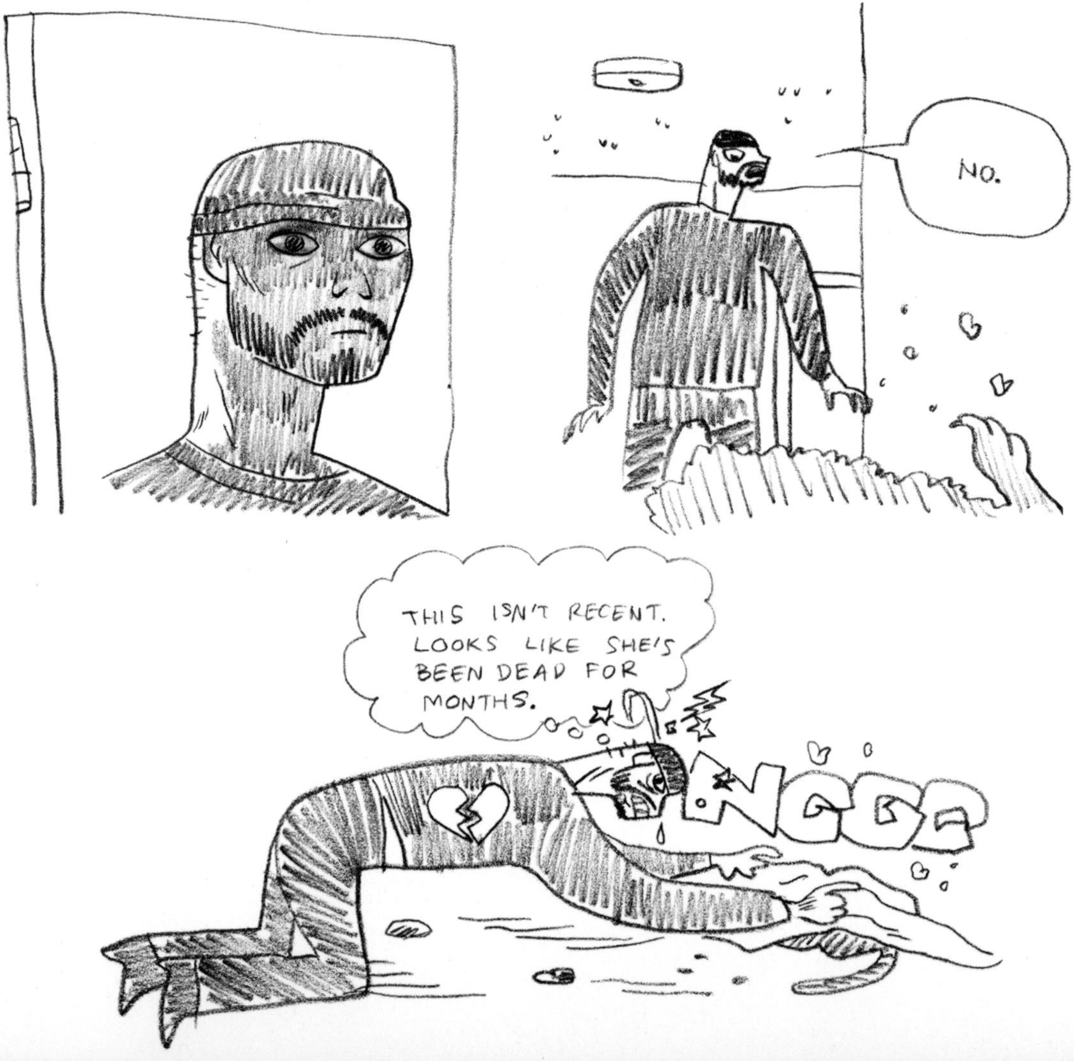
NO.
THIS ISN'T RECENT. LOOKS LIKE SHE'S BEEN DEAD FOR MONTHS.

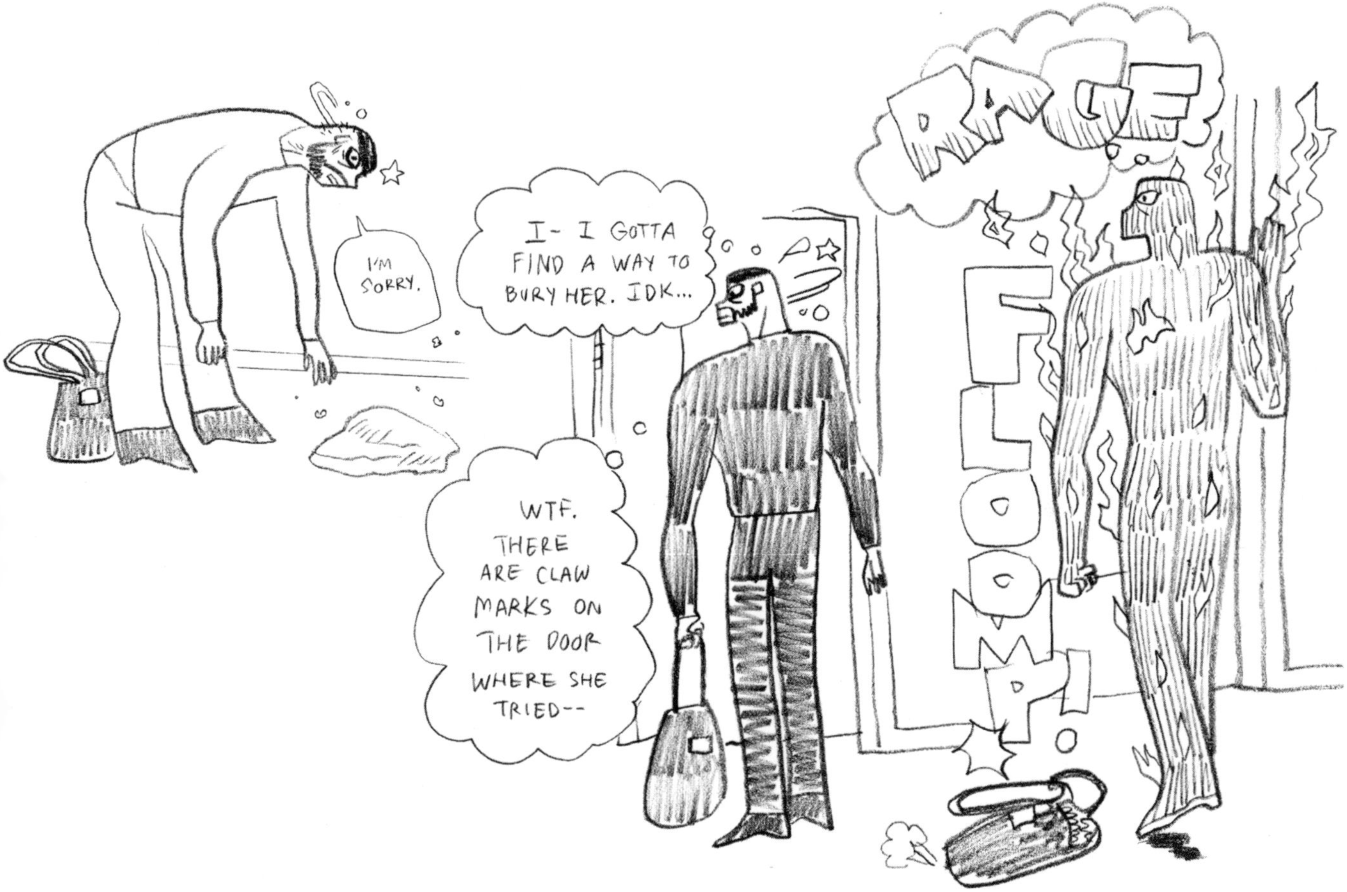
I'M SORRY.
I- I GOTTA FIND A WAY TO BURY HER. IDK...
WTF. THERE ARE CLAW MARKS ON THE DOOR WHERE SHE TRIED--
RAGE
FLLOOMP!

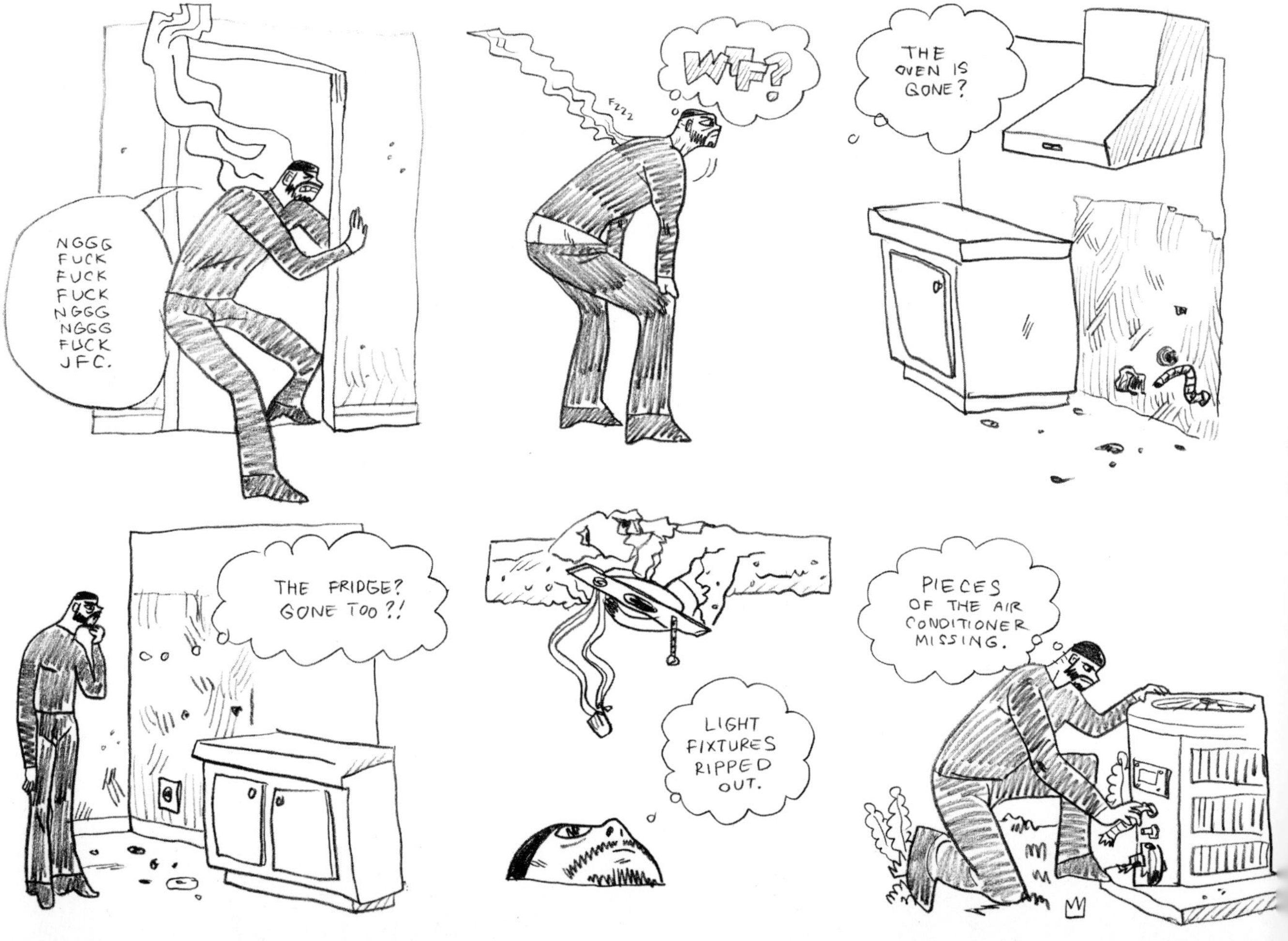
NGGG
FUCK
FUCK
FUCK
NGGG
NGGG
FUCK
JFC.
FZZZ
WTF?
THE OVEN IS GONE?
THE FRIDGE? GONE TOO?!
LIGHT FIXTURES RIPPED OUT.
PIECES OF THE AIR CONDITIONER MISSING.

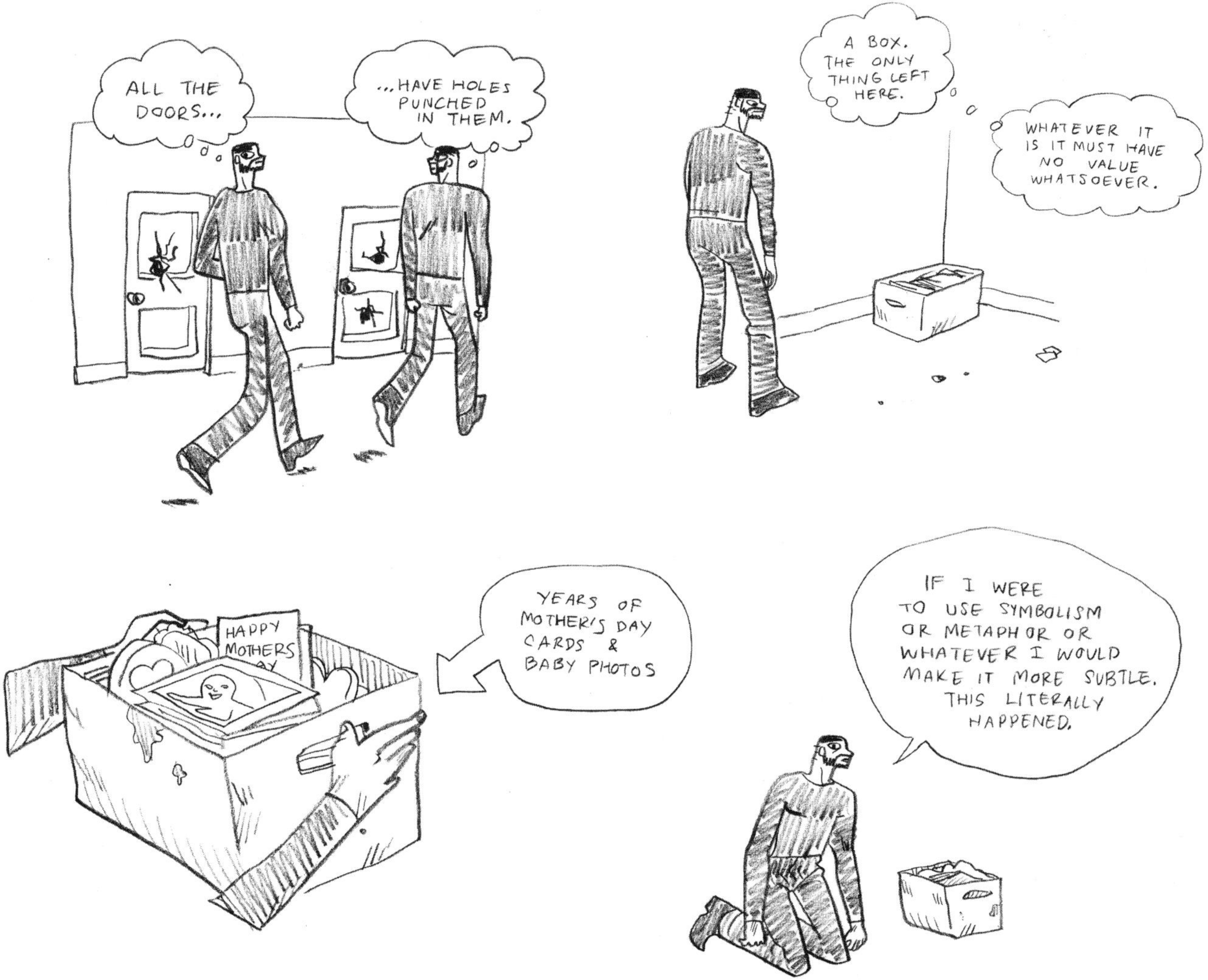
ALL THE DOORS...
...HAVE HOLES PUNCHED IN THEM.
A BOX. THE ONLY THING LEFT HERE.
WHATEVER IT IS IT MUST HAVE NO VALUE WHATSOEVER.
HAPPY MOTHERS
YEARS OF MOTHER'S DAY CARDS & BABY PHOTOS
IF I WERE TO USE SYMBOLISM OR METAPHOR OR WHATEVER I WOULD MAKE IT MORE SUBTLE. THIS LITERALLY HAPPENED.

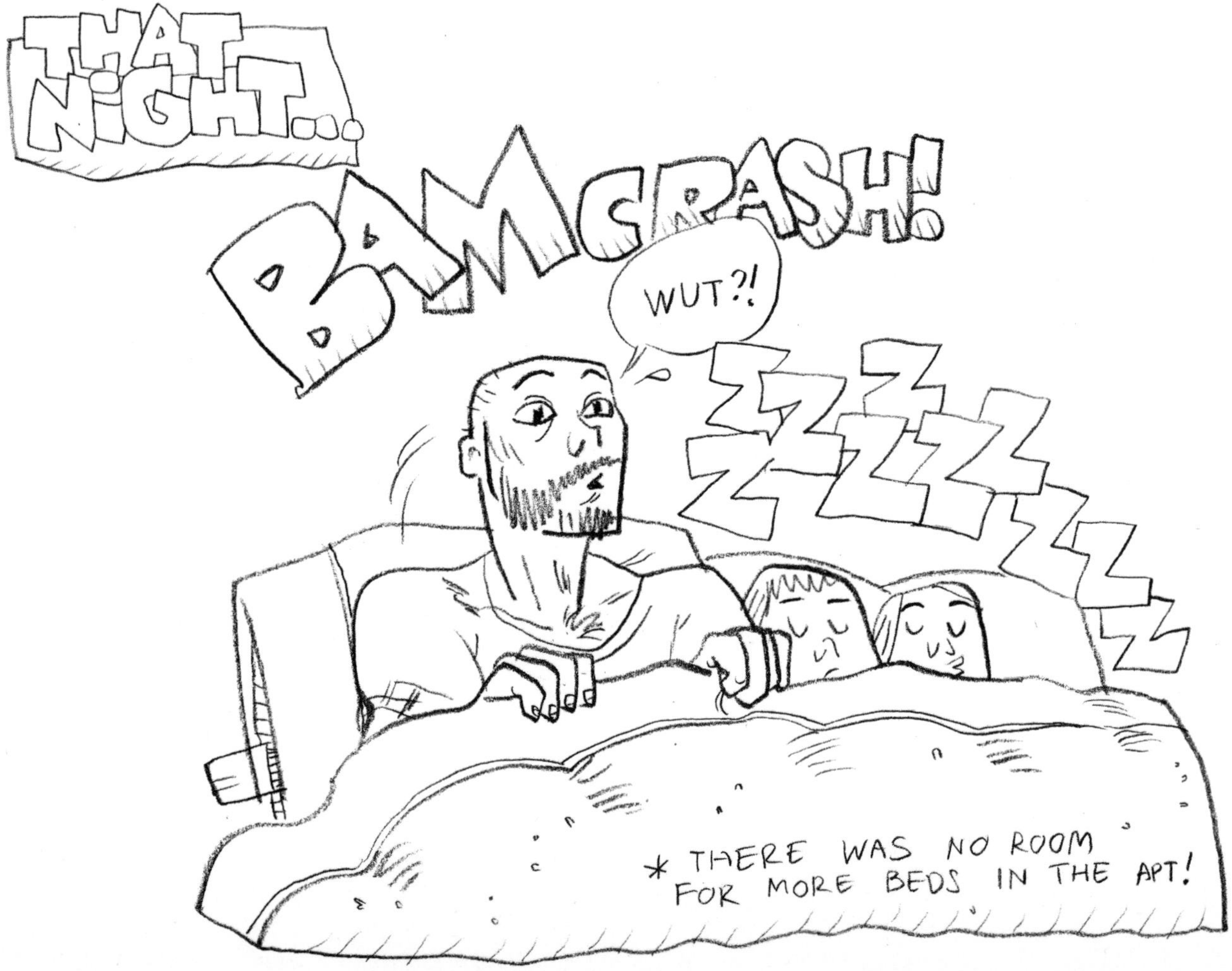
THAT NIGHT...
BAMCRASH!
WUT?!
ZZZZZZZZZZ
* THERE WAS NO ROOM FOR MORE BEDS IN THE APT!

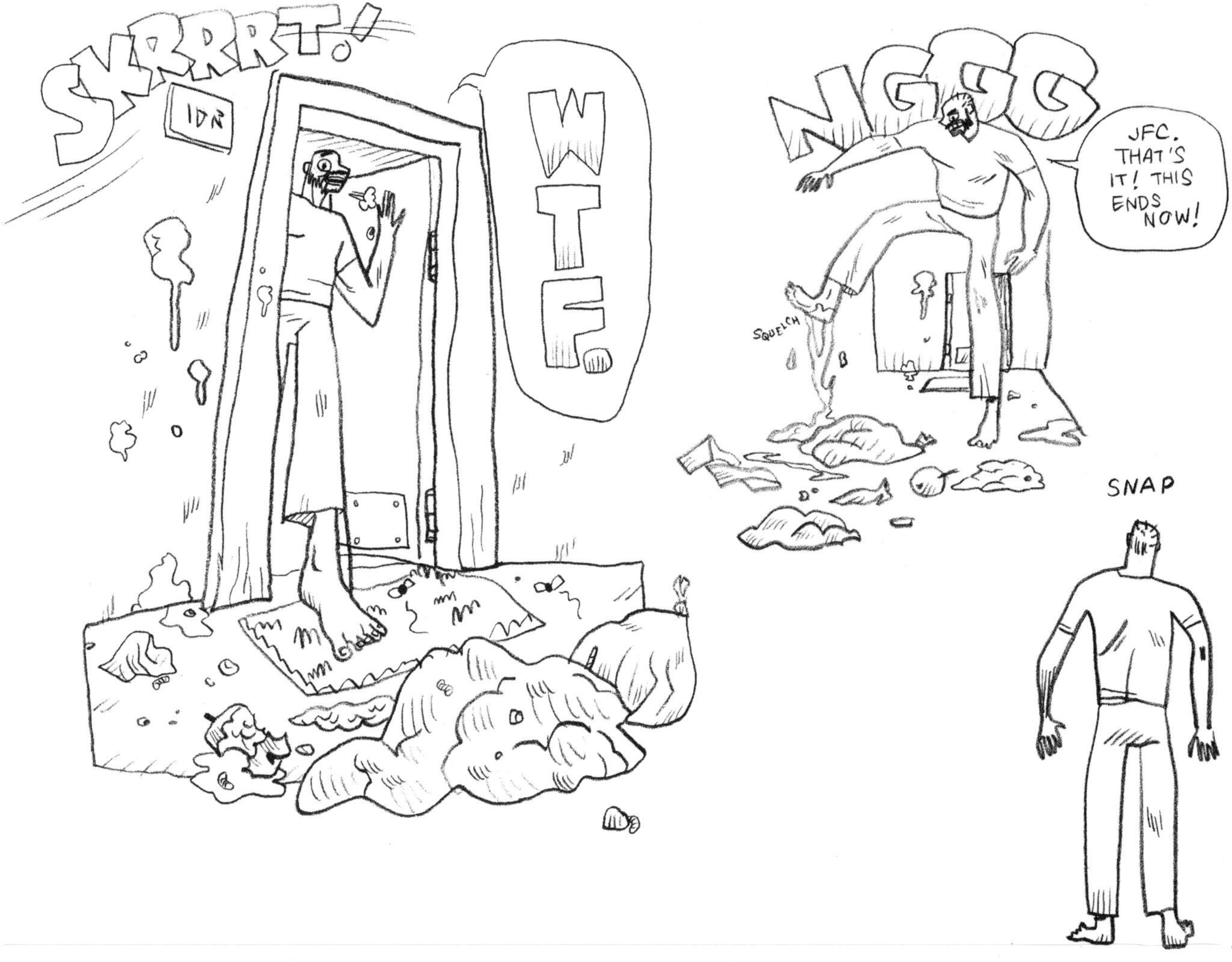
SKRRRT!
WTF.
NGGG
JFC. THAT'S IT! THIS ENDS NOW!
SQUELCH
SNAP

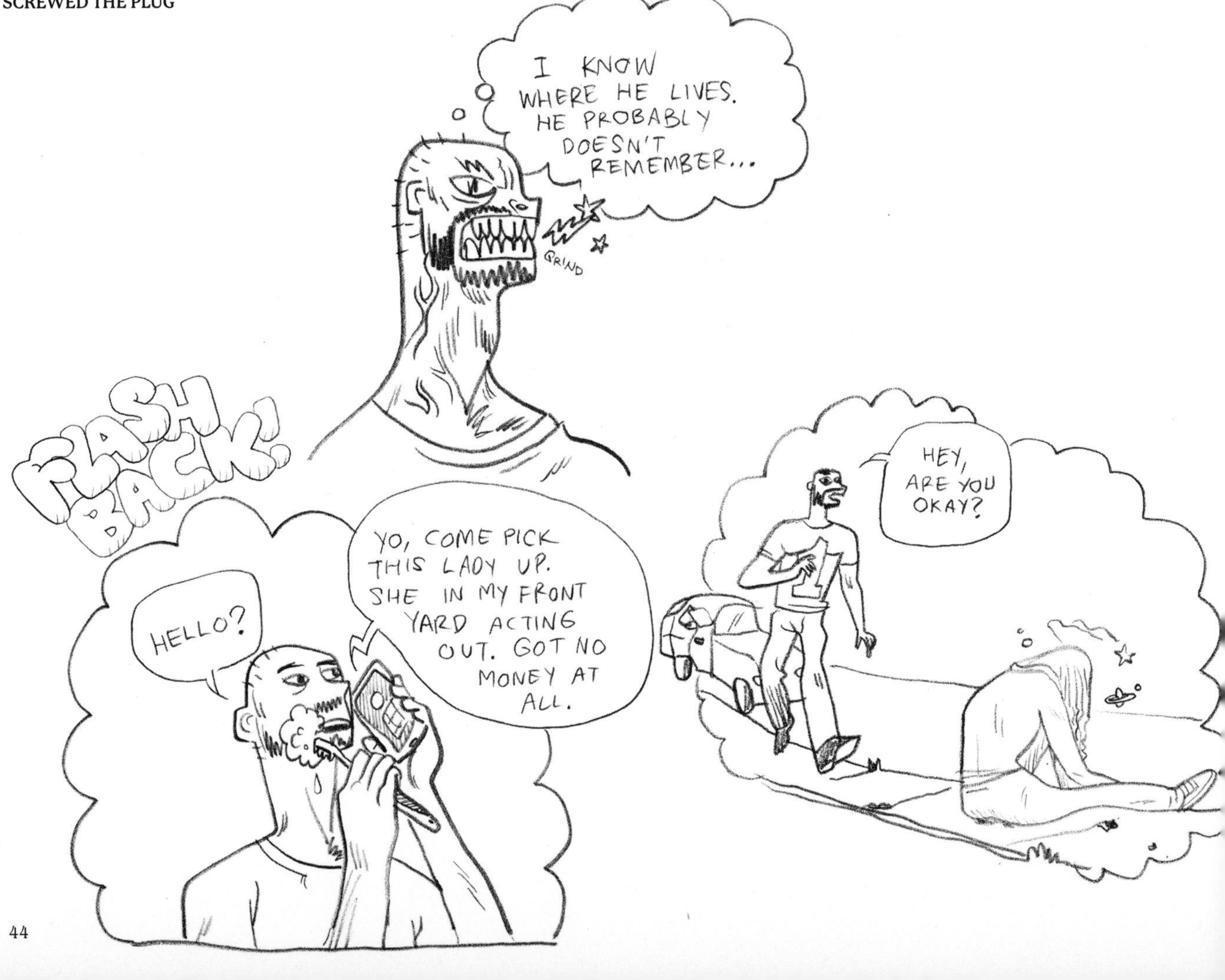
I KNOW WHERE HE LIVES. HE PROBABLY DOESN'T REMEMBER...
GRIND
FLASH BACK!
HELLO?
YO, COME PICK THIS LADY UP. SHE IN MY FRONT YARD ACTING OUT. GOT NO MONEY AT ALL.
HEY, ARE YOU OKAY?

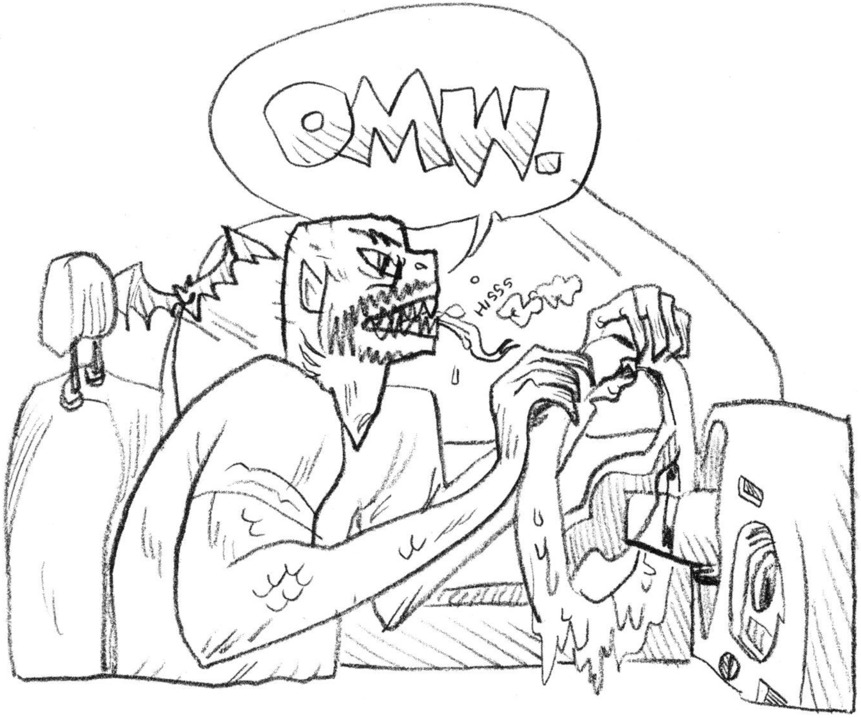
OMW.
HISSS
SSSSH

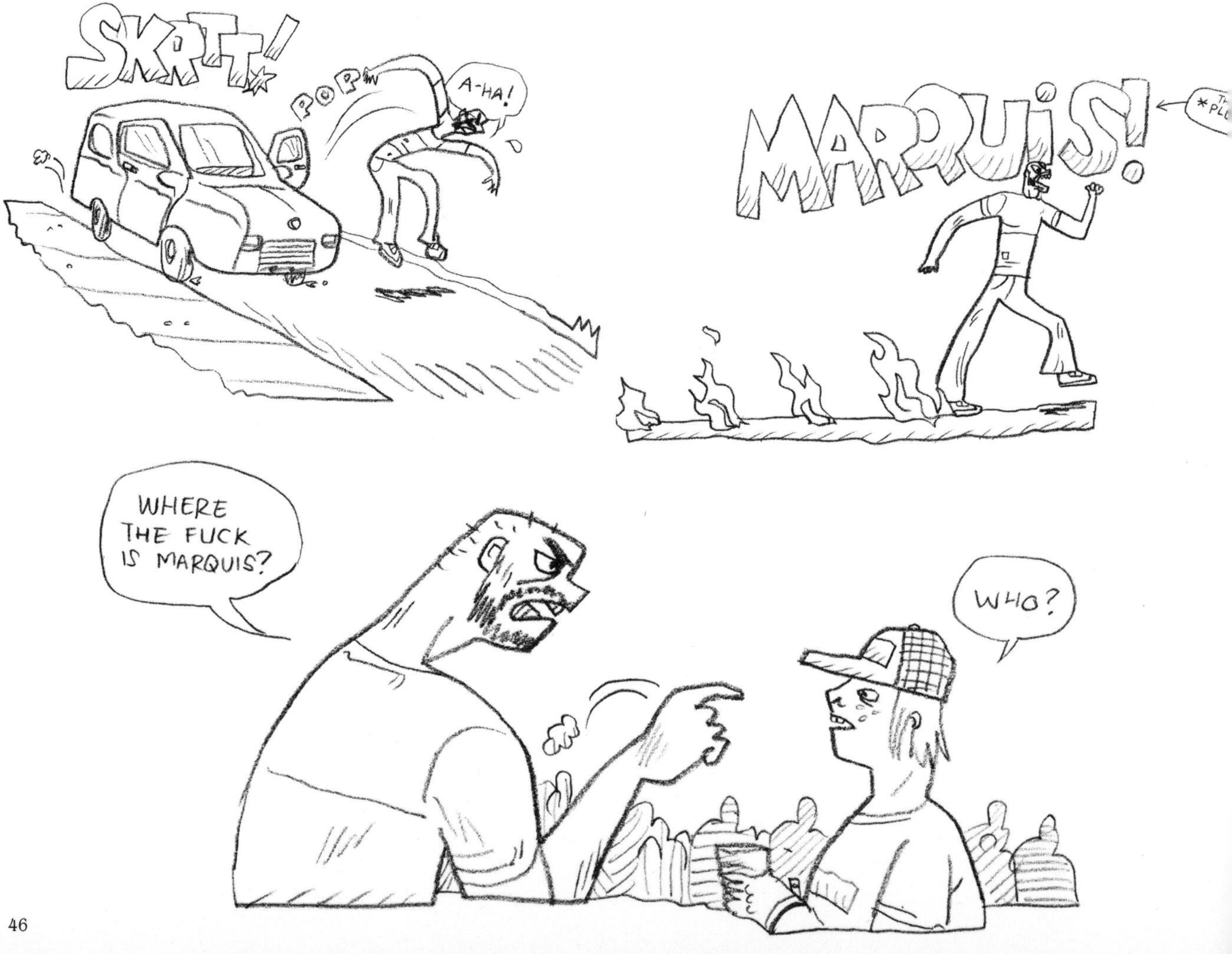
SKRTT!
POP
A-HA!
MARQUIS!
WHERE THE FUCK IS MARQUIS?
WHO?

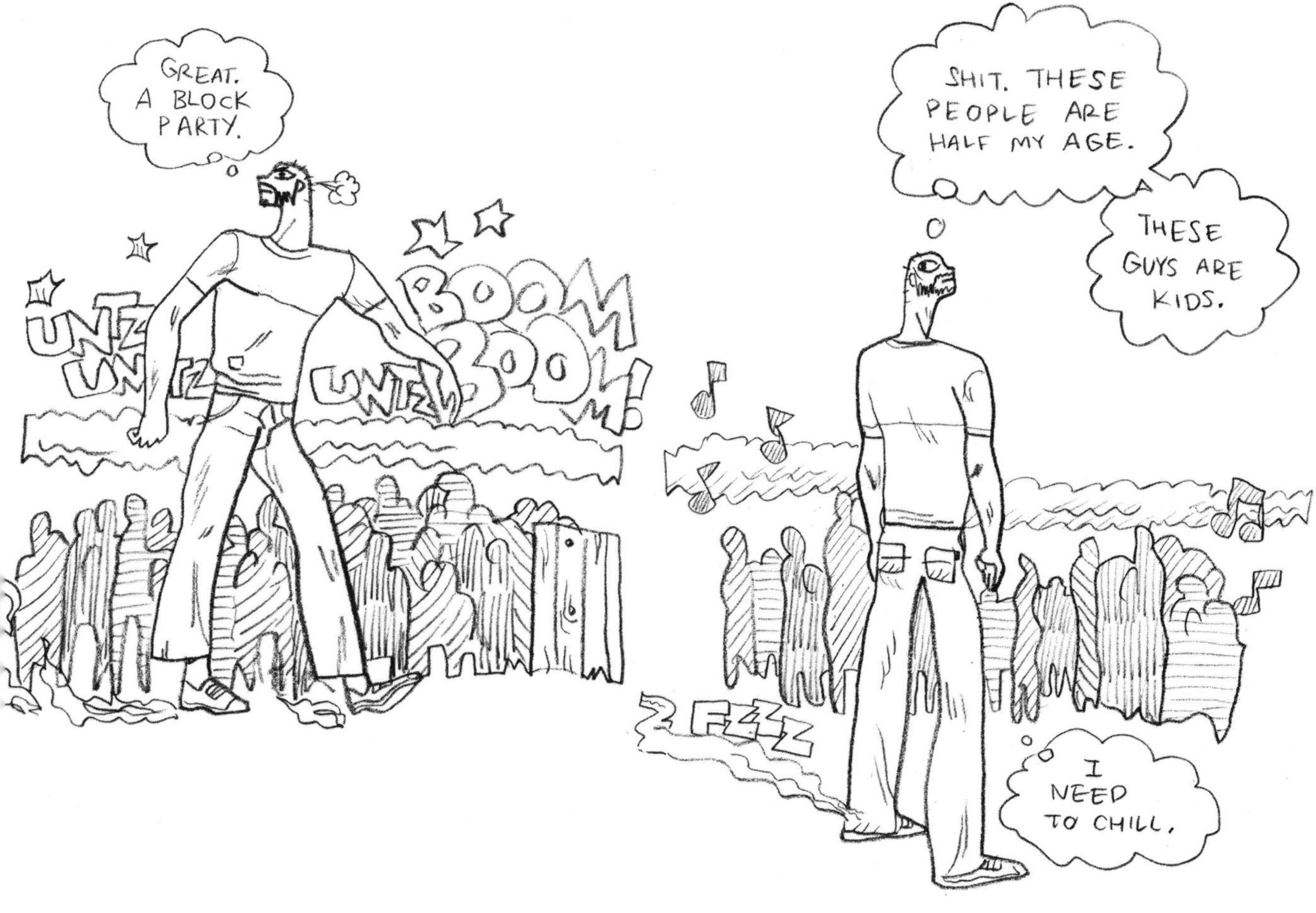
GREAT. A BLOCK PARTY.
UNTZ UNTZ
UNTZ
BOOM BOOM!
SHIT. THESE PEOPLE ARE HALF MY AGE.
THESE GUYS ARE KIDS.
ZFZZZ
I NEED TO CHILL.

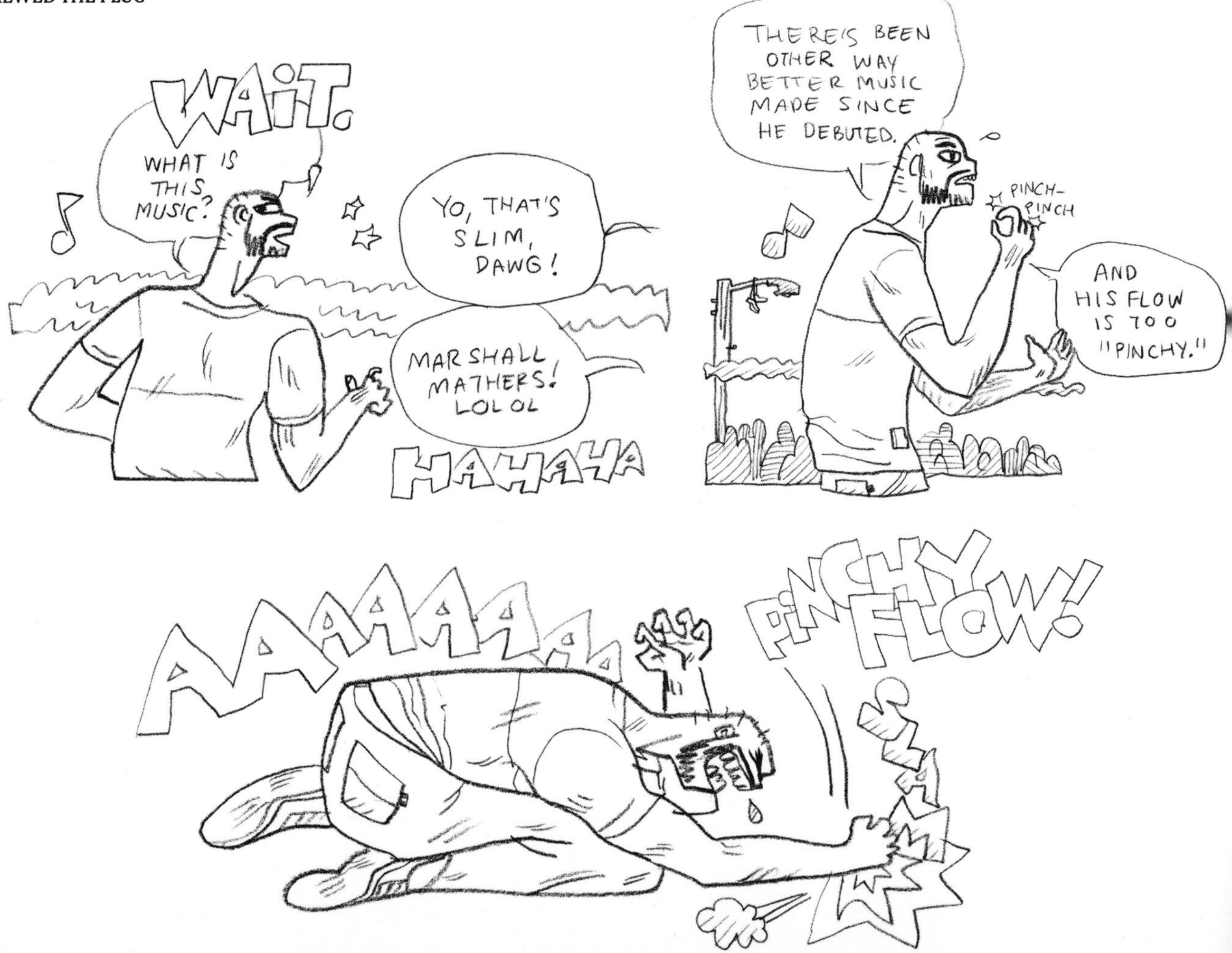
WAIT.
WHAT IS THIS MUSIC?
YO, THAT'S SLIM, DAWG!
MARSHALL MATHERS! LOL OL
HAHAHA
THERE'S BEEN OTHER WAY BETTER MUSIC MADE SINCE HE DEBUTED.
PINCH-PINCH
AND HIS FLOW IS TOO "PINCHY."
AAAAAAA
PINCHY FLOW!

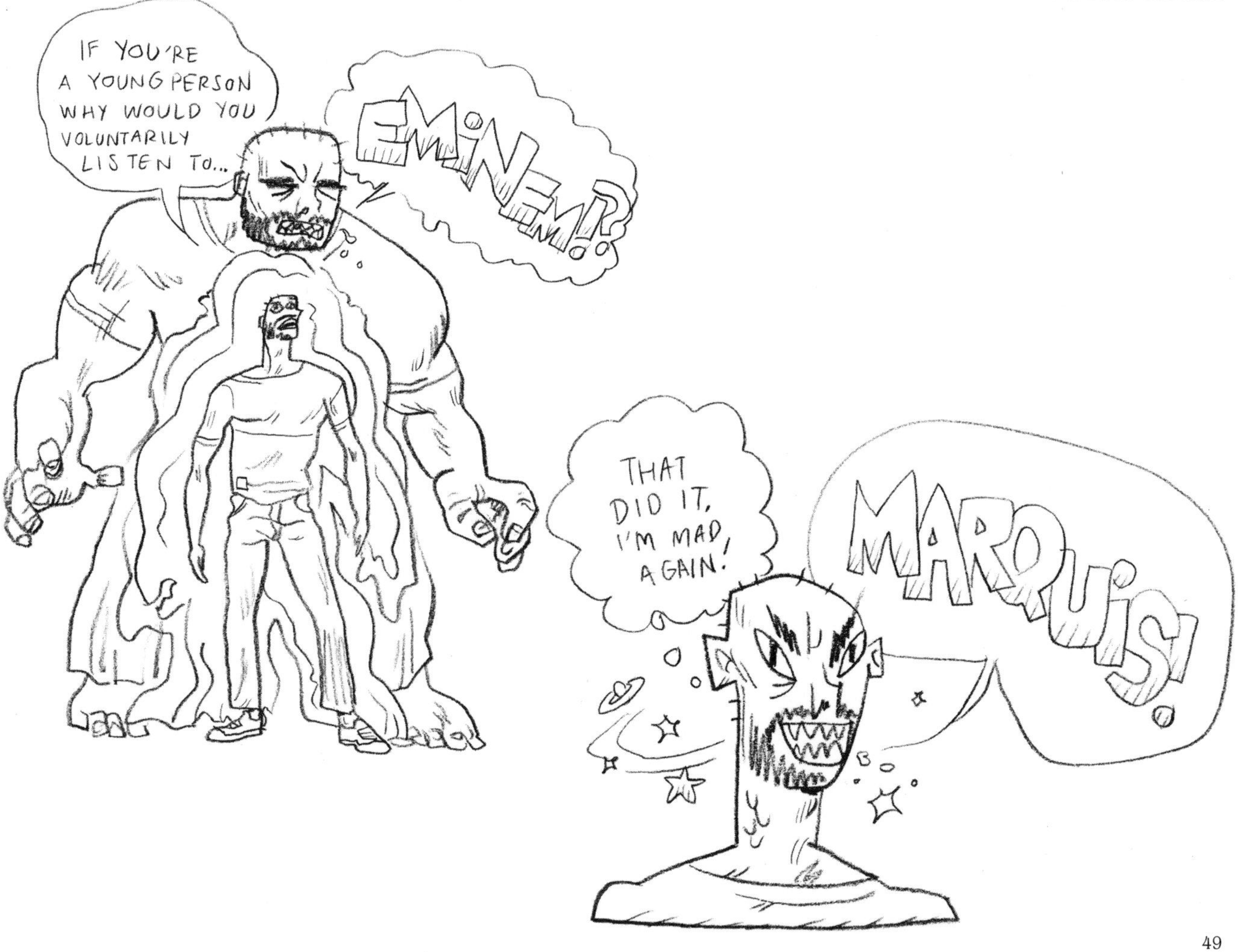
IF YOU'RE A YOUNG PERSON WHY WOULD YOU VOLUNTARILY LISTEN TO...
EMINEM!?
THAT DID IT, I'M MAD, AGAIN!
MARQUIS!

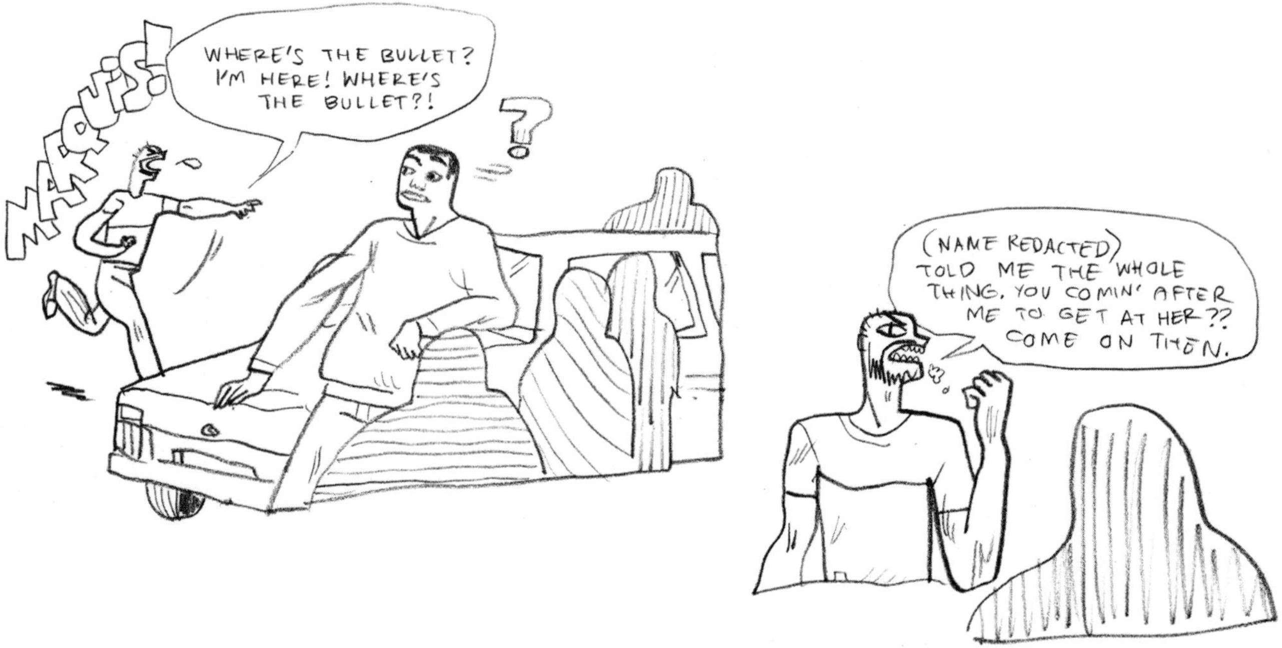
MARQUIS!
WHERE'S THE BULLET? I'M HERE! WHERE'S THE BULLET?!
?
(NAME REDACTED) TOLD ME THE WHOLE THING. YOU COMIN' AFTER ME TO GET AT HER?? COME ON THEN.

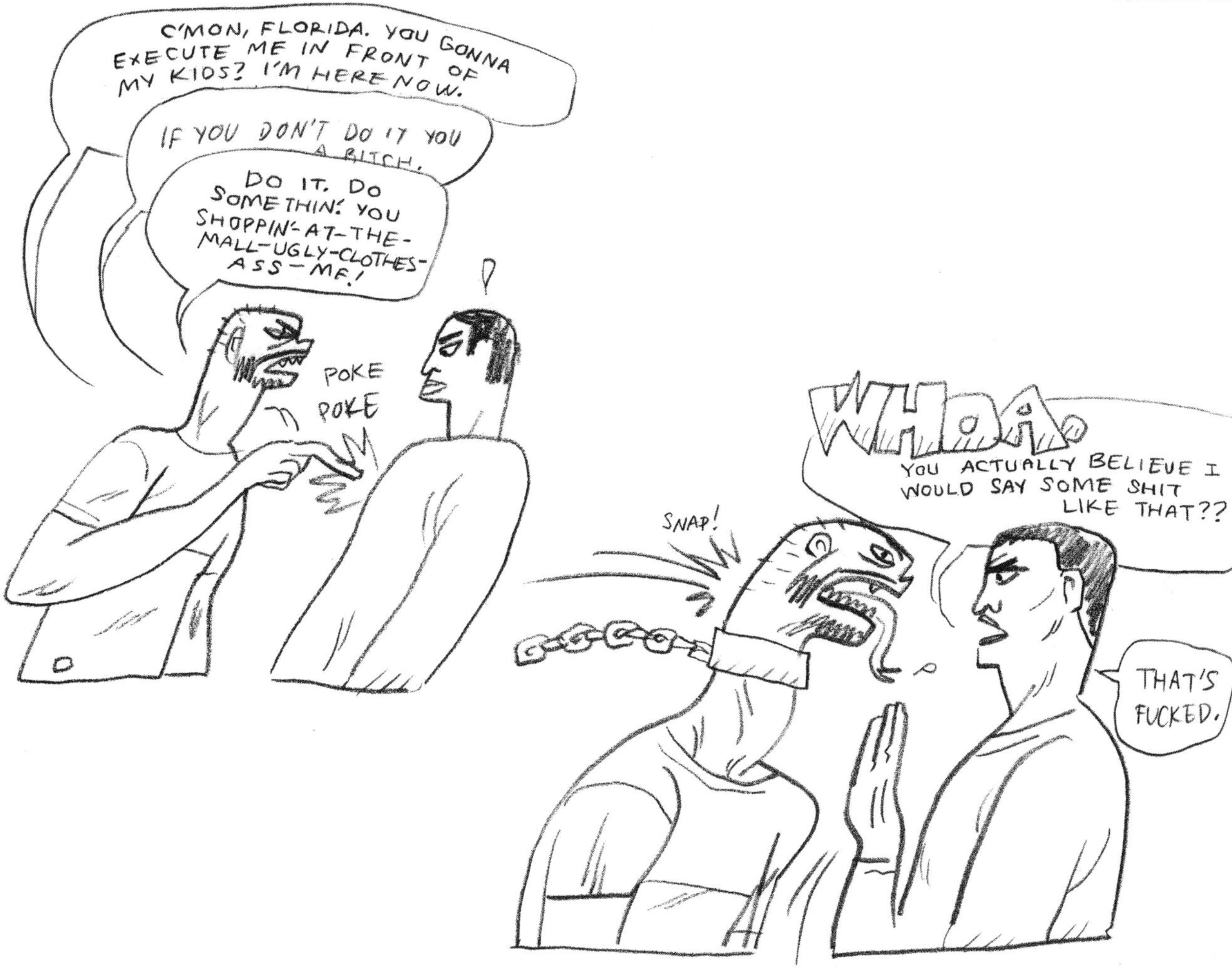
C'MON, FLORIDA. YOU GONNA EXECUTE ME IN FRONT OF MY KIDS? I'M HERE NOW.
IF YOU DON'T DO IT YOU A BITCH.
DO IT. DO SOMETHIN'! YOU SHOPPIN'-AT-THE-MALL-UGLY-CLOTHES-ASS-MF!
POKE
POKE
WHOA.
YOU ACTUALLY BELIEVE I WOULD SAY SOME SHIT LIKE THAT??
SNAP!
THAT'S FUCKED.

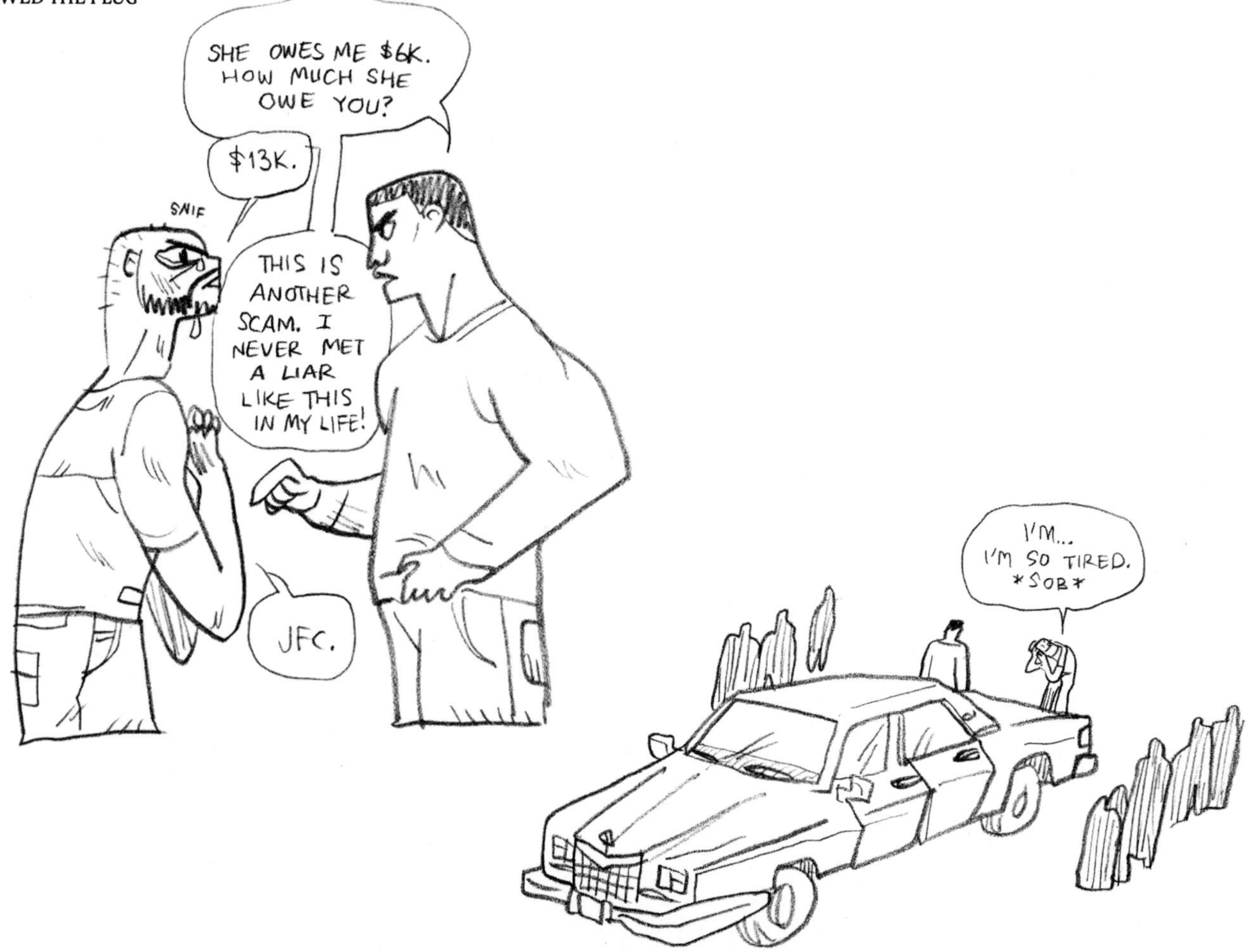
SHE OWES ME $6K. HOW MUCH SHE OWE YOU?
$13K.
SNIF
THIS IS ANOTHER SCAM. I NEVER MET A LIAR LIKE THIS IN MY LIFE!
JFC.
I'M... I'M SO TIRED. *SOB*

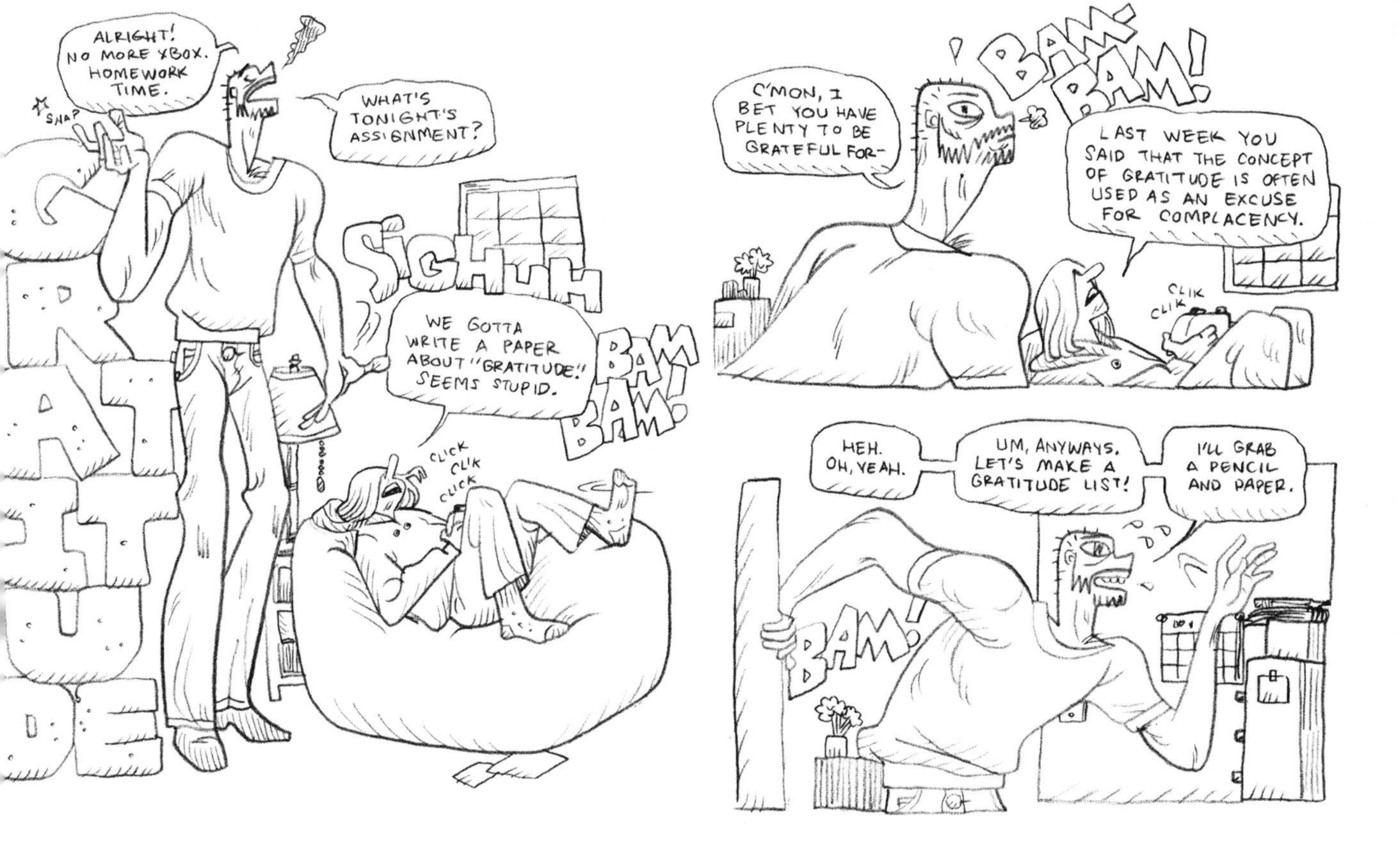
GRATITUDE
ALRIGHT! NO MORE XBOX. HOMEWORK TIME.
SNAP
WHAT'S TONIGHT'S ASSIGNMENT?
SIGHUH
WE GOTTA WRITE A PAPER ABOUT "GRATITUDE." SEEMS STUPID.
BAM BAM!
CLICK CLIK CLICK
C'MON, I BET YOU HAVE PLENTY TO BE GRATEFUL FOR-
BAM BAM!
LAST WEEK YOU SAID THAT THE CONCEPT OF GRATITUDE IS OFTEN USED AS AN EXCUSE FOR COMPLACENCY.
CLIK CLIK
HEH. OH, YEAH.
UM, ANYWAYS. LET'S MAKE A GRATITUDE LIST!
I'LL GRAB A PENCIL AND PAPER.
BAM!

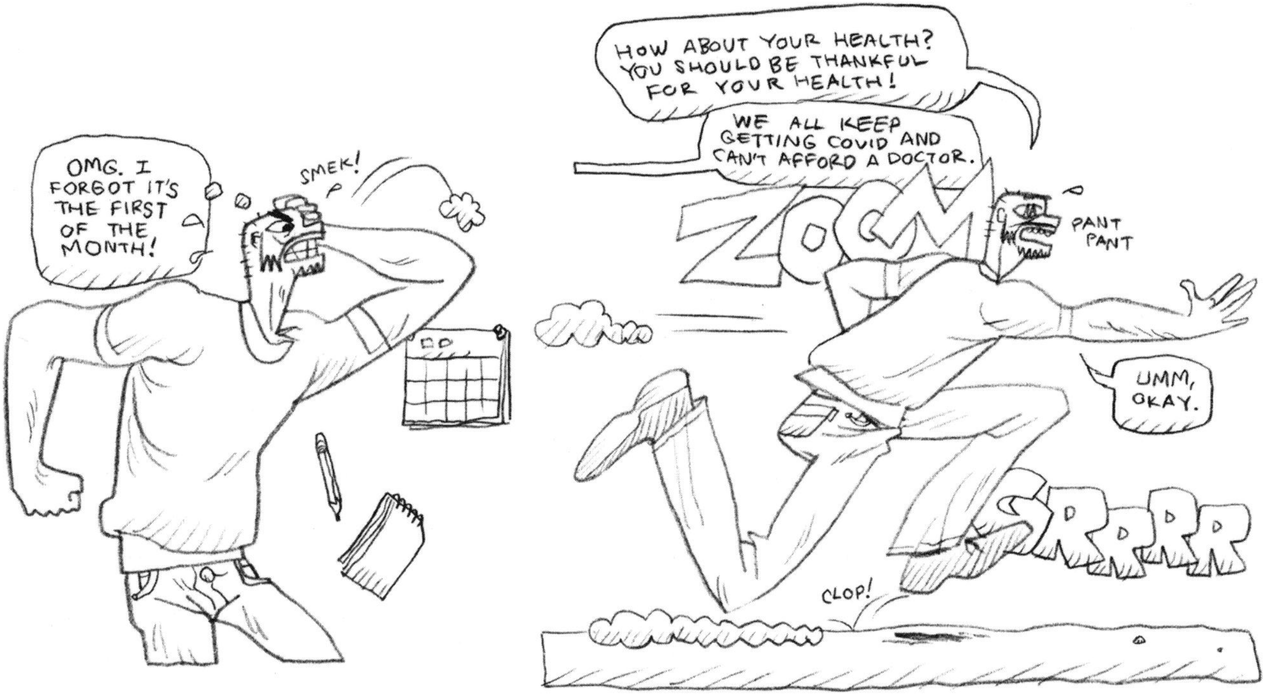
OMG. I FORGOT IT'S THE FIRST OF THE MONTH!
SMEK!
HOW ABOUT YOUR HEALTH? YOU SHOULD BE THANKFUL FOR YOUR HEALTH!
WE ALL KEEP GETTING COVID AND CAN'T AFFORD A DOCTOR.
ZOOM
PANT PANT
UMM, OKAY.
SRRRR
CLOP!

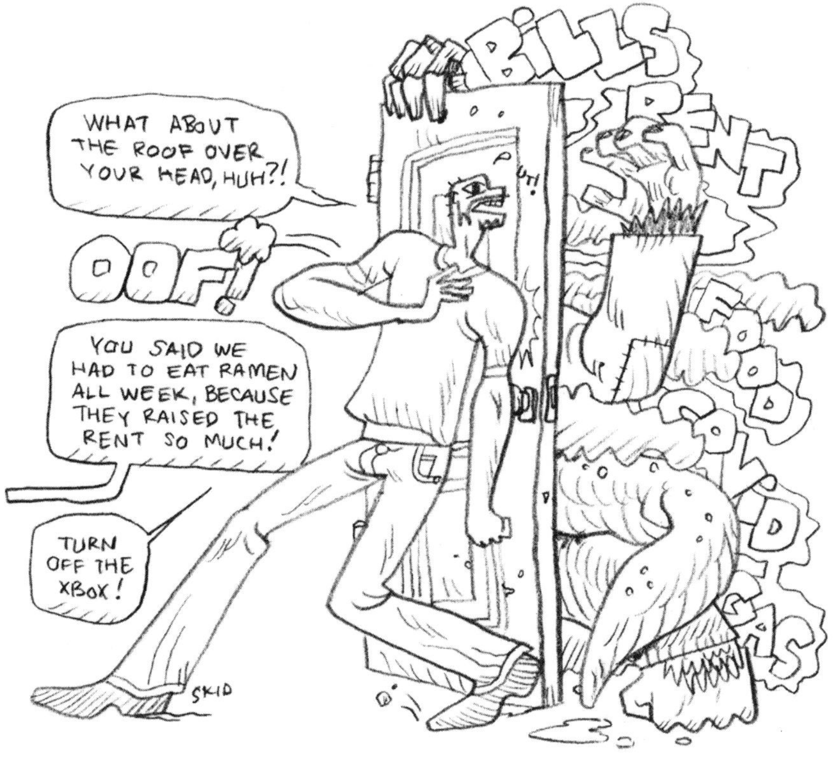
WHAT ABOUT THE ROOF OVER YOUR HEAD, HUH?!
OOF!
YOU SAID WE HAD TO EAT RAMEN ALL WEEK, BECAUSE THEY RAISED THE RENT SO MUCH!
TURN OFF THE XBOX!
BILLS
RENT
FOOD
COVID
GAS
SKID

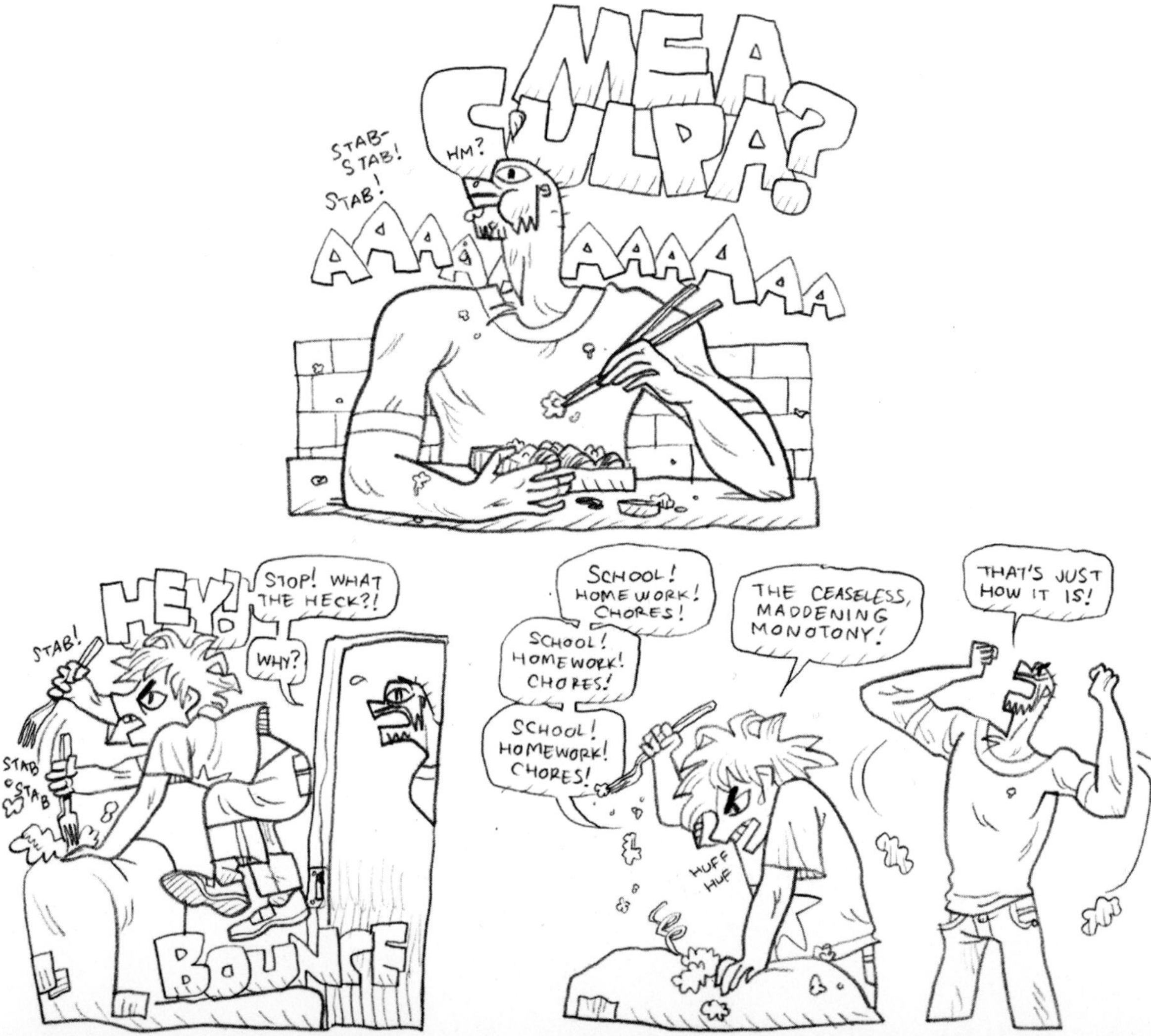
MEA CULPA?
HM?
STAB-STAB!
STAB!
AAAAAAAAAAA
HEY!
STOP! WHAT THE HECK?!
WHY?
STAB!
STAB STAB
BOUNCE
SCHOOL! HOMEWORK! CHORES!
SCHOOL! HOMEWORK! CHORES!
SCHOOL! HOMEWORK! CHORES!
THE CEASELESS, MADDENING MONOTONY!
HUFF HUF
THAT'S JUST HOW IT IS!

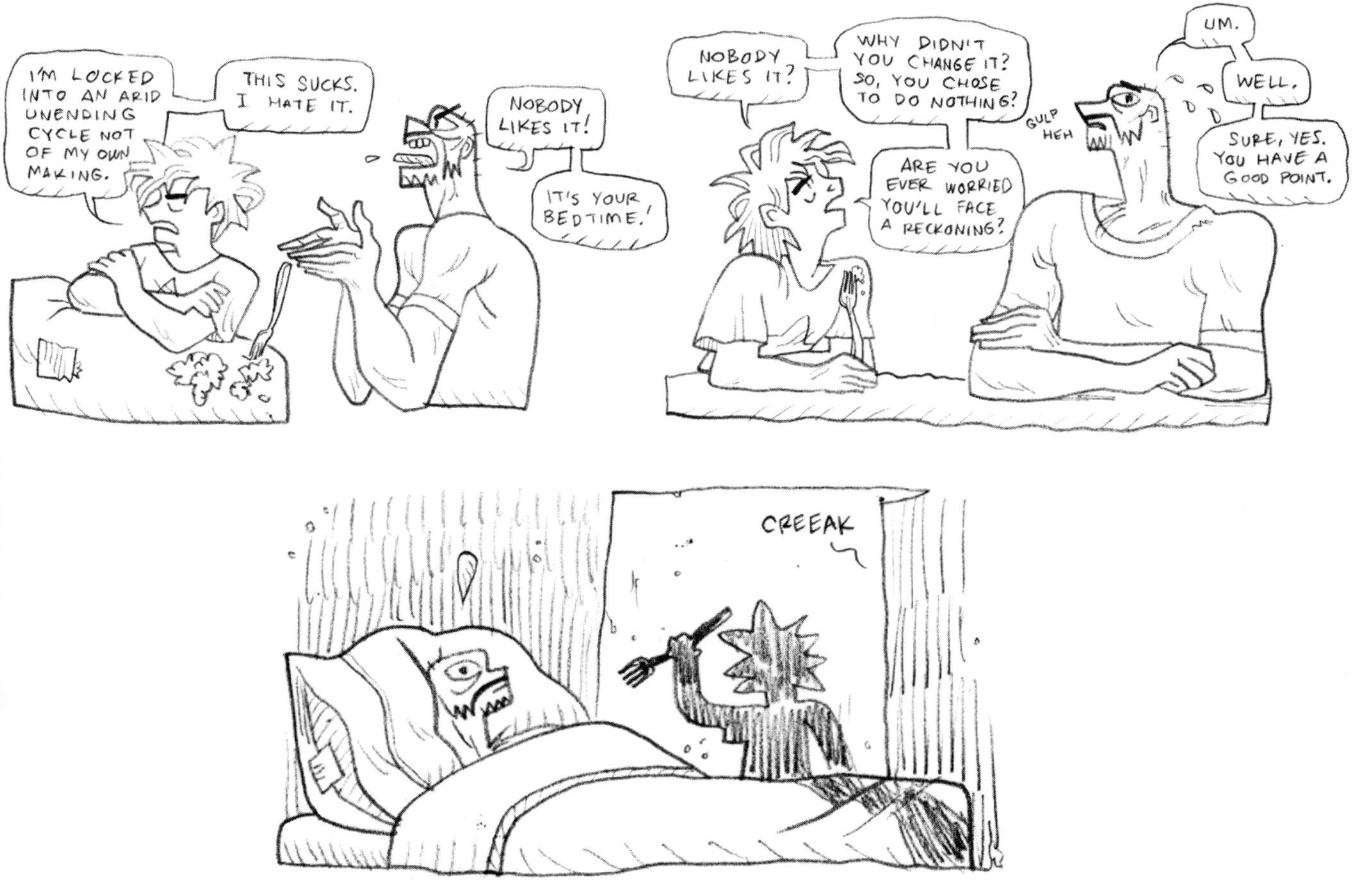
I'M LOCKED INTO AN ARID UNENDING CYCLE NOT OF MY OWN MAKING.
THIS SUCKS. I HATE IT.
NOBODY LIKES IT!
IT'S YOUR BEDTIME!
NOBODY LIKES IT?
WHY DIDN'T YOU CHANGE IT? SO, YOU CHOSE TO DO NOTHING?
ARE YOU EVER WORRIED YOU'LL FACE A RECKONING?
GULP
HEH
UM.
WELL.
SURE, YES. YOU HAVE A GOOD POINT.
CREEAK

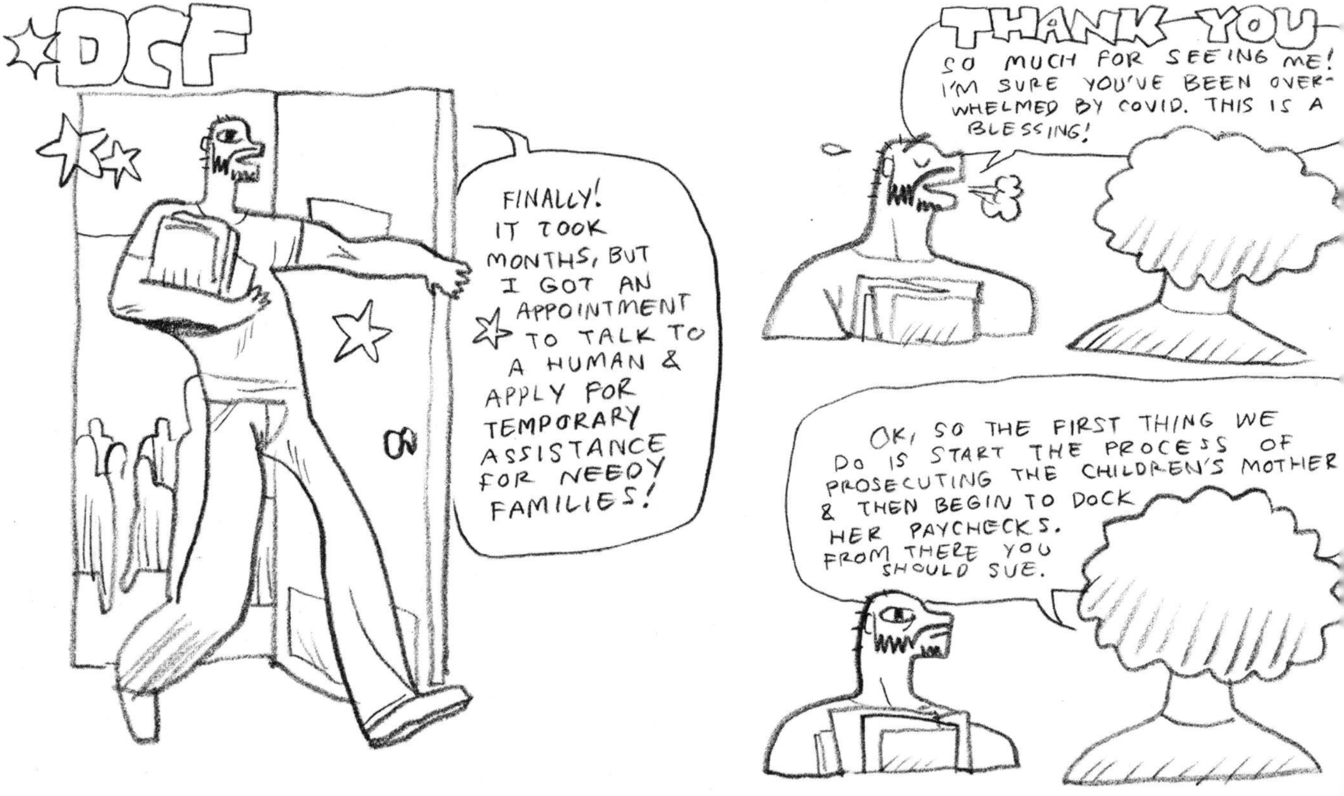
DCF
FINALLY! IT TOOK MONTHS, BUT I GOT AN APPOINTMENT TO TALK TO A HUMAN & APPLY FOR TEMPORARY ASSISTANCE FOR NEEDY FAMILIES!
THANK YOU SO MUCH FOR SEEING ME! I'M SURE YOU'VE BEEN OVER-WHELMED BY COVID. THIS IS A BLESSING!
OK, SO THE FIRST THING WE DO IS START THE PROCESS OF PROSECUTING THE CHILDREN'S MOTHER & THEN BEGIN TO DOCK HER PAYCHECKS. FROM THERE YOU SHOULD SUE.

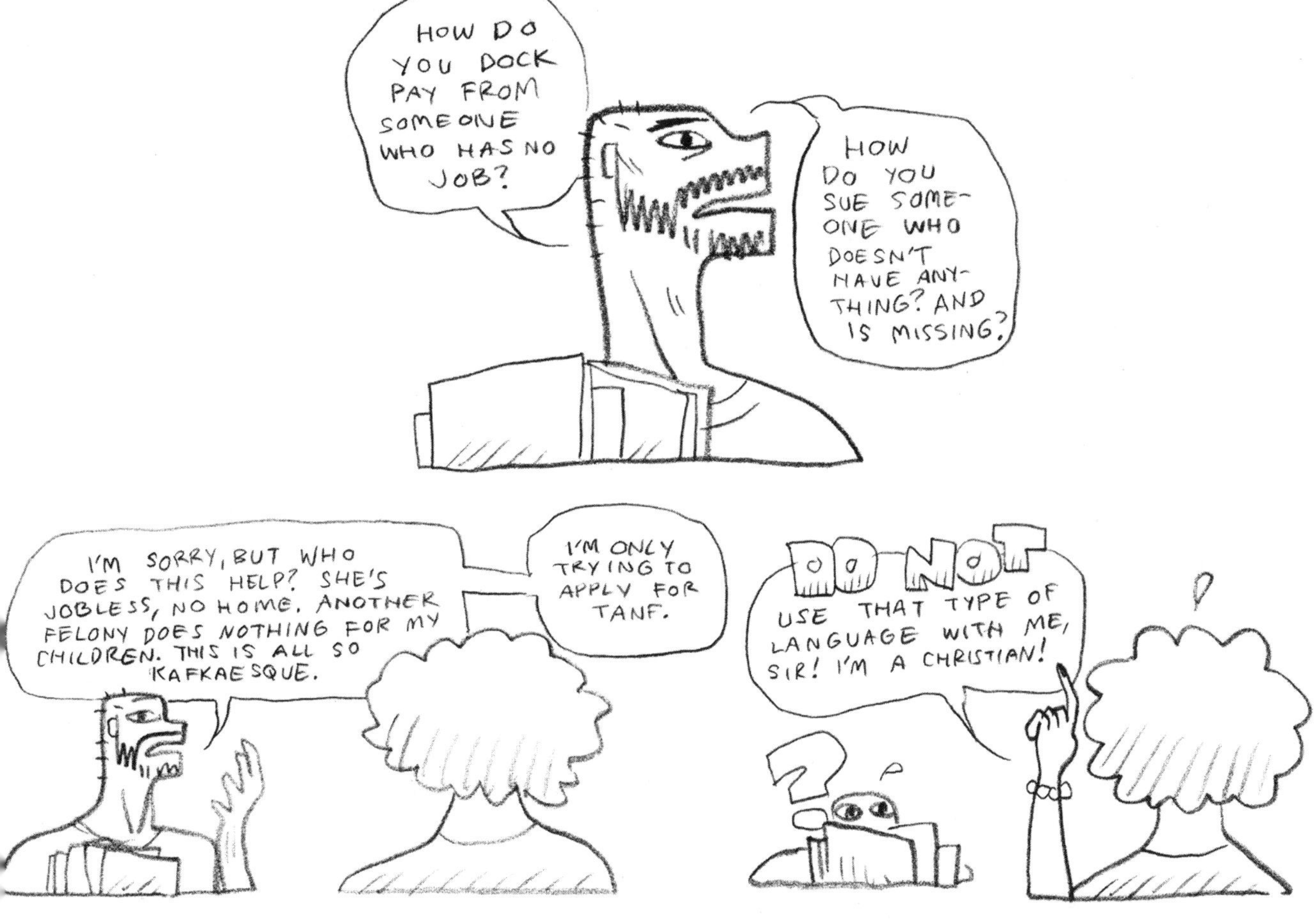
HOW DO YOU DOCK PAY FROM SOMEONE WHO HAS NO JOB?
HOW DO YOU SUE SOMEONE WHO DOESN'T HAVE ANYTHING? AND IS MISSING?
I'M SORRY, BUT WHO DOES THIS HELP? SHE'S JOBLESS, NO HOME. ANOTHER FELONY DOES NOTHING FOR MY CHILDREN. THIS IS ALL SO KAFKAESQUE.
I'M ONLY TRYING TO APPLY FOR TANF.
DO NOT
USE THAT TYPE OF LANGUAGE WITH ME, SIR! I'M A CHRISTIAN!

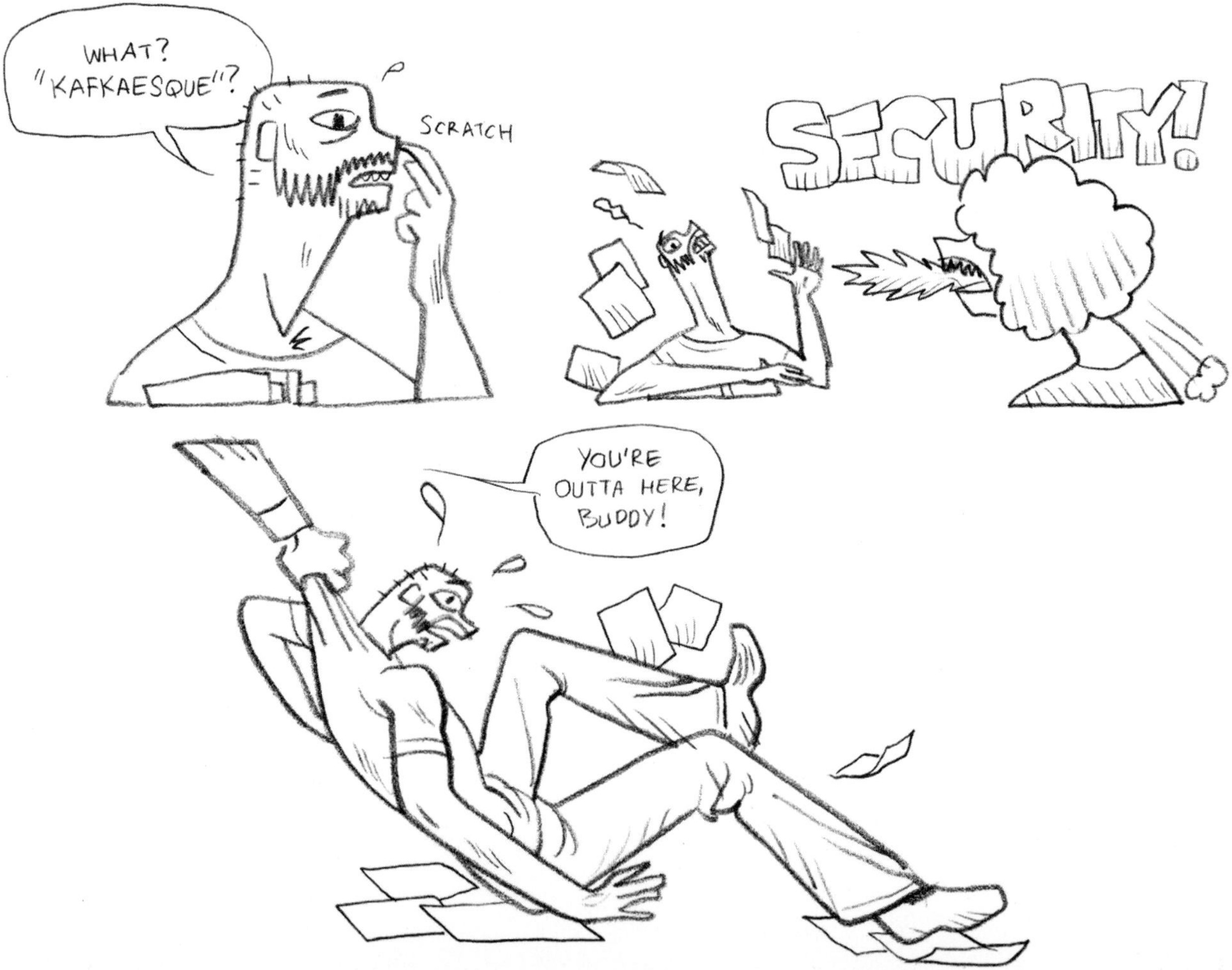
WHAT? "KAFKAESQUE"?
SCRATCH
SECURITY!
YOU'RE OUTTA HERE, BUDDY!

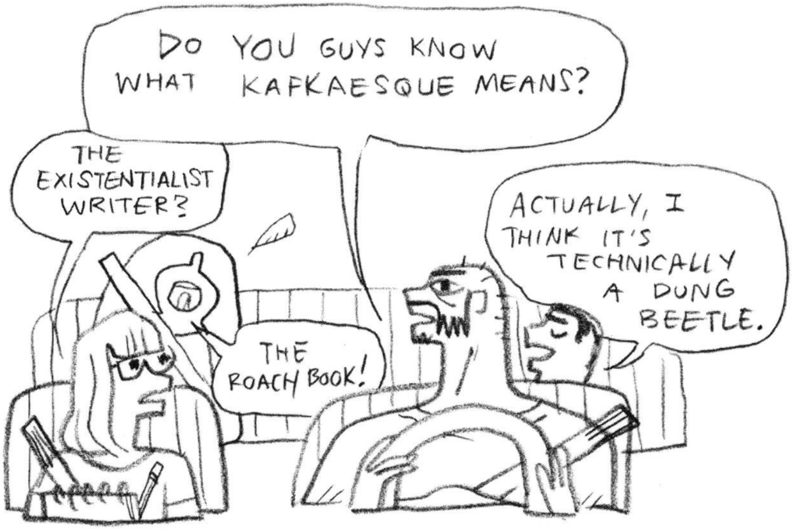
DO YOU GUYS KNOW WHAT KAFKAESQUE MEANS?
THE EXISTENTIALIST WRITER?
THE ROACH BOOK!
ACTUALLY, I THINK IT'S TECHNICALLY A DUNG BEETLE.

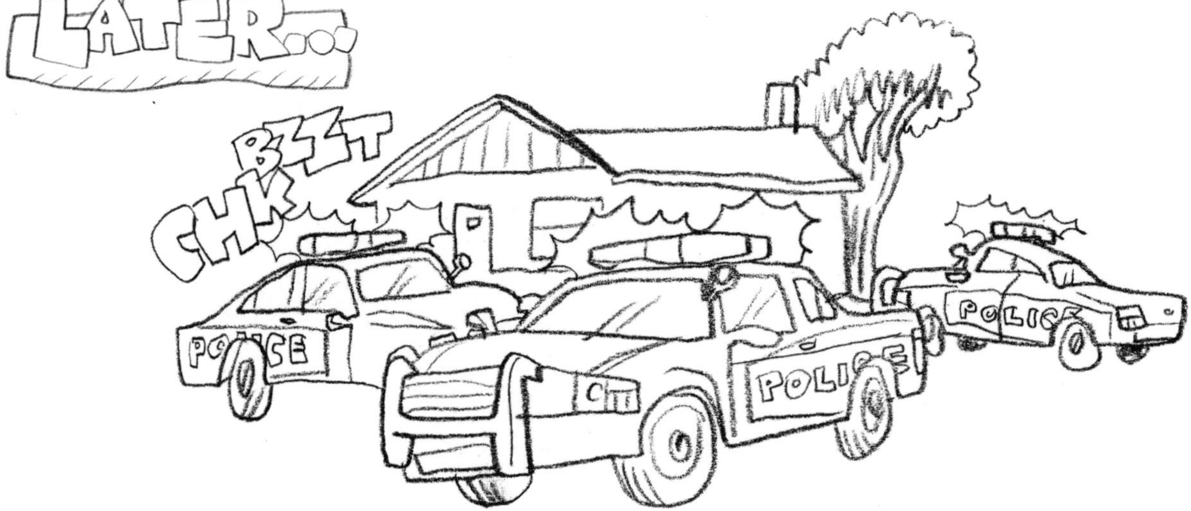
LATER...
CHK
BZZZT

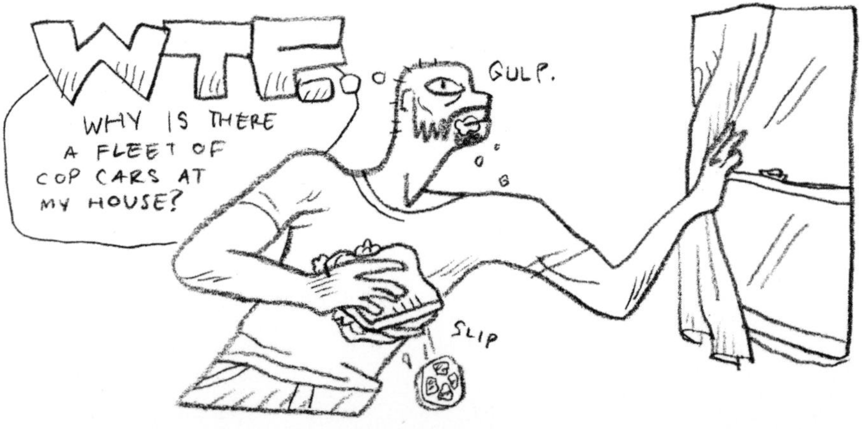
WTF...
WHY IS THERE A FLEET OF COP CARS AT MY HOUSE?
GULP.
SLIP

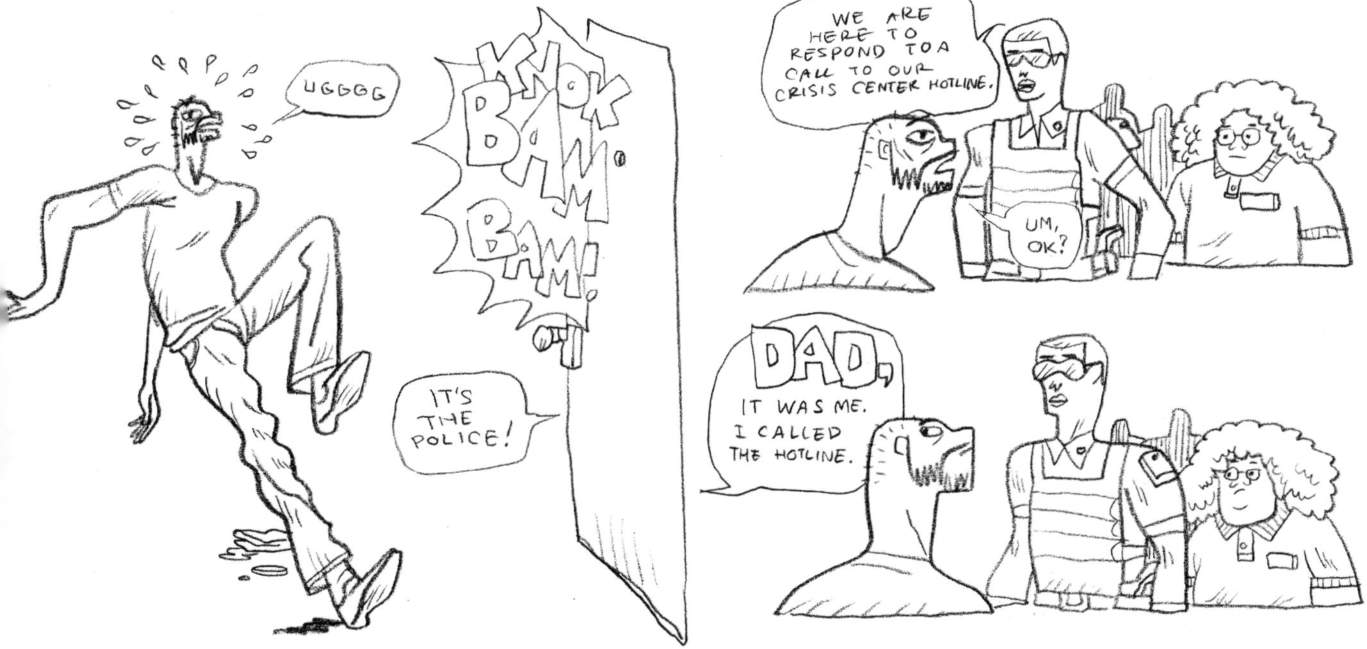
UGGGG
KNOK
BAMM
BAMM!
IT'S THE POLICE!
WE ARE HERE TO RESPOND TO A CALL TO OUR CRISIS CENTER HOTLINE.
UM, OK?
DAD,
IT WAS ME. I CALLED THE HOTLINE.

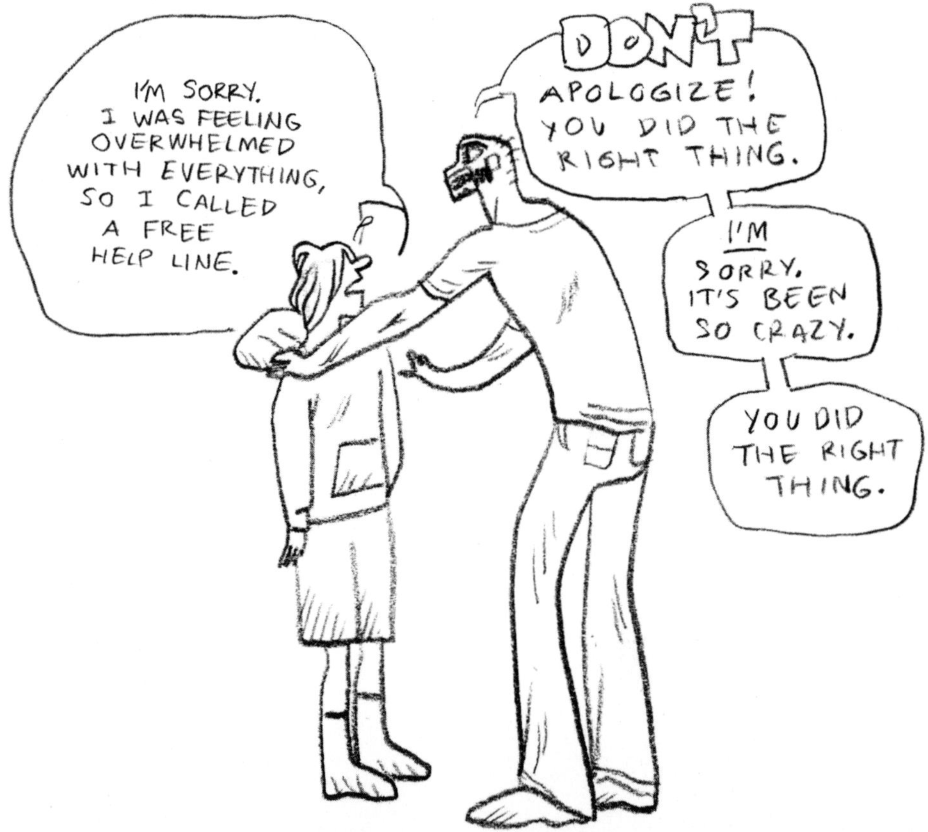
I'M SORRY. I WAS FEELING OVERWHELMED WITH EVERYTHING, SO I CALLED A FREE HELP LINE.
DON'T APOLOGIZE! YOU DID THE RIGHT THING.
I'M SORRY. IT'S BEEN SO CRAZY.
YOU DID THE RIGHT THING.

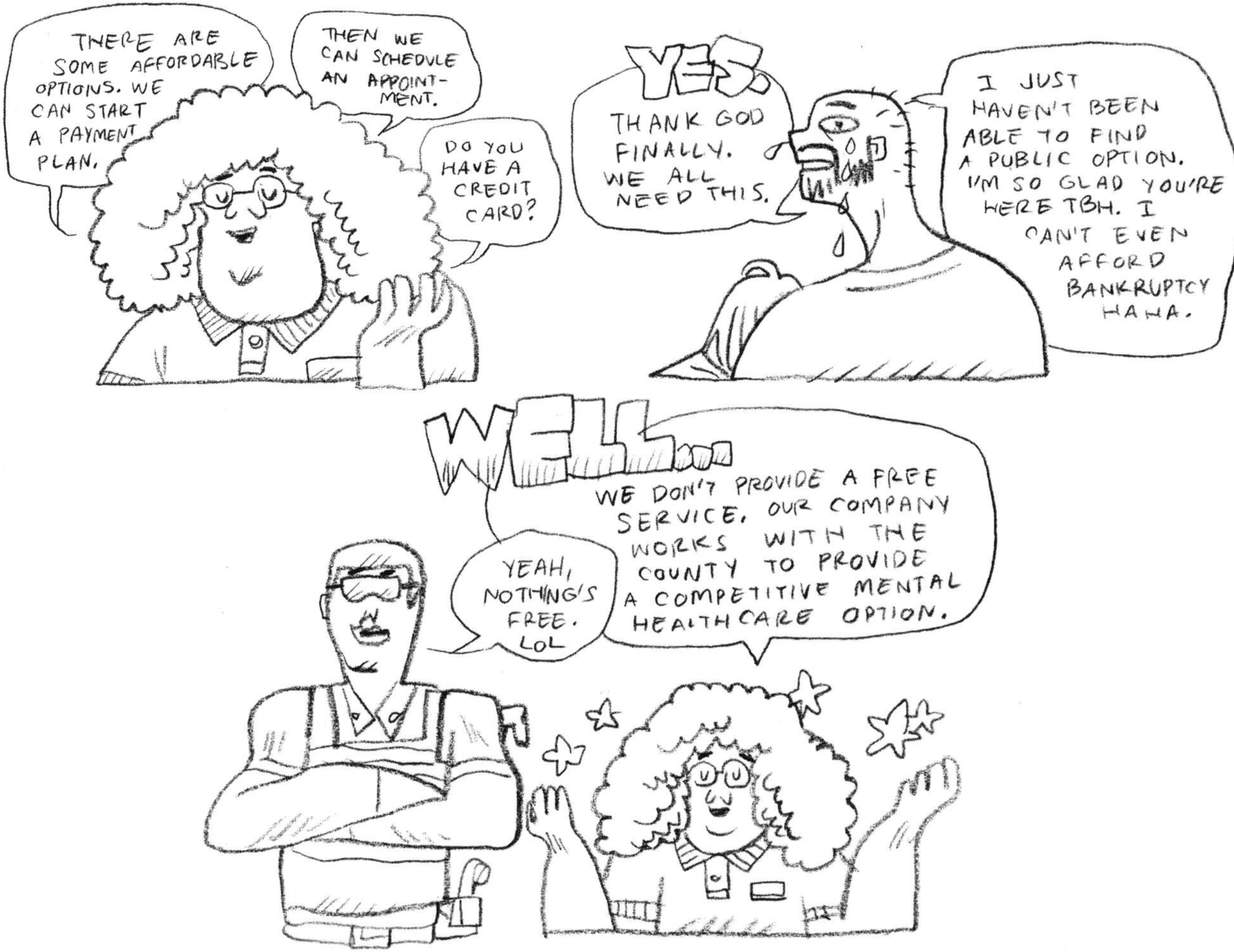
THERE ARE SOME AFFORDABLE OPTIONS. WE CAN START A PAYMENT PLAN.
THEN WE CAN SCHEDULE AN APPOINTMENT.
DO YOU HAVE A CREDIT CARD?
YES.
THANK GOD FINALLY. WE ALL NEED THIS.
I JUST HAVEN'T BEEN ABLE TO FIND A PUBLIC OPTION. I'M SO GLAD YOU'RE HERE TBH. I CAN'T EVEN AFFORD BANKRUPTCY HAHA.
WELL...
WE DON'T PROVIDE A FREE SERVICE. OUR COMPANY WORKS WITH THE COUNTY TO PROVIDE A COMPETITIVE MENTAL HEALTHCARE OPTION.
YEAH, NOTHING'S FREE. LOL

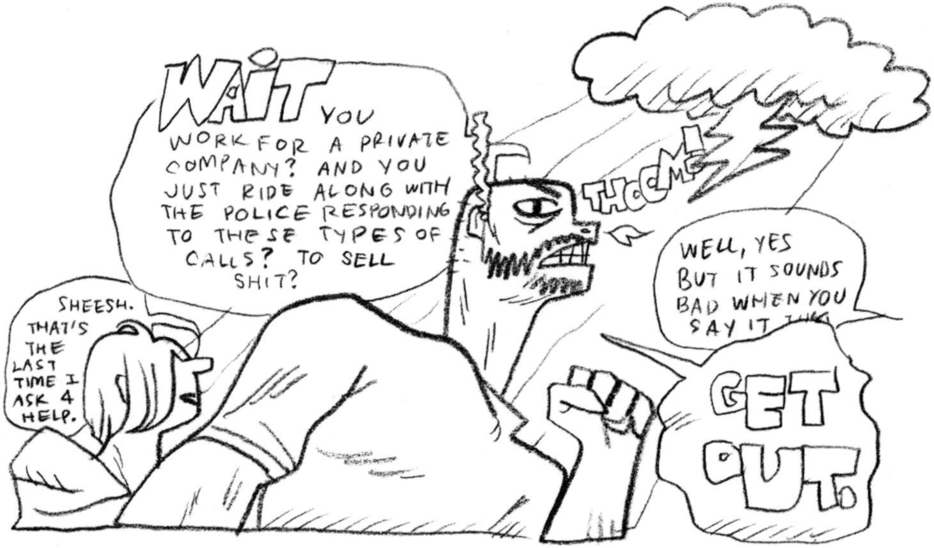
WAIT YOU WORK FOR A PRIVATE COMPANY? AND YOU JUST RIDE ALONG WITH THE POLICE RESPONDING TO THESE TYPES OF CALLS? TO SELL SHIT?
WELL, YES BUT IT SOUNDS BAD WHEN YOU SAY IT
THOOM!
GET OUT.
SHEESH. THAT'S THE LAST TIME I ASK 4 HELP.

AND SO...
ALACHUA COUNTY CRIMINAL JUSTICE CENTER

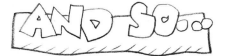

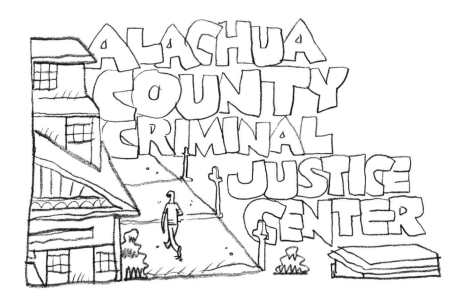

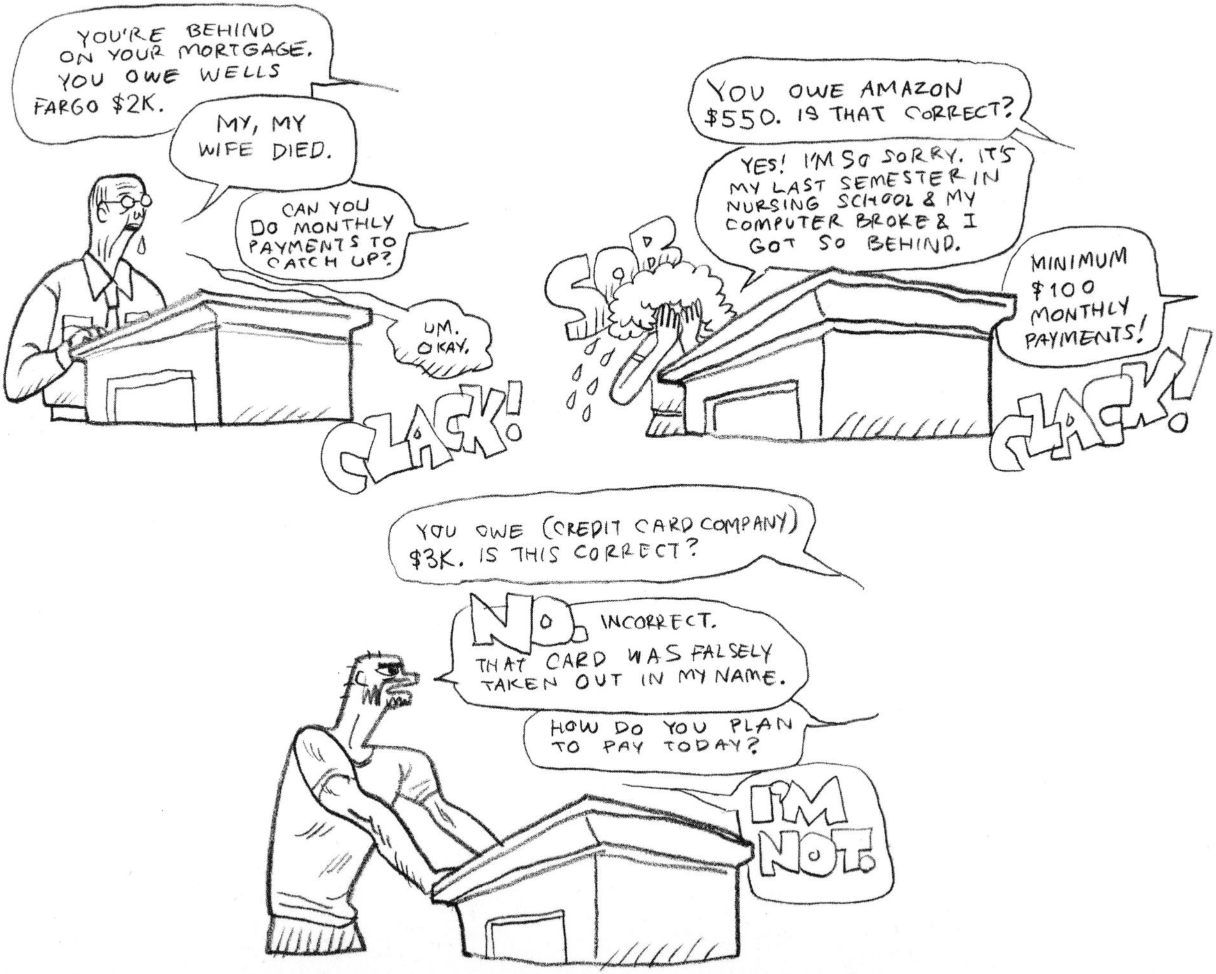
YOU'RE BEHIND ON YOUR MORTGAGE. YOU OWE WELLS FARGO $2K.
MY, MY WIFE DIED.
CAN YOU DO MONTHLY PAYMENTS TO CATCH UP?
UM. OKAY.
CLACK!
YOU OWE AMAZON $550. IS THAT CORRECT?
YES! I'M SO SORRY. IT'S MY LAST SEMESTER IN NURSING SCHOOL & MY COMPUTER BROKE & I GOT SO BEHIND.
SOB
MINIMUM $100 MONTHLY PAYMENTS!
CLACK!
YOU OWE (CREDIT CARD COMPANY) $3K. IS THIS CORRECT?
NO. INCORRECT. THAT CARD WAS FALSELY TAKEN OUT IN MY NAME.
HOW DO YOU PLAN TO PAY TODAY?
I'M NOT.

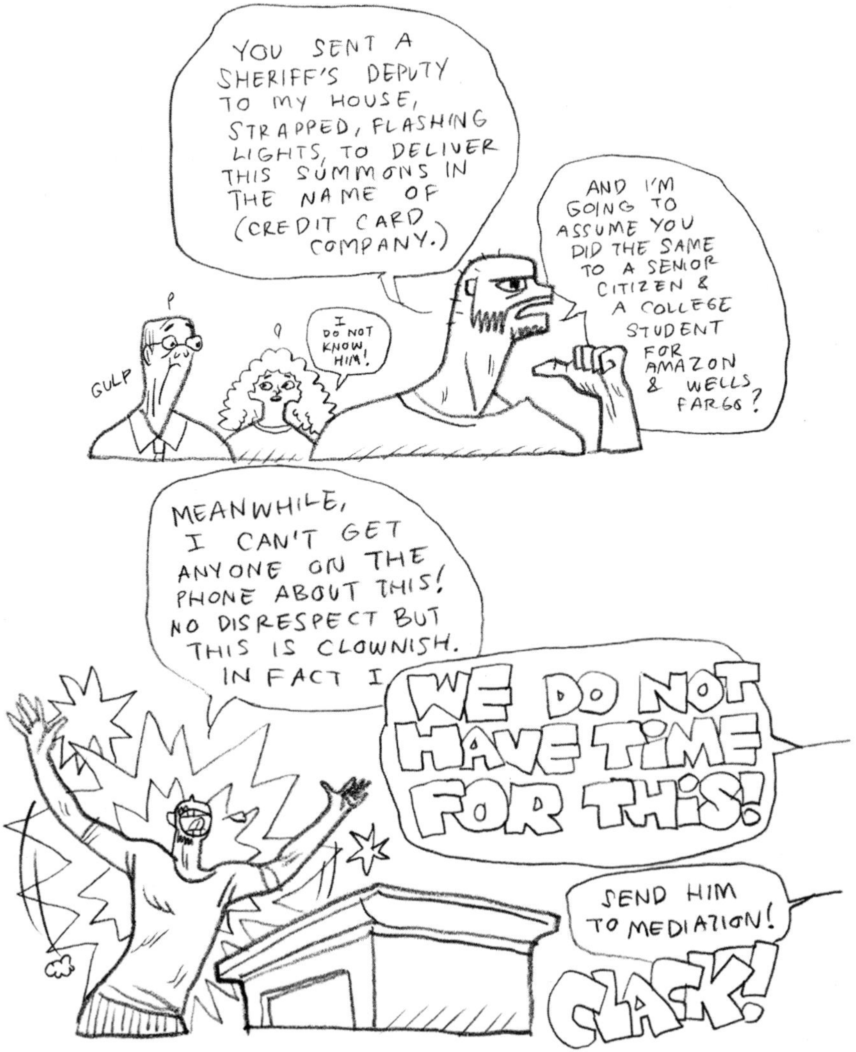
YOU SENT A SHERIFF'S DEPUTY TO MY HOUSE, STRAPPED, FLASHING LIGHTS, TO DELIVER THIS SUMMONS IN THE NAME OF (CREDIT CARD COMPANY.)
AND I'M GOING TO ASSUME YOU DID THE SAME TO A SENIOR CITIZEN & A COLLEGE STUDENT FOR AMAZON & WELLS FARGO?
GULP
I DO NOT KNOW HIM!
MEANWHILE, I CAN'T GET ANYONE ON THE PHONE ABOUT THIS! NO DISRESPECT BUT THIS IS CLOWNISH. IN FACT I
WE DO NOT HAVE TIME FOR THIS!
SEND HIM TO MEDIATION!
CLACK!

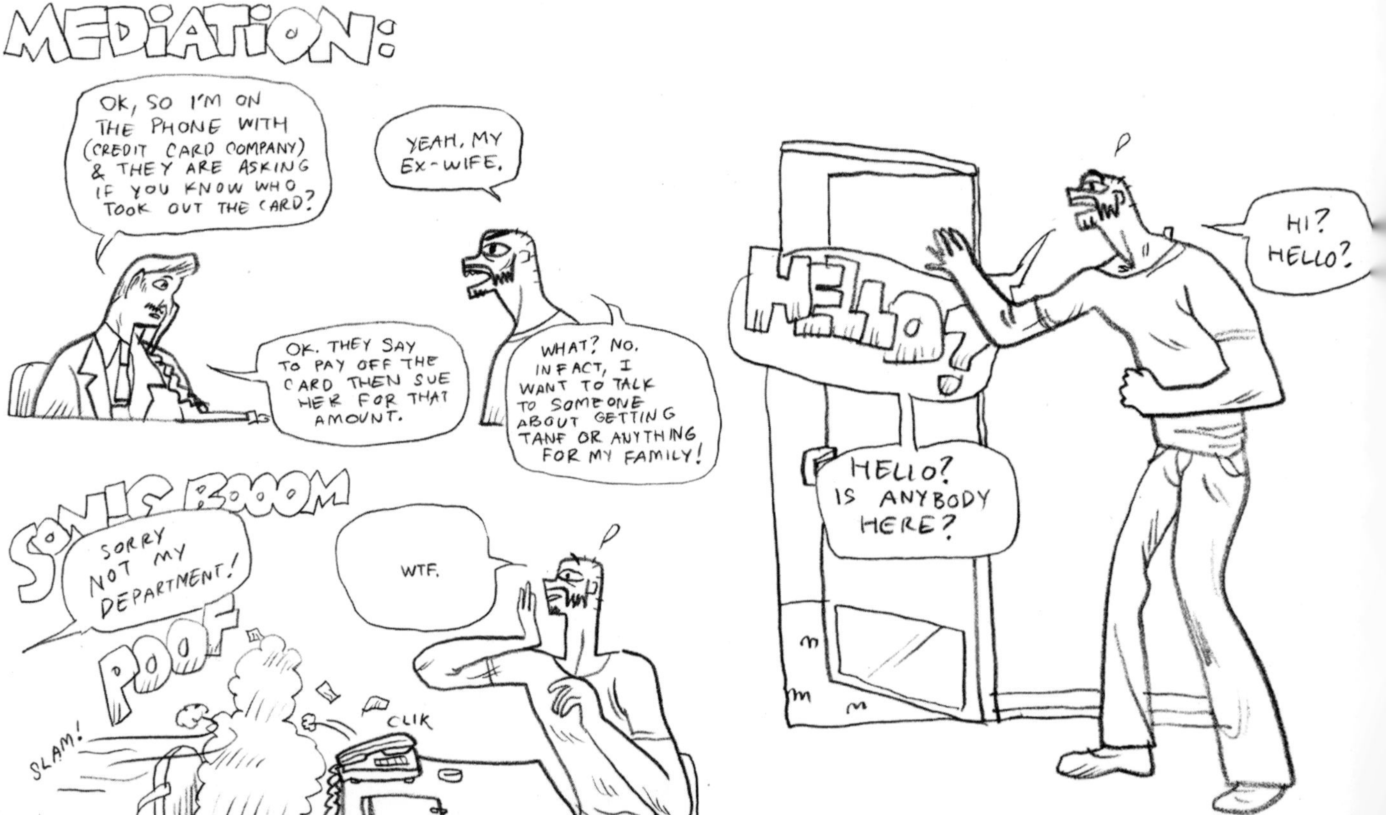
MEDIATION:
OK, SO I'M ON THE PHONE WITH (CREDIT CARD COMPANY) & THEY ARE ASKING IF YOU KNOW WHO TOOK OUT THE CARD?
YEAH, MY EX-WIFE.
OK. THEY SAY TO PAY OFF THE CARD THEN SUE HER FOR THAT AMOUNT.
WHAT? NO. IN FACT, I WANT TO TALK TO SOMEONE ABOUT GETTING TANF OR ANYTHING FOR MY FAMILY!
SONIC BOOOOM
SORRY NOT MY DEPARTMENT!
POOF
SLAM!
CLIK
WTF.
HELLO?
HELLO? IS ANYBODY HERE?
HI? HELLO?

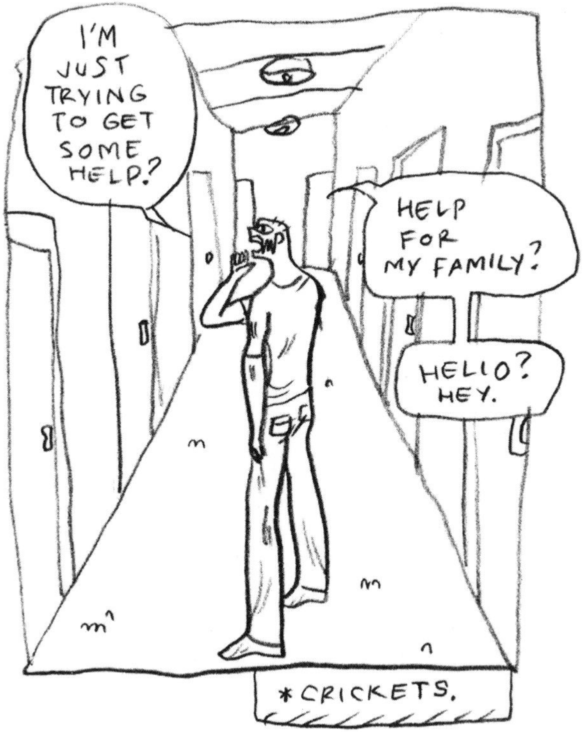
I'M JUST TRYING TO GET SOME HELP?
HELP FOR MY FAMILY?
HELLO? HEY.
*CRICKETS.

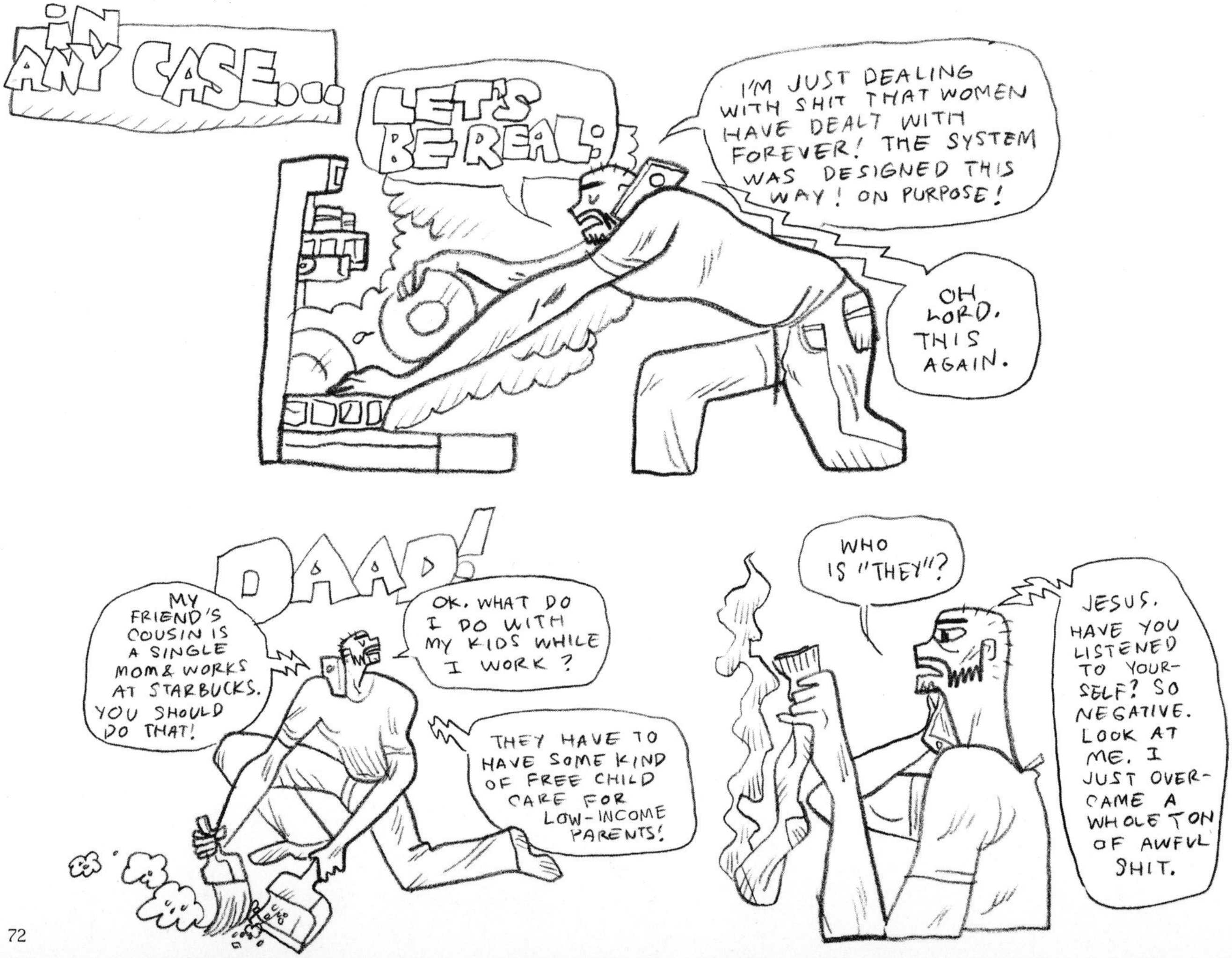
IN ANY CASE...
LET'S BE REAL:
I'M JUST DEALING WITH SHIT THAT WOMEN HAVE DEALT WITH FOREVER! THE SYSTEM WAS DESIGNED THIS WAY! ON PURPOSE!
OH LORD. THIS AGAIN.
DAAD!
MY FRIEND'S COUSIN IS A SINGLE MOM & WORKS AT STARBUCKS. YOU SHOULD DO THAT!
OK. WHAT DO I DO WITH MY KIDS WHILE I WORK?
THEY HAVE TO HAVE SOME KIND OF FREE CHILD CARE FOR LOW-INCOME PARENTS!
WHO IS "THEY"?
JESUS. HAVE YOU LISTENED TO YOUR-SELF? SO NEGATIVE. LOOK AT ME. I JUST OVER-CAME A WHOLE TON OF AWFUL SHIT.

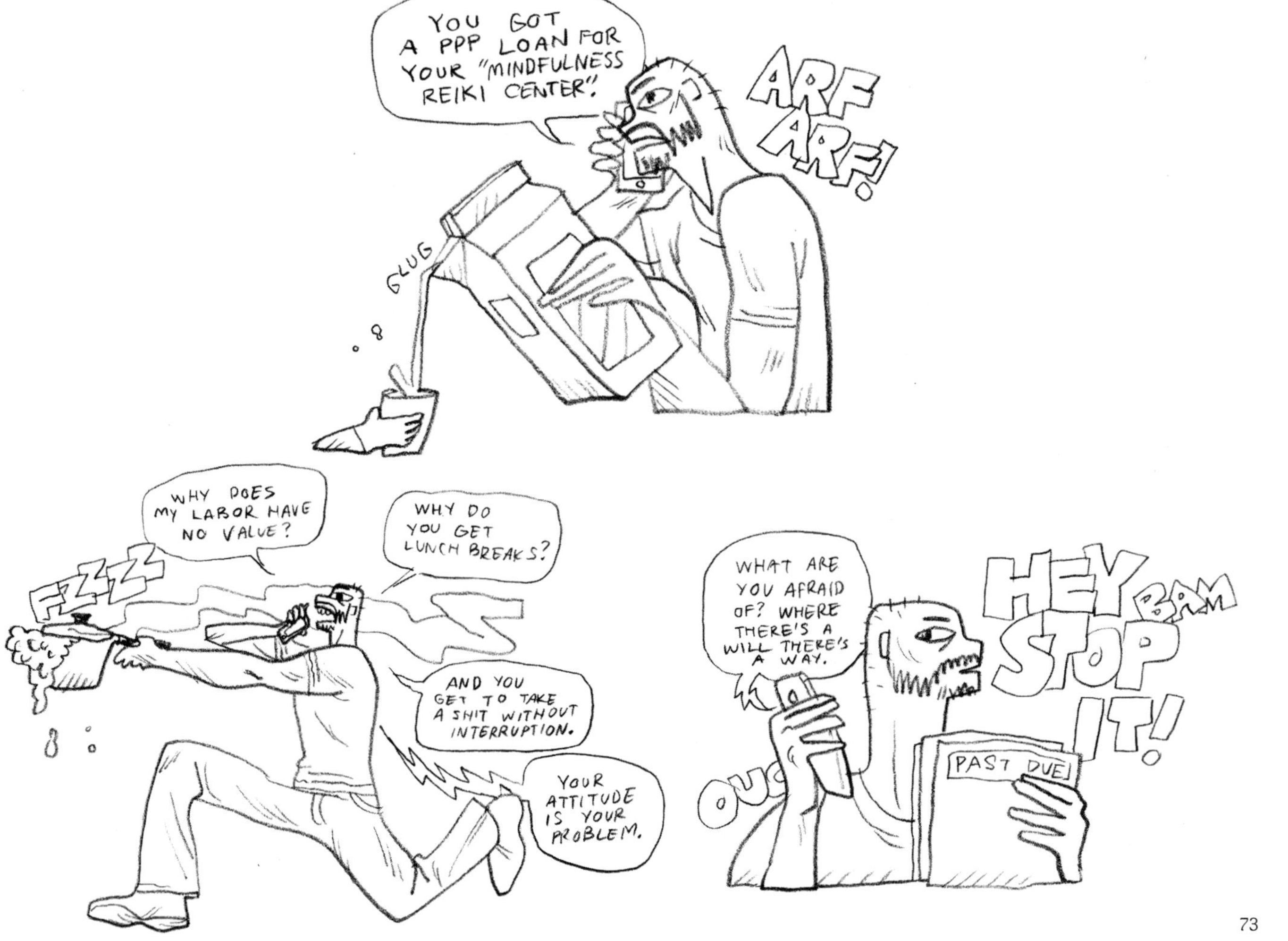
YOU GOT A PPP LOAN FOR YOUR "MINDFULNESS REIKI CENTER".
ARF ARF!
GLUG
FZZZZ
WHY DOES MY LABOR HAVE NO VALUE?
WHY DO YOU GET LUNCH BREAKS?
AND YOU GET TO TAKE A SHIT WITHOUT INTERRUPTION.
YOUR ATTITUDE IS YOUR PROBLEM.
WHAT ARE YOU AFRAID OF? WHERE THERE'S A WILL THERE'S A WAY.
HEY
BAM
STOP IT!
OUC
PAST DUE

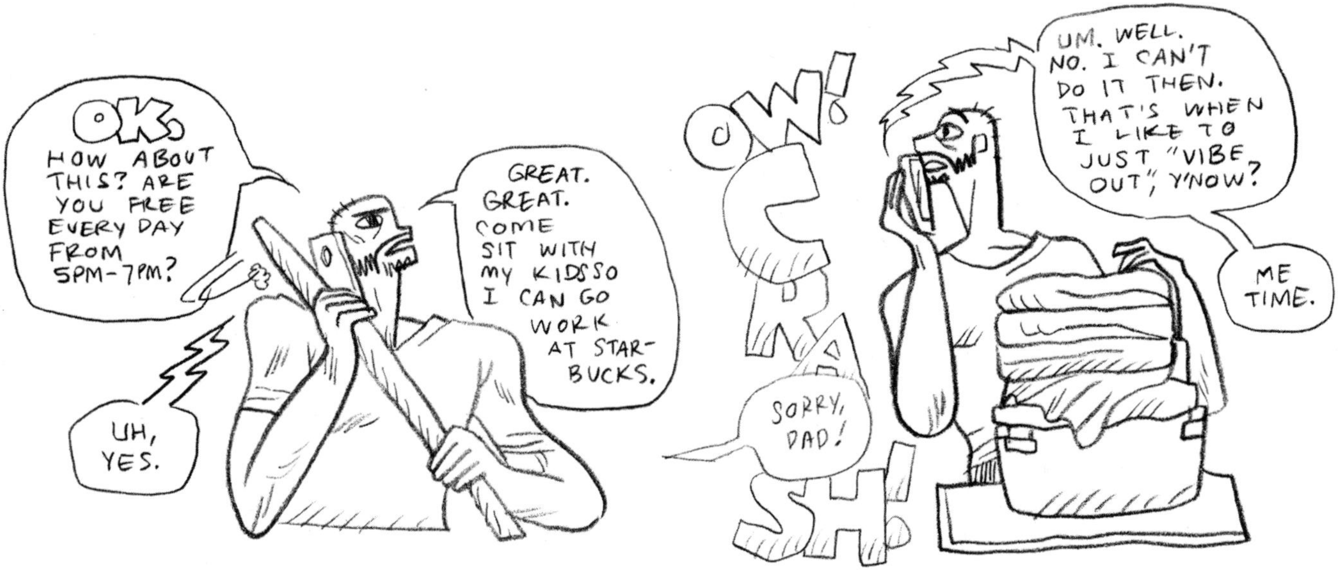
OK. HOW ABOUT THIS? ARE YOU FREE EVERY DAY FROM 5PM-7PM?
UH, YES.
GREAT. GREAT. COME SIT WITH MY KIDS SO I CAN GO WORK AT STAR-BUCKS.
OW!
CRASH!
SORRY, DAD!
UM. WELL. NO. I CAN'T DO IT THEN. THAT'S WHEN I LIKE TO JUST "VIBE OUT," Y'NOW?
ME TIME.

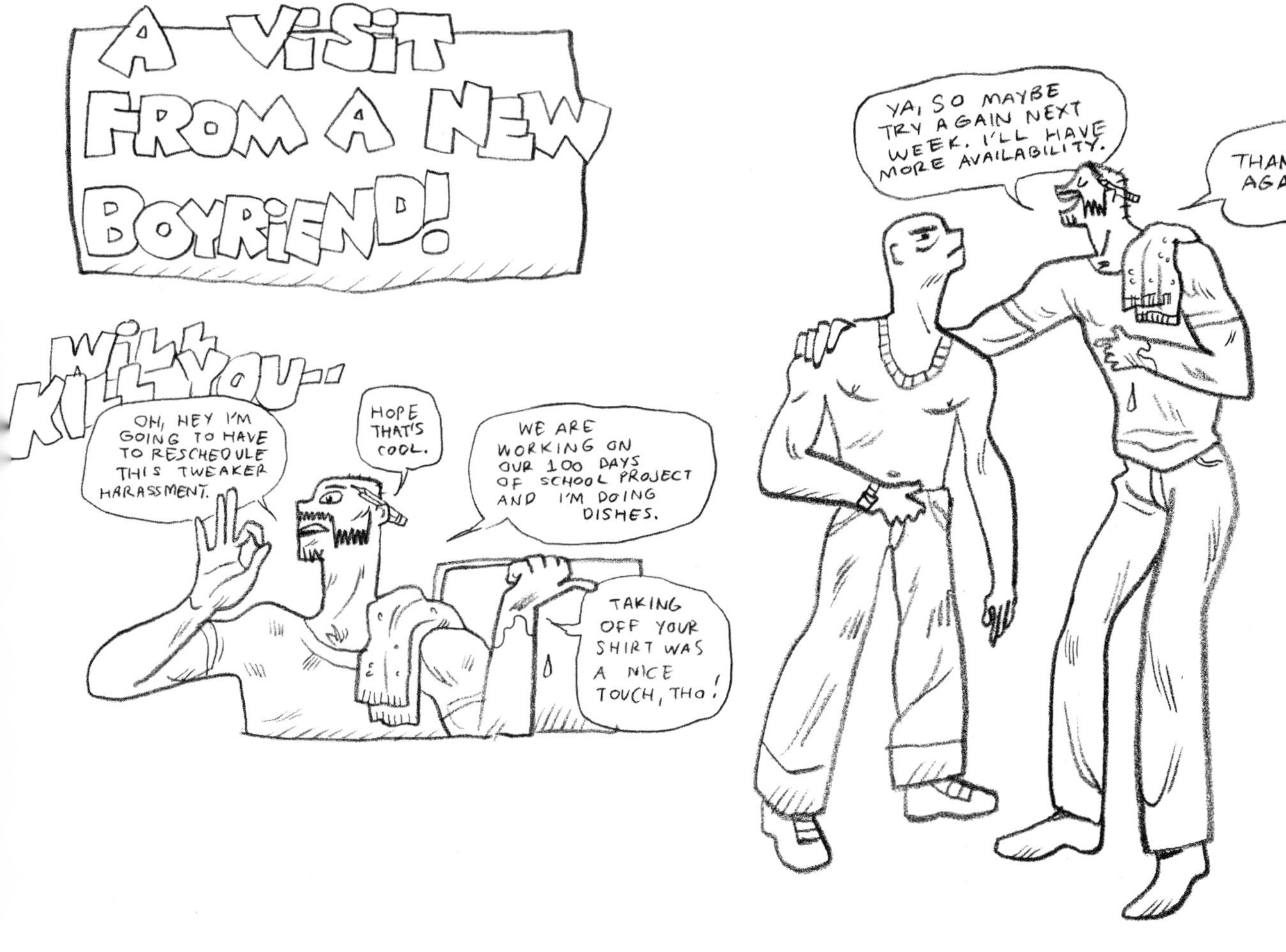
A VISIT FROM A NEW BOYRIEND!
WILL KILL YOU..
OH, HEY I'M GOING TO HAVE TO RESCHEDULE THIS TWEAKER HARASSMENT.
HOPE THAT'S COOL.
WE ARE WORKING ON OUR 100 DAYS OF SCHOOL PROJECT AND I'M DOING DISHES.
TAKING OFF YOUR SHIRT WAS A NICE TOUCH, THO!
YA, SO MAYBE TRY AGAIN NEXT WEEK. I'LL HAVE MORE AVAILABILITY.
THANKS, AGAIN.

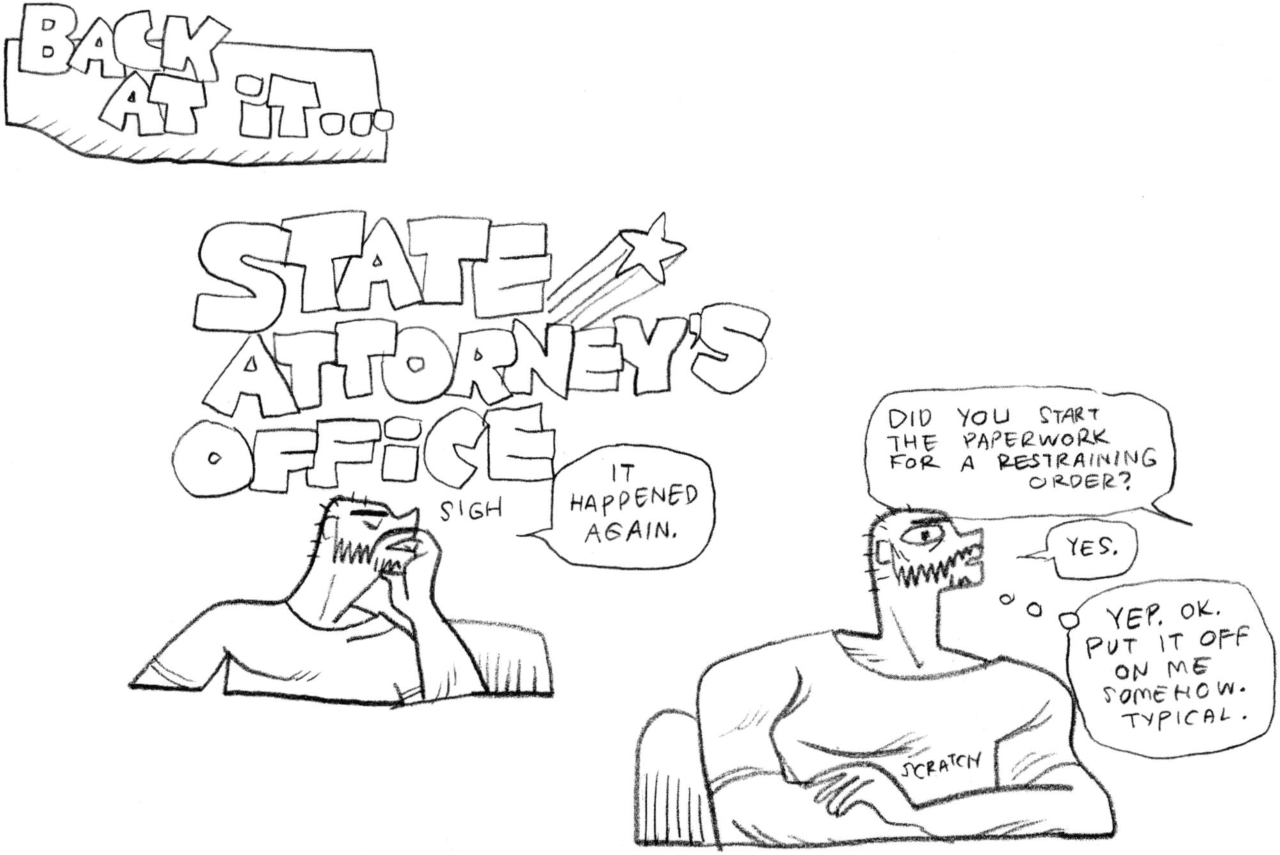
BACK AT IT...
STATE ATTORNEY'S OFFICE
SIGH
IT HAPPENED AGAIN.
DID YOU START THE PAPERWORK FOR A RESTRAINING ORDER?
YES.
YEP. OK. PUT IT OFF ON ME SOMEHOW. TYPICAL.
SCRATCH

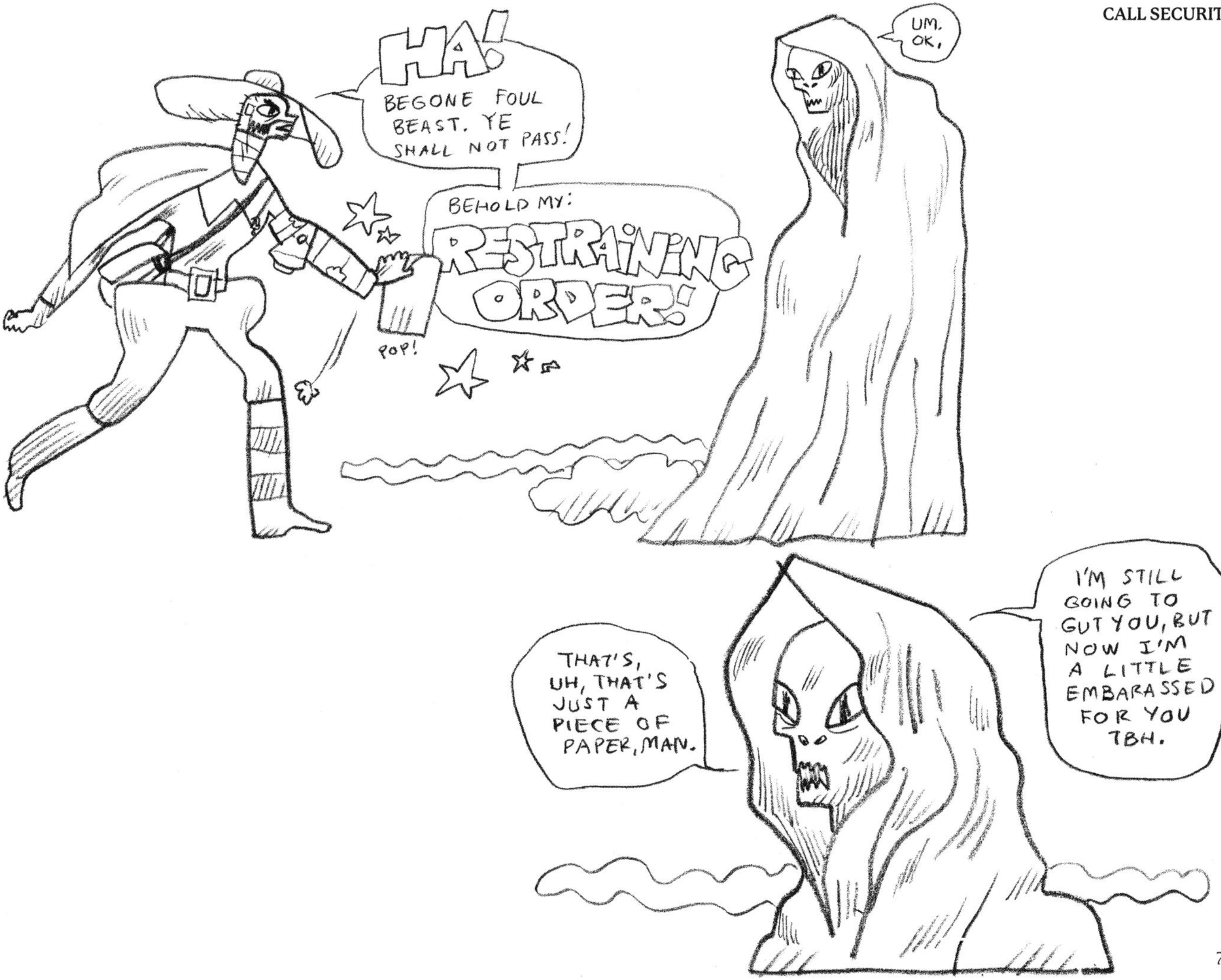
HA! BEGONE FOUL BEAST. YE SHALL NOT PASS!
BEHOLD MY: RESTRAINING ORDER!
POP!
UM, OK,
THAT'S, UH, THAT'S JUST A PIECE OF PAPER, MAN.
I'M STILL GOING TO GUT YOU, BUT NOW I'M A LITTLE EMBARASSED FOR YOU TBH.

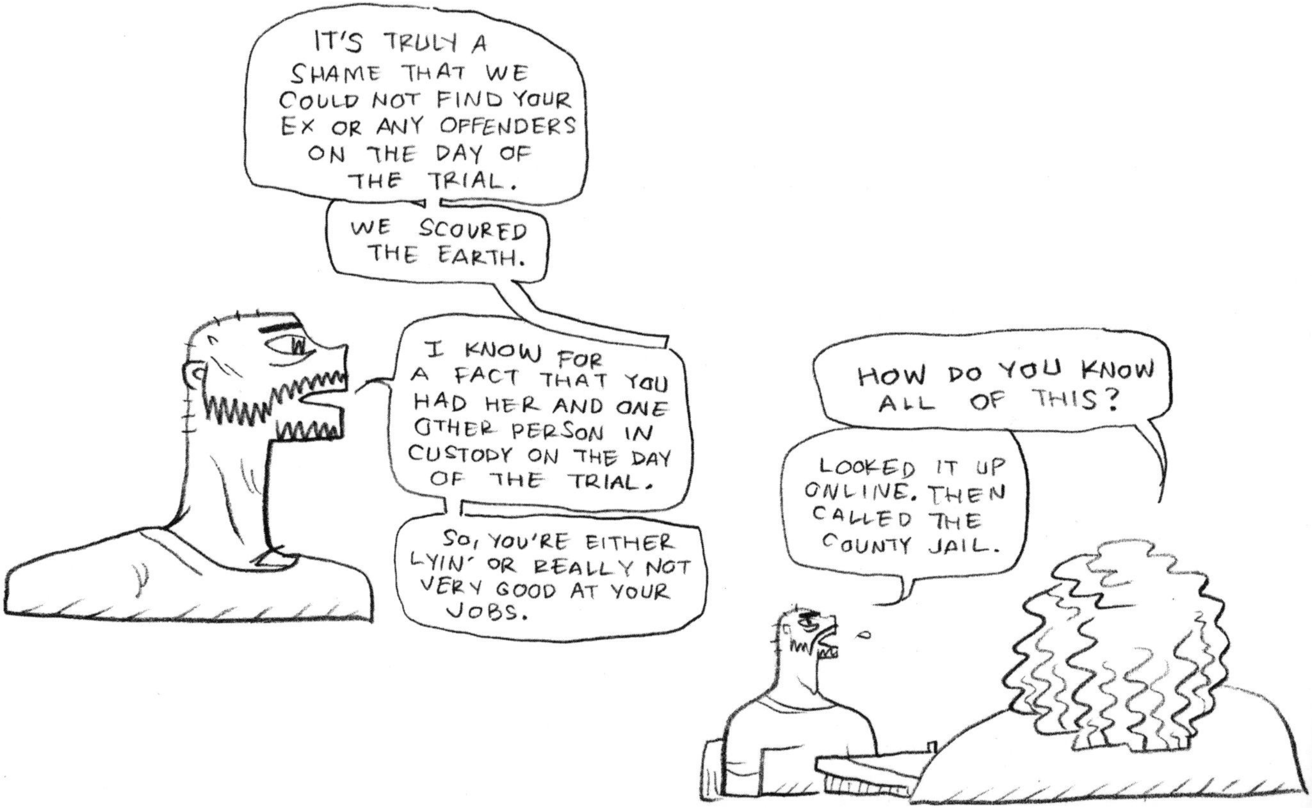
IT'S TRULY A SHAME THAT WE COULD NOT FIND YOUR EX OR ANY OFFENDERS ON THE DAY OF THE TRIAL.
WE SCOURED THE EARTH.
I KNOW FOR A FACT THAT YOU HAD HER AND ONE OTHER PERSON IN CUSTODY ON THE DAY OF THE TRIAL.
SO, YOU'RE EITHER LYIN' OR REALLY NOT VERY GOOD AT YOUR JOBS.
HOW DO YOU KNOW ALL OF THIS?
LOOKED IT UP ONLINE. THEN CALLED THE COUNTY JAIL.

WELL, MR. BALLARD, THE STATE ATTORNEY'S OFFICE WOULD LOVE TO KNOW THIS "MAGIC" WEBSITE THAT YOU USE. I'LL WRITE IT DOWN.
OKAY.
GOOGLE.
* LAUGH TRACK

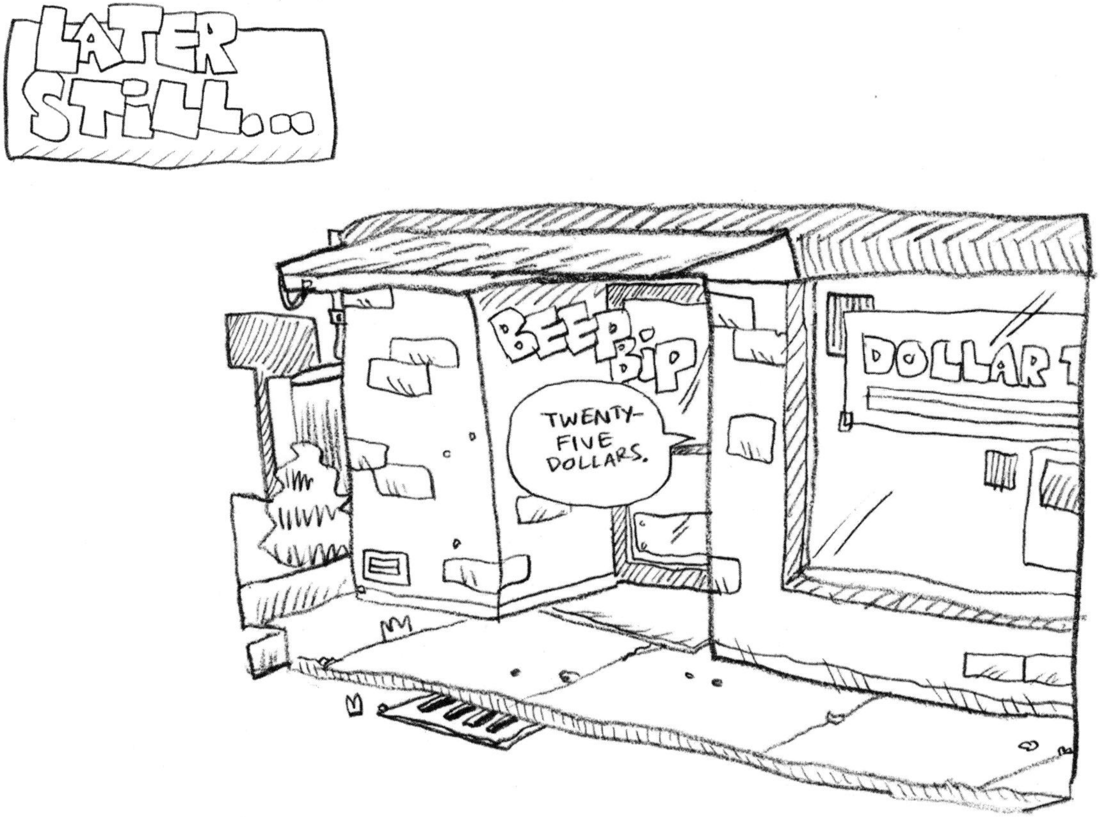
LATER STILL...
BEEP BIP
TWENTY-FIVE DOLLARS.
DOLLAR

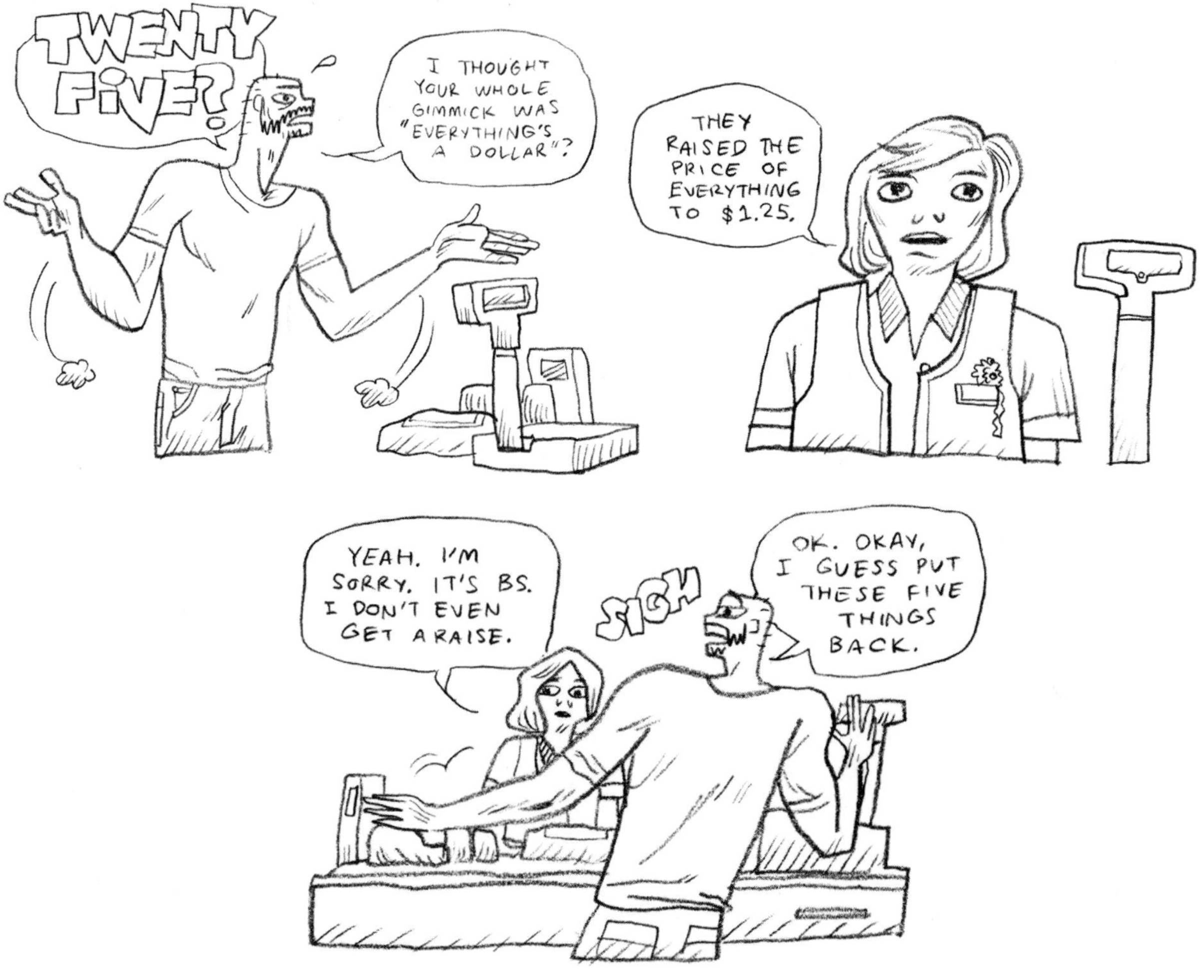
TWENTY FIVE?
I THOUGHT YOUR WHOLE GIMMICK WAS "EVERYTHING'S A DOLLAR"?
THEY RAISED THE PRICE OF EVERYTHING TO $1.25.
YEAH. I'M SORRY. IT'S BS. I DON'T EVEN GET A RAISE.
SIGH
OK. OKAY, I GUESS PUT THESE FIVE THINGS BACK.

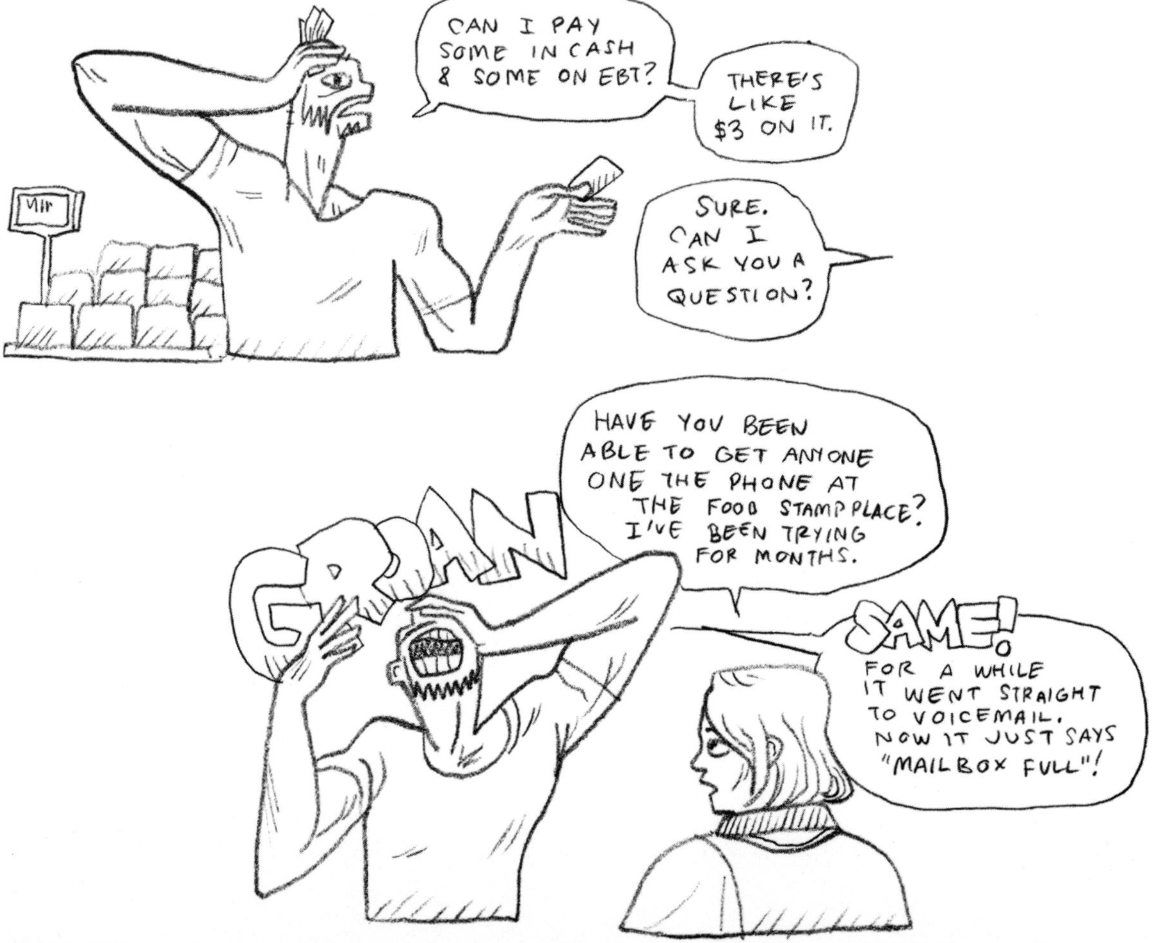
CAN I PAY SOME IN CASH & SOME ON EBT?
THERE'S LIKE $3 ON IT.
SURE. CAN I ASK YOU A QUESTION?
HAVE YOU BEEN ABLE TO GET ANYONE ONE THE PHONE AT THE FOOD STAMP PLACE? I'VE BEEN TRYING FOR MONTHS.
GROAN
SAME! FOR A WHILE IT WENT STRAIGHT TO VOICEMAIL. NOW IT JUST SAYS "MAILBOX FULL"!

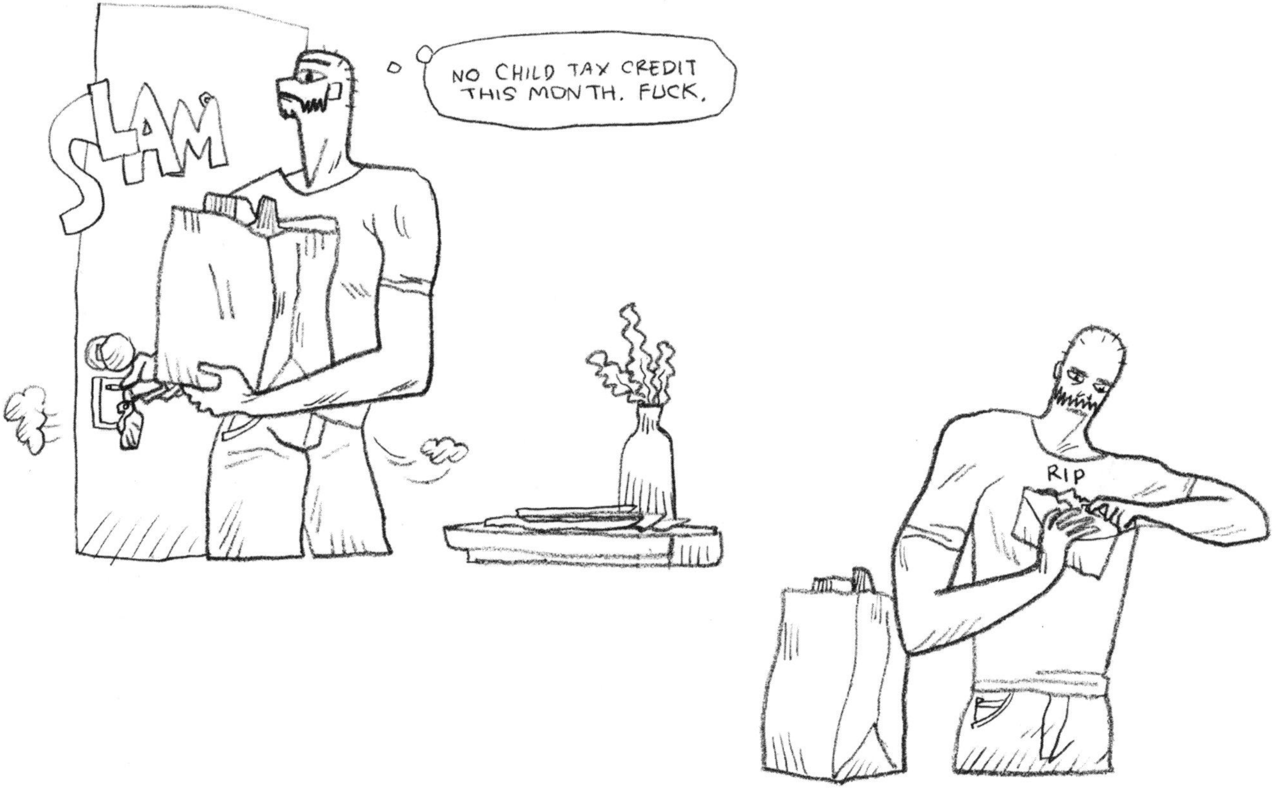
SLAM
NO CHILD TAX CREDIT THIS MONTH. FUCK.
RIP

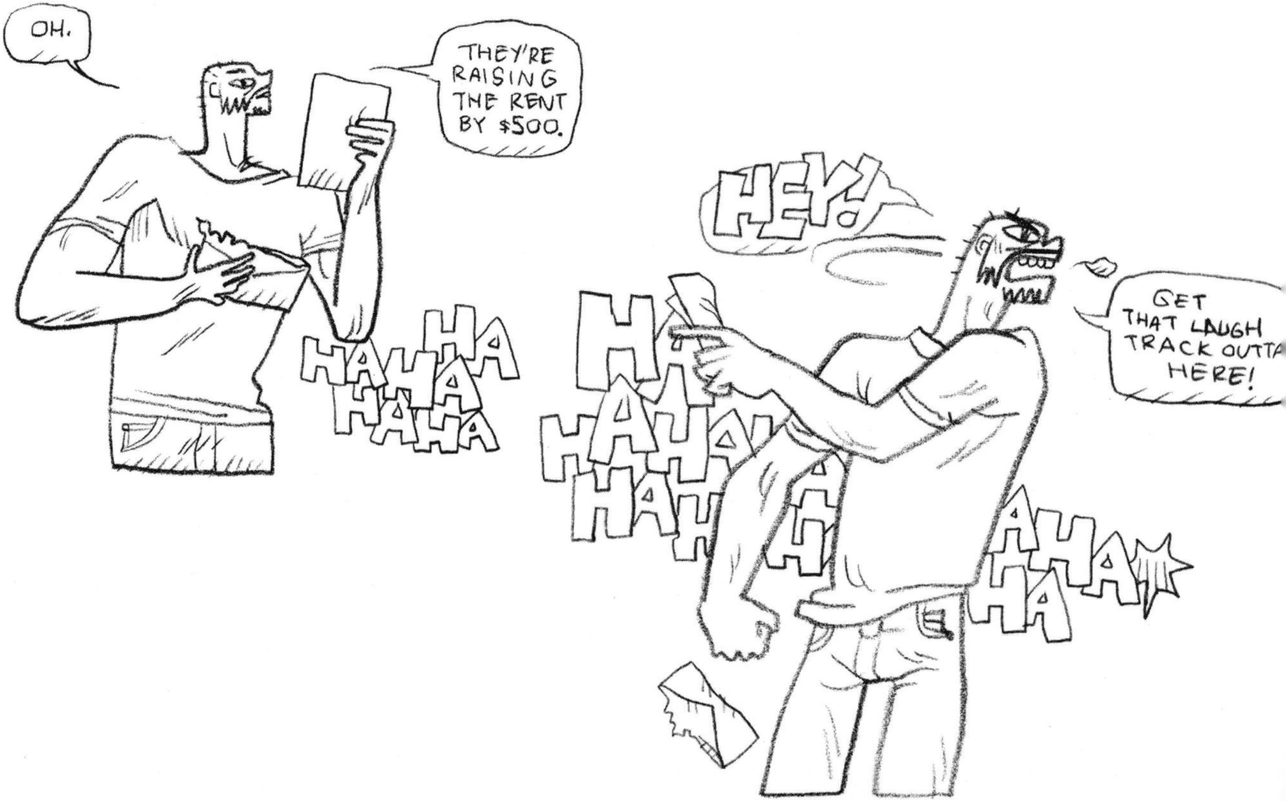
OH.
THEY'RE RAISING THE RENT BY $500.
HAHAHA HAHAHA
HEY!
GET THAT LAUGH TRACK OUTTA HERE!

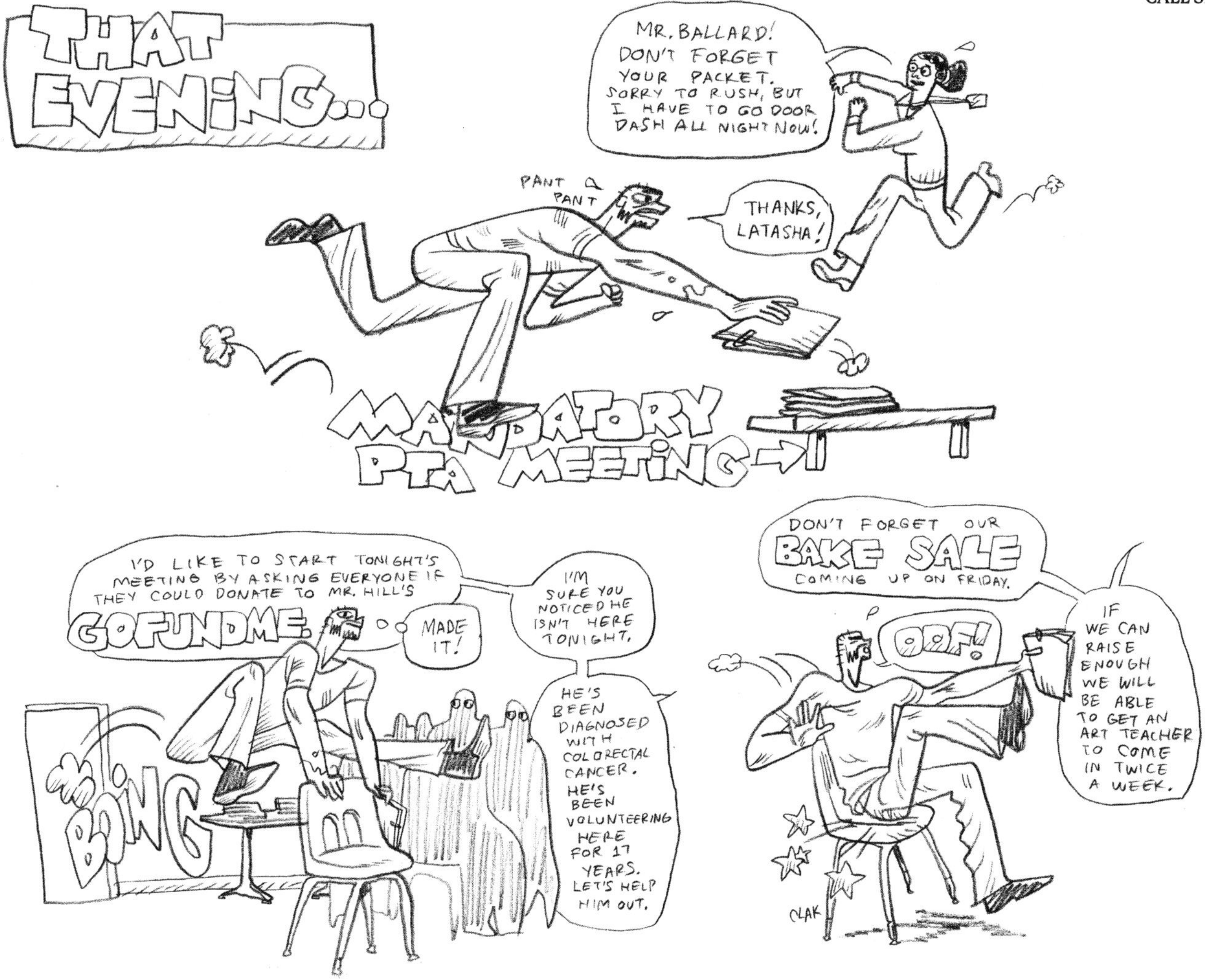
THAT EVENING...
MR. BALLARD! DON'T FORGET YOUR PACKET. SORRY TO RUSH, BUT I HAVE TO GO DOOR DASH ALL NIGHT NOW!
PANT PANT
THANKS, LATASHA!
MANDATORY PTA MEETING
I'D LIKE TO START TONIGHT'S MEETING BY ASKING EVERYONE IF THEY COULD DONATE TO MR. HILL'S GOFUNDME.
MADE IT!
BOING
I'M SURE YOU NOTICED HE ISN'T HERE TONIGHT.
HE'S BEEN DIAGNOSED WITH COLORECTAL CANCER. HE'S BEEN VOLUNTEERING HERE FOR 17 YEARS. LET'S HELP HIM OUT.
DON'T FORGET OUR BAKE SALE COMING UP ON FRIDAY.
OOF!
IF WE CAN RAISE ENOUGH WE WILL BE ABLE TO GET AN ART TEACHER TO COME IN TWICE A WEEK.
CLAK

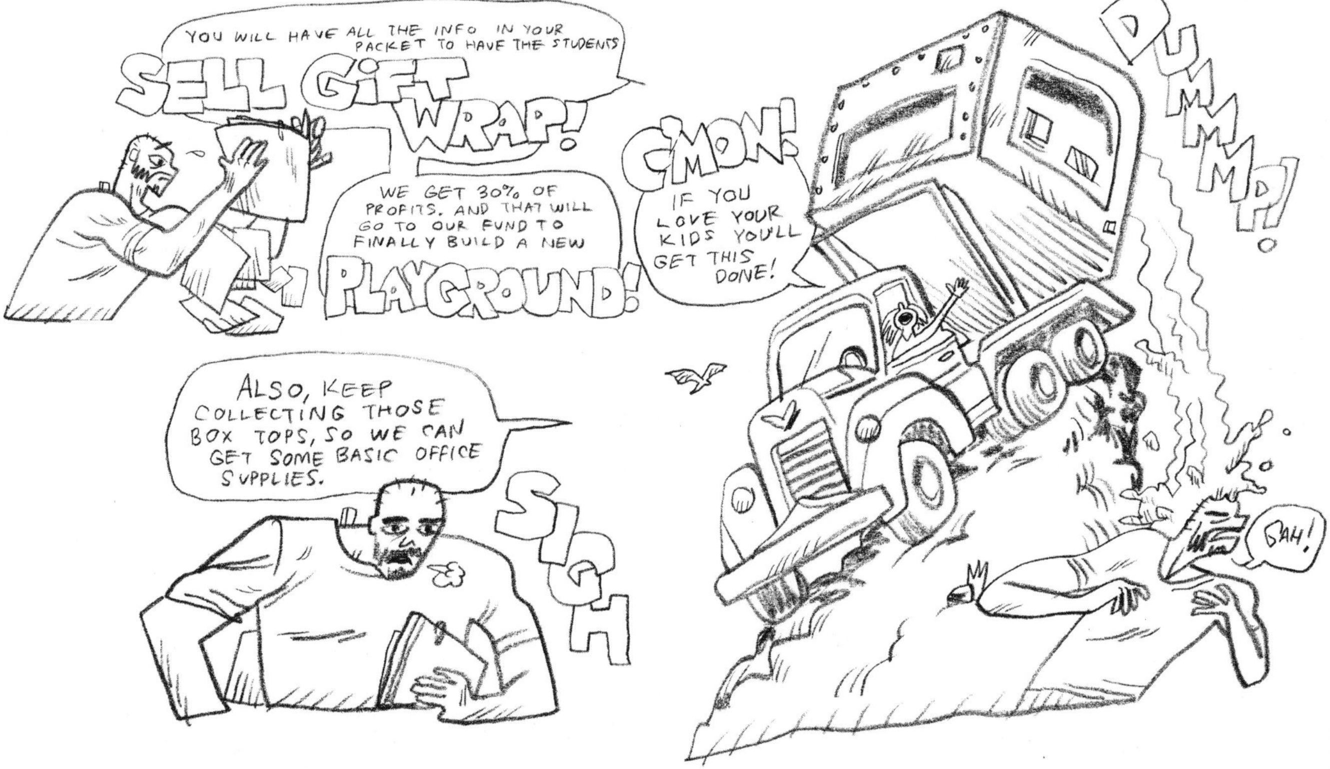
YOU WILL HAVE ALL THE INFO IN YOUR PACKET TO HAVE THE STUDENTS
SELL GIFT WRAP!
WE GET 30% OF PROFITS. AND THAT WILL GO TO OUR FUND TO FINALLY BUILD A NEW
PLAYGROUND!
C'MON!
IF YOU LOVE YOUR KIDS YOU'LL GET THIS DONE!
DUMMMP!
ALSO, KEEP COLLECTING THOSE BOX TOPS, SO WE CAN GET SOME BASIC OFFICE SUPPLIES.
SIGH
GAH!

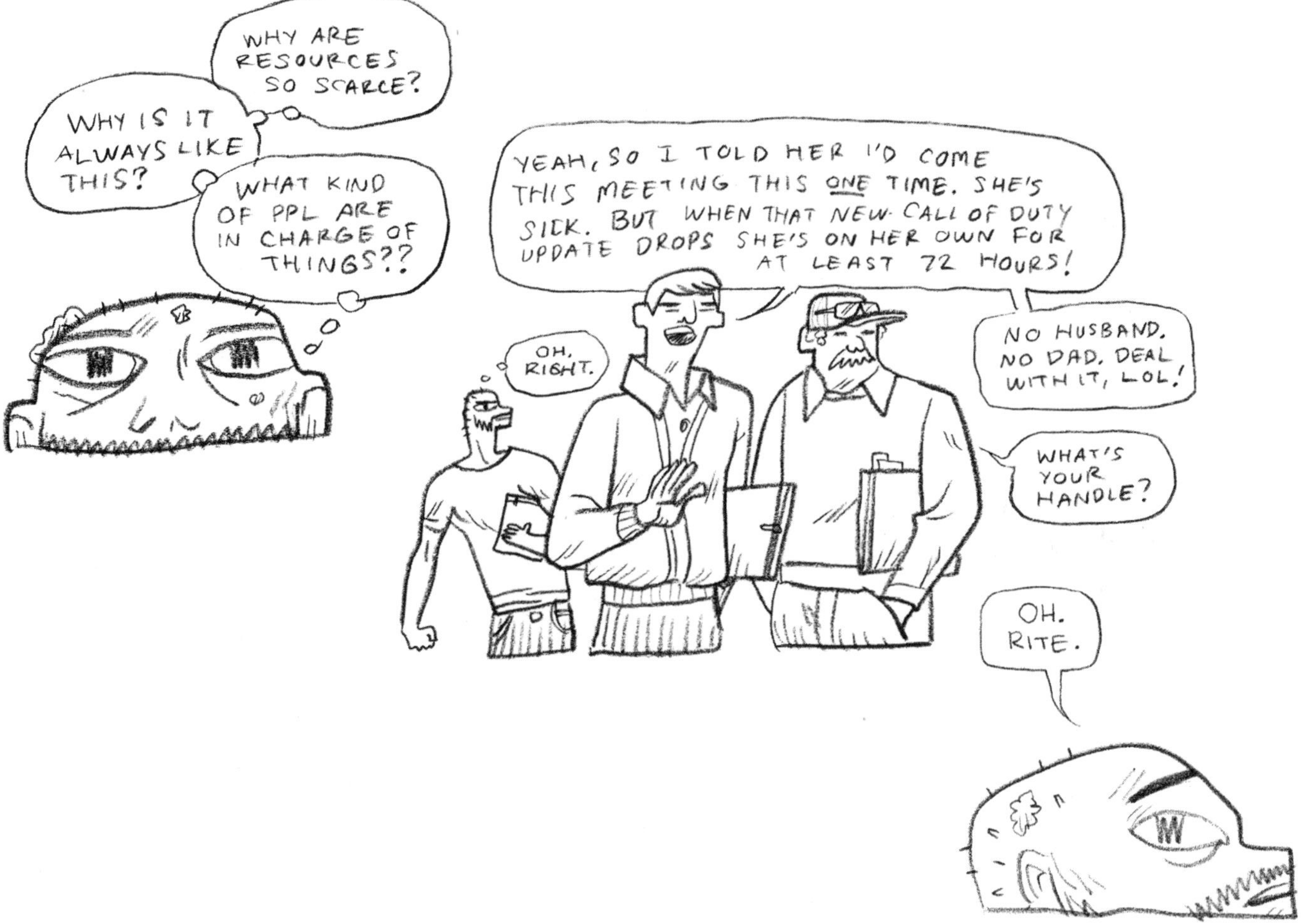
WHY IS IT ALWAYS LIKE THIS?
WHY ARE RESOURCES SO SCARCE?
WHAT KIND OF PPL ARE IN CHARGE OF THINGS??
YEAH, SO I TOLD HER I'D COME THIS MEETING THIS ONE TIME. SHE'S SICK. BUT WHEN THAT NEW CALL OF DUTY UPDATE DROPS SHE'S ON HER OWN FOR AT LEAST 72 HOURS!
NO HUSBAND. NO DAD. DEAL WITH IT, LOL!
OH, RIGHT.
WHAT'S YOUR HANDLE?
OH. RITE.

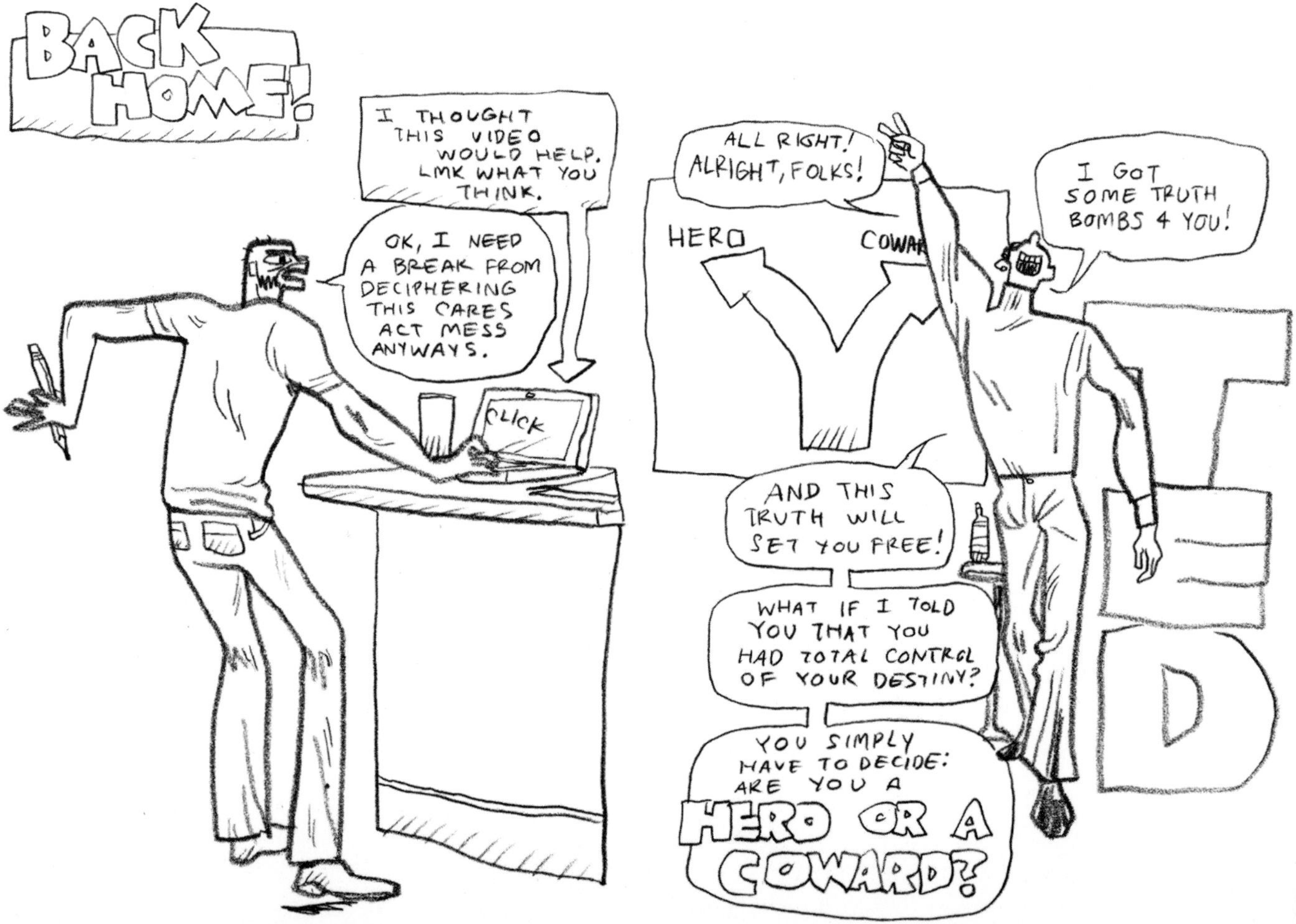
BACK HOME!
I THOUGHT THIS VIDEO WOULD HELP. LMK WHAT YOU THINK.
OK, I NEED A BREAK FROM DECIPHERING THIS CARES ACT MESS ANYWAYS.
CLICK
ALL RIGHT! ALRIGHT, FOLKS!
I GOT SOME TRUTH BOMBS 4 YOU!
HERO
AND THIS TRUTH WILL SET YOU FREE!
WHAT IF I TOLD YOU THAT YOU HAD TOTAL CONTROL OF YOUR DESTINY?
YOU SIMPLY HAVE TO DECIDE: ARE YOU A HERO OR A COWARD?

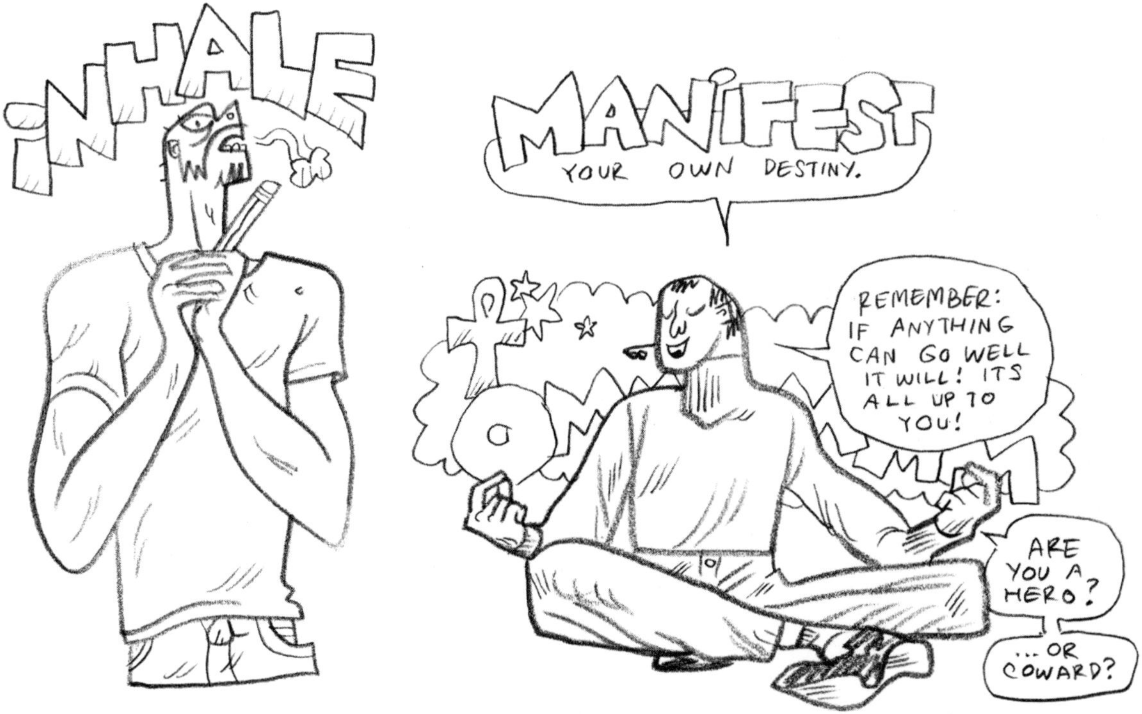
INHALE
MANIFEST YOUR OWN DESTINY.
REMEMBER: IF ANYTHING CAN GO WELL IT WILL! ITS ALL UP TO YOU!
ARE YOU A HERO?
...OR COWARD?

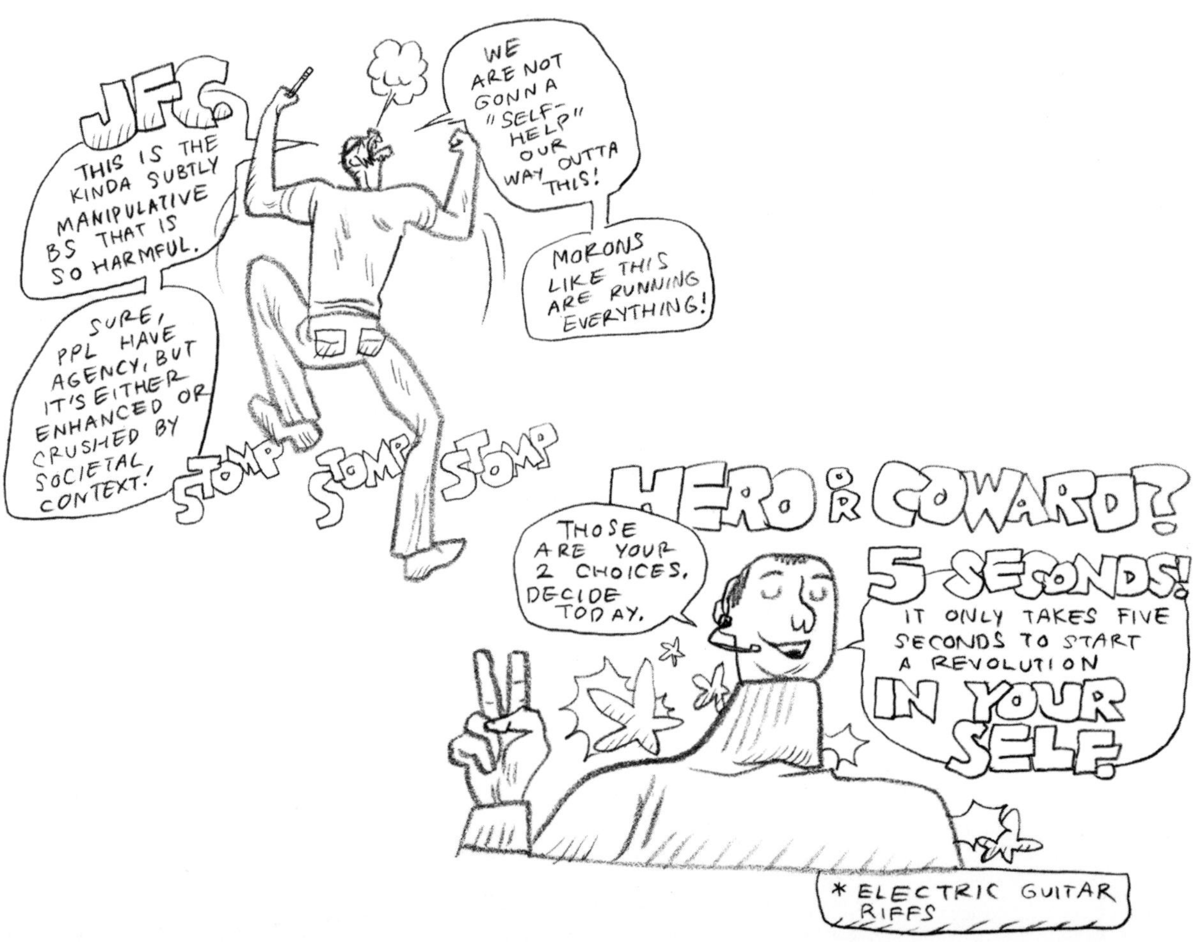
JFC
THIS IS THE KINDA SUBTLY MANIPULATIVE BS THAT IS SO HARMFUL.
SURE, PPL HAVE AGENCY, BUT IT'S EITHER ENHANCED OR CRUSHED BY SOCIETAL CONTEXT!
WE ARE NOT GONNA "SELF-HELP" OUR WAY OUTTA THIS!
MORONS LIKE THIS ARE RUNNING EVERYTHING!
STOMP STOMP STOMP
HERO OR COWARD?
THOSE ARE YOUR 2 CHOICES. DECIDE TODAY.
5 SECONDS!
IT ONLY TAKES FIVE SECONDS TO START A REVOLUTION IN YOUR SELF.
* ELECTRIC GUITAR RIFFS

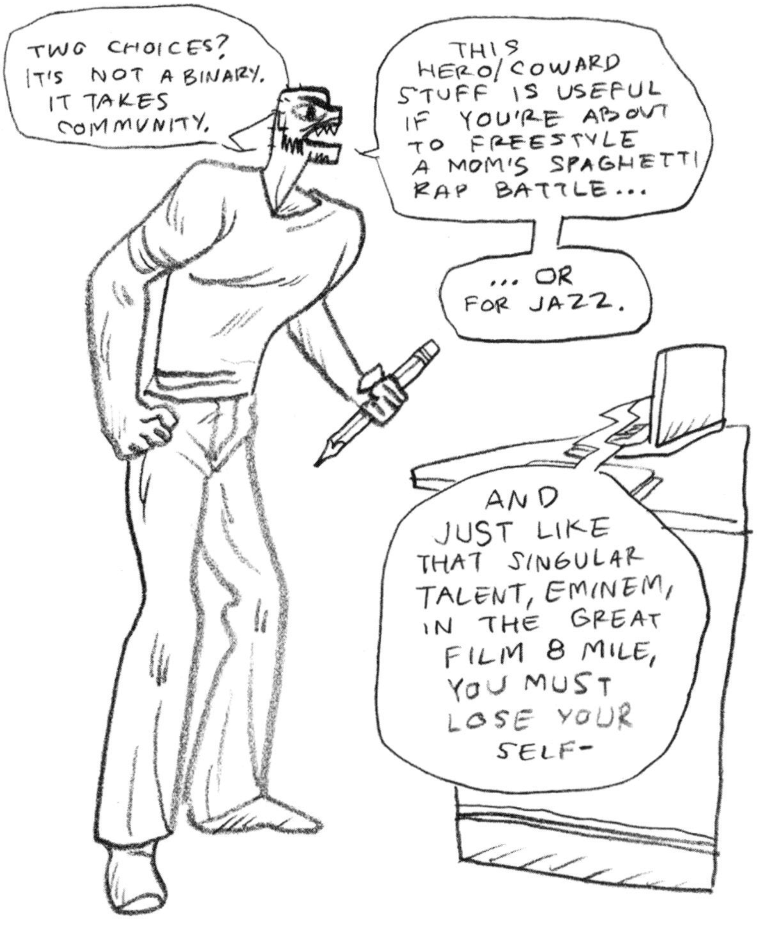
TWO CHOICES? IT'S NOT A BINARY. IT TAKES COMMUNITY.
THIS HERO/COWARD STUFF IS USEFUL IF YOU'RE ABOUT TO FREESTYLE A MOM'S SPAGHETTI RAP BATTLE...
... OR FOR JAZZ.
AND JUST LIKE THAT SINGULAR TALENT, EMINEM, IN THE GREAT FILM 8 MILE, YOU MUST LOSE YOUR SELF-

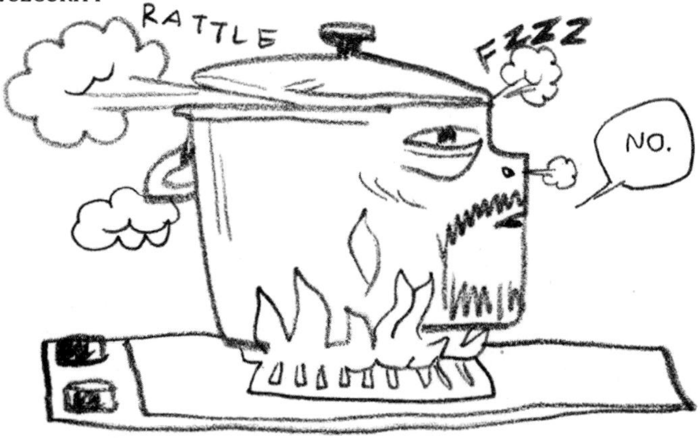
RATTLE
FZZZ
NO.

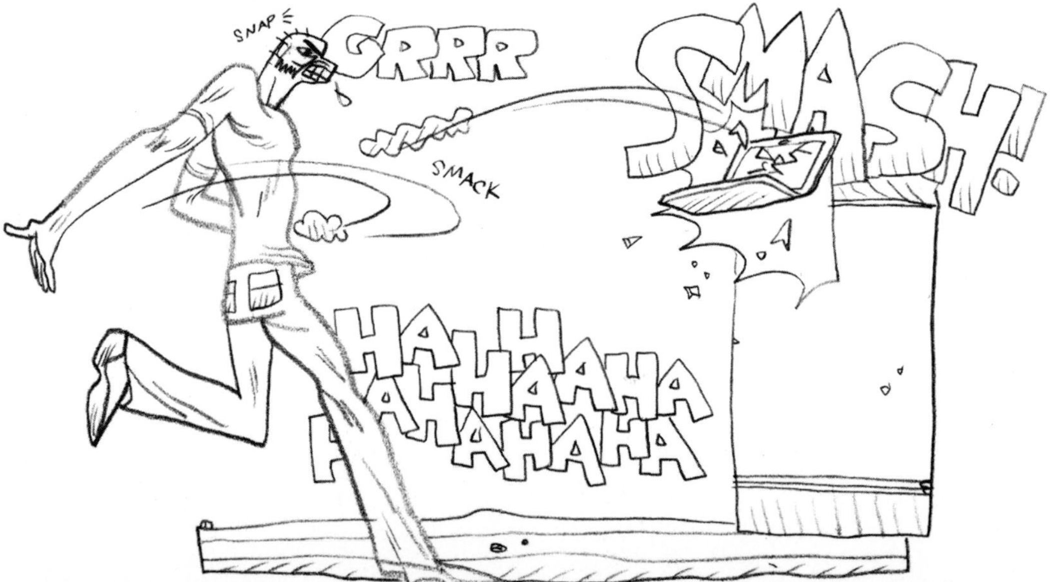
SNAP
GRRR
SMASH!
SMACK
HAHAH
HAHAHAHA
HAHAHAHA

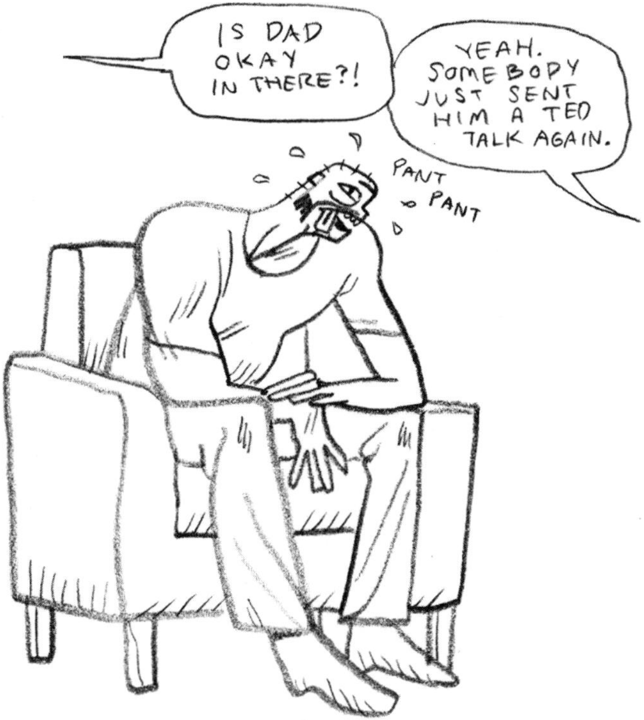
IS DAD OKAY IN THERE?!
YEAH. SOMEBODY JUST SENT HIM A TED TALK AGAIN.
PANT PANT

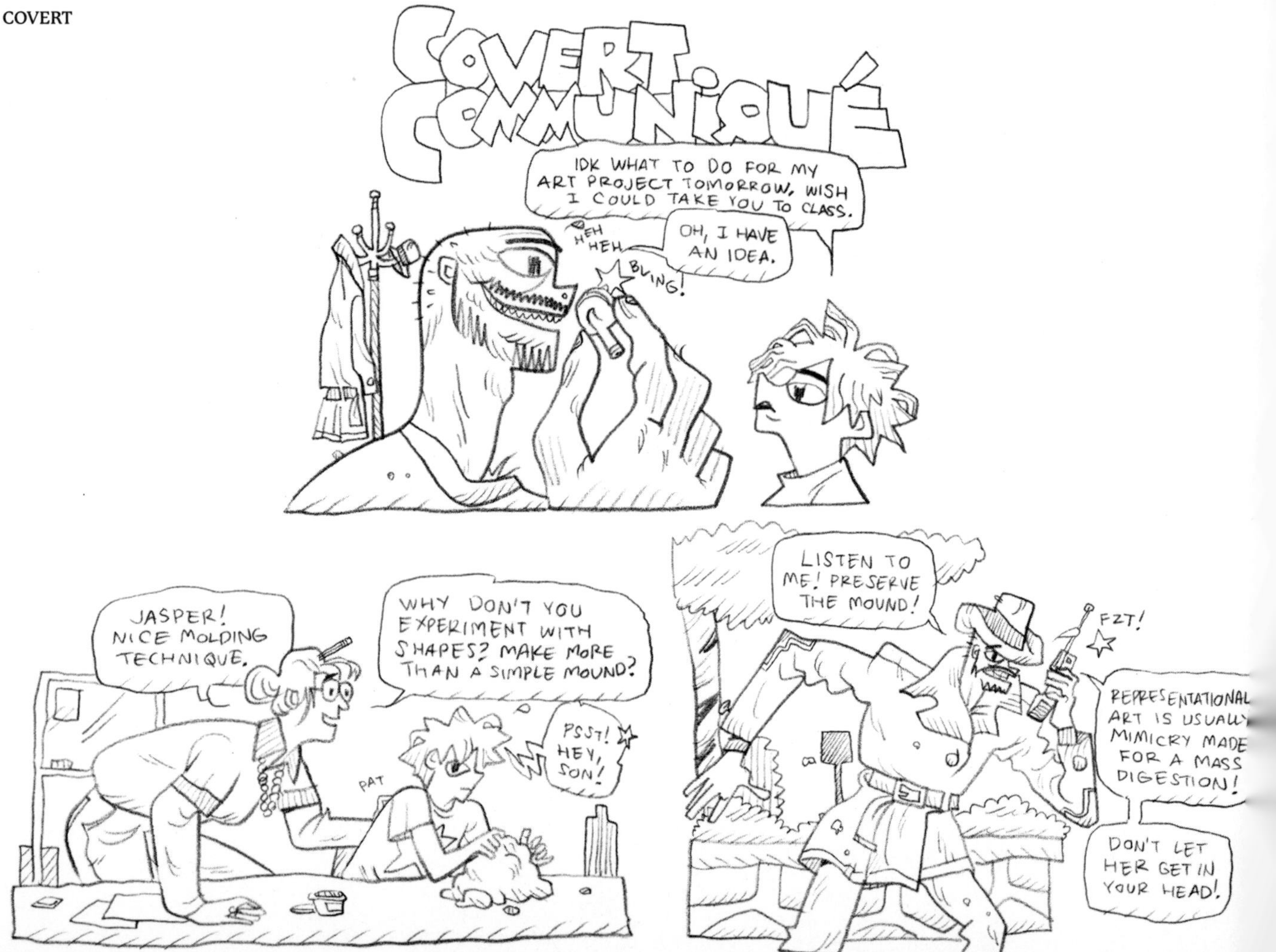
COVERT COMMUNIQUÉ
IDK WHAT TO DO FOR MY ART PROJECT TOMORROW, WISH I COULD TAKE YOU TO CLASS.
HEH HEH
OH, I HAVE AN IDEA.
BLING!
JASPER! NICE MOLDING TECHNIQUE.
WHY DON'T YOU EXPERIMENT WITH SHAPES? MAKE MORE THAN A SIMPLE MOUND?
PAT
PSST! HEY, SON!
LISTEN TO ME! PRESERVE THE MOUND!
FZT!
REPRESENTATIONAL ART IS USUALL MIMICRY MADE FOR A MASS DIGESTION!
DON'T LET HER GET IN YOUR HEAD!

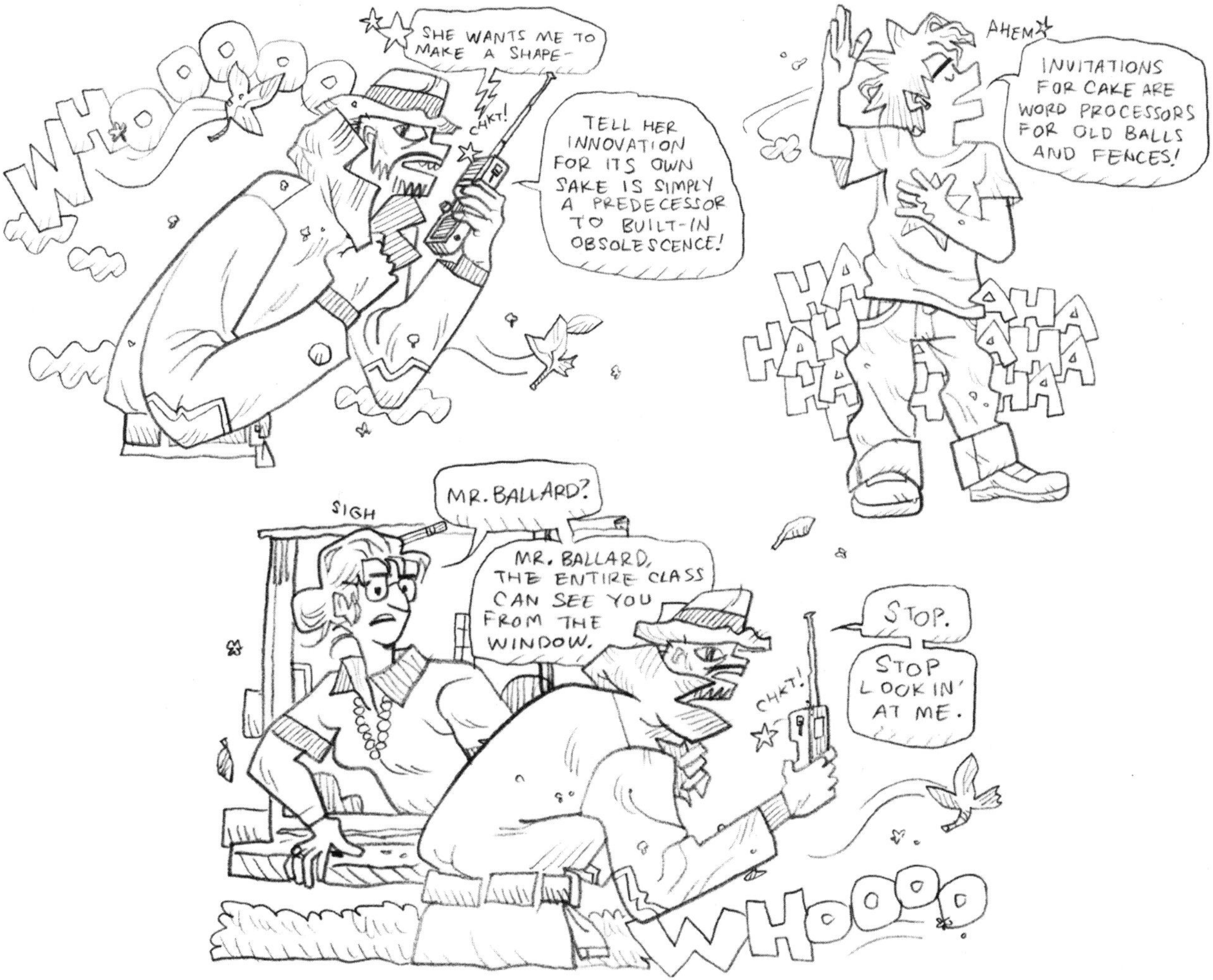
WHOOOOO
SHE WANTS ME TO MAKE A SHAPE-
CHKT!
TELL HER INNOVATION FOR ITS OWN SAKE IS SIMPLY A PREDECESSOR TO BUILT-IN OBSOLESCENCE!
AHEM
INVITATIONS FOR CAKE ARE WORD PROCESSORS FOR OLD BALLS AND FENCES!
HAHAHAHA HAHAHAHA
SIGH
MR. BALLARD?
MR. BALLARD, THE ENTIRE CLASS CAN SEE YOU FROM THE WINDOW.
CHKT!
STOP.
STOP LOOKIN' AT ME.
WHOOOO

SUSPENDED!
SOMETIMES REAL LIFE TAKES PRECEDENT.
TODAY'S REGULAR COMIC WILL BE PUT ON HOLD.
I'VE BEEN CALLED TO A PARENT-TEACHER MEETING.
AND I THOUGHT IT'D BE FUN IF YOU ALL CAME ALONG!
STRAP IN! LET'S ROLL UP OUR SLEEVES AND GET INTO SOME REAL LIFE LEGIT PARENTIN'!
MR. BALLARD, LIAM IS BEING SUSPENDED.
YOUR SON PUNCHED ANOTHER STUDENT IN CLASS TODAY.
HE BROKE HIS NOSE. THE FAMILY MIGHT PRESS CHARGES.
WAT.

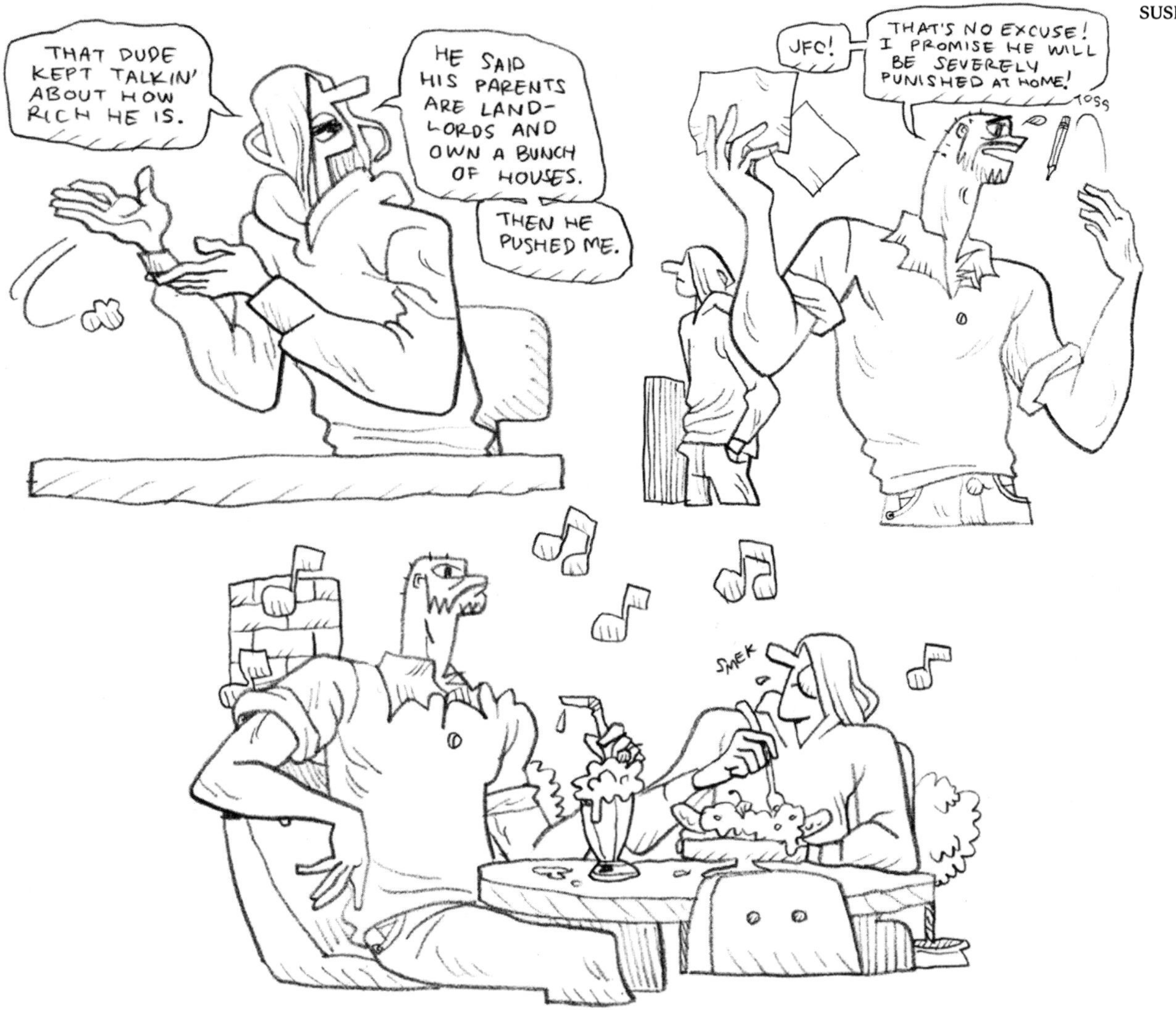
THAT DUDE KEPT TALKIN' ABOUT HOW RICH HE IS.
HE SAID HIS PARENTS ARE LANDLORDS AND OWN A BUNCH OF HOUSES.
THEN HE PUSHED ME.
JFC!
THAT'S NO EXCUSE! I PROMISE HE WILL BE SEVERELY PUNISHED AT HOME!
TOSS
SMEK

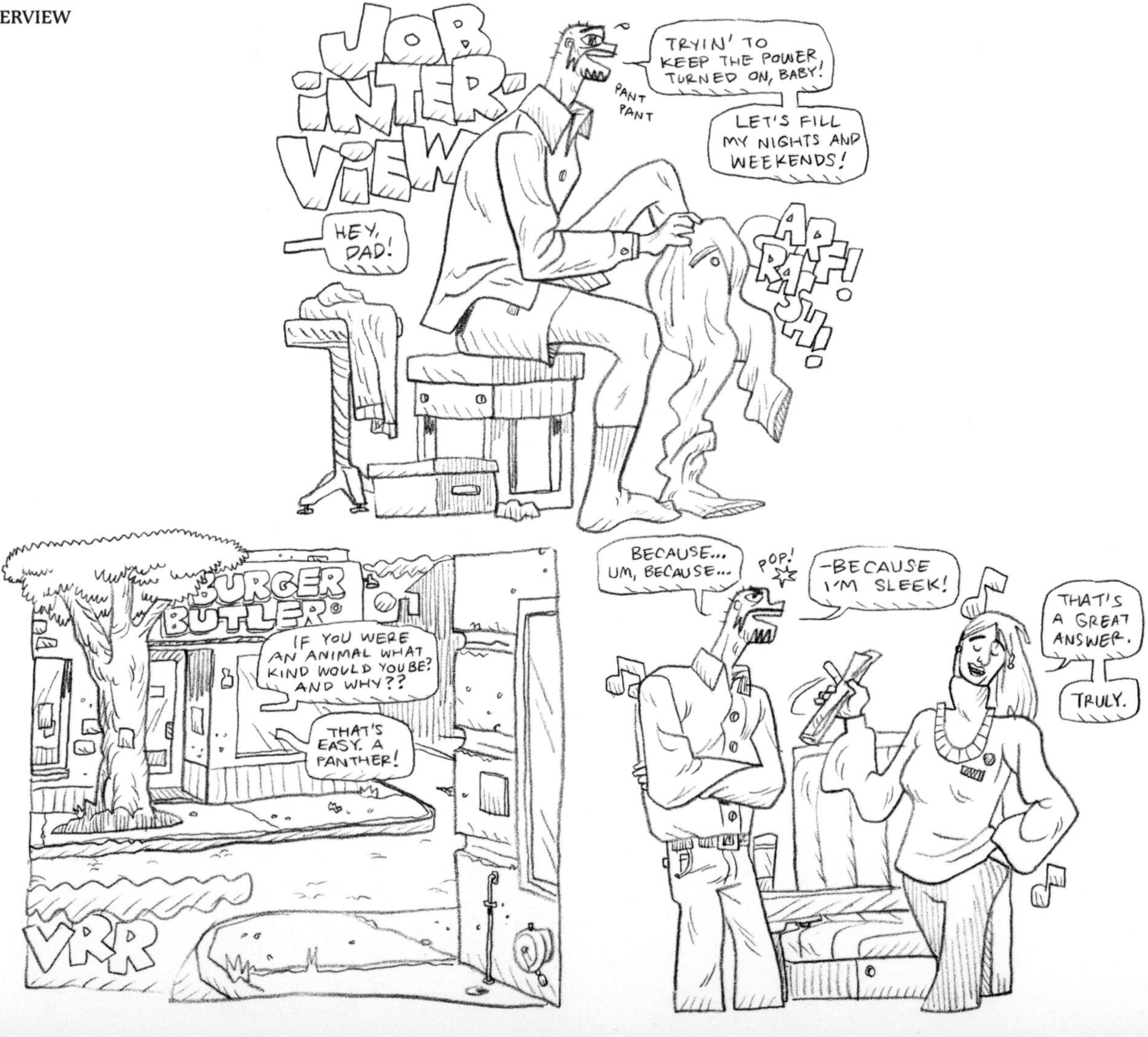
JOB INTER-VIEW
TRYIN' TO KEEP THE POWER TURNED ON, BABY!
PANT PANT
LET'S FILL MY NIGHTS AND WEEKENDS!
HEY, DAD!
ARF! RAFF! RASH!
BURGER BUTLER®
IF YOU WERE AN ANIMAL WHAT KIND WOULD YOU BE? AND WHY??
THAT'S EASY. A PANTHER!
VRR
BECAUSE... UM, BECAUSE...
POP!
-BECAUSE I'M SLEEK!
THAT'S A GREAT ANSWER.
TRULY.

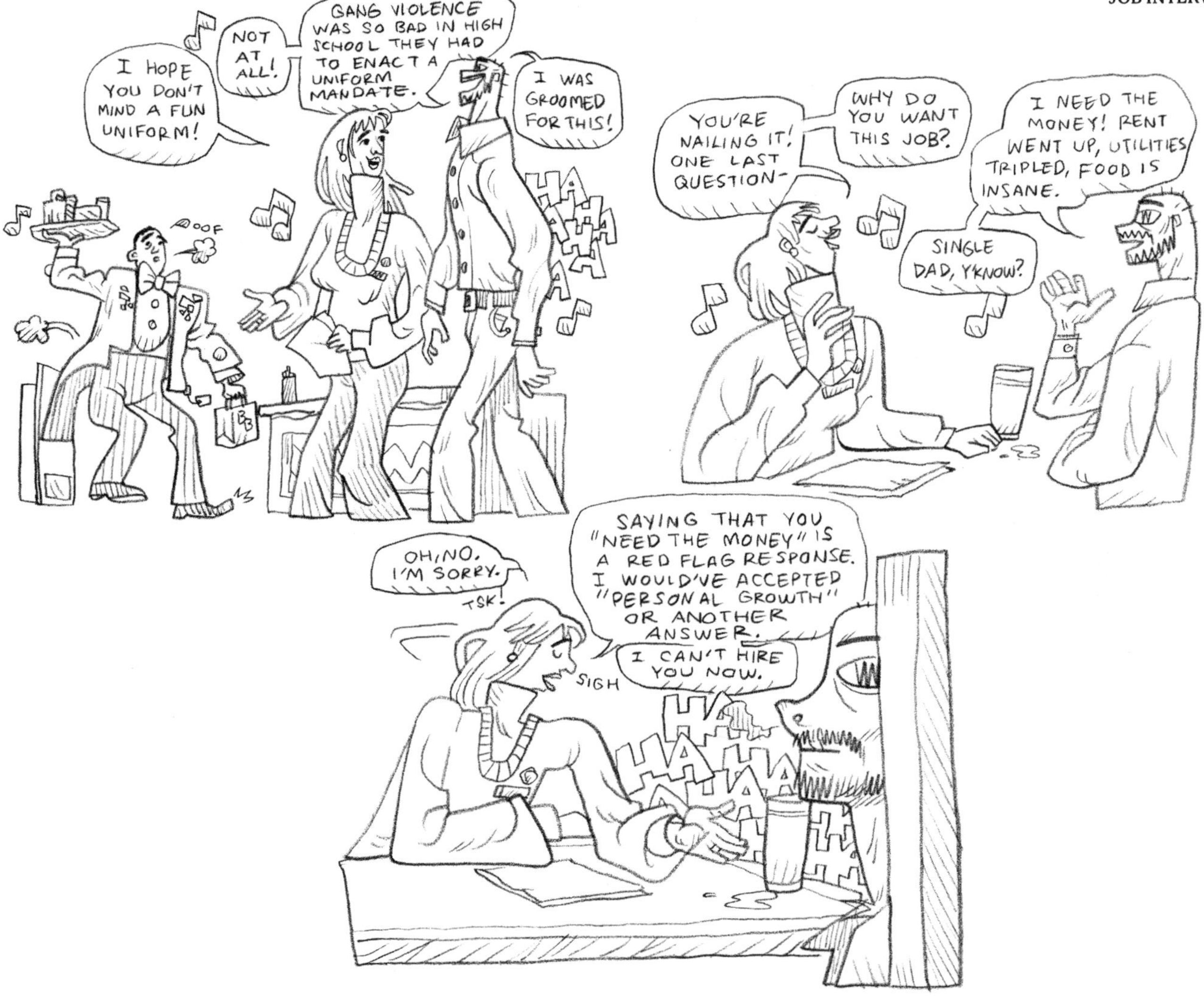
I HOPE YOU DON'T MIND A FUN UNIFORM!
NOT AT ALL!
GANG VIOLENCE WAS SO BAD IN HIGH SCHOOL THEY HAD TO ENACT A UNIFORM MANDATE.
I WAS GROOMED FOR THIS!
OOF
YOU'RE NAILING IT! ONE LAST QUESTION-
WHY DO YOU WANT THIS JOB?
I NEED THE MONEY! RENT WENT UP, UTILITIES TRIPLED, FOOD IS INSANE.
SINGLE DAD, Y'KNOW?
OH, NO. I'M SORRY.
TSK!
SAYING THAT YOU "NEED THE MONEY" IS A RED FLAG RESPONSE. I WOULD'VE ACCEPTED "PERSONAL GROWTH" OR ANOTHER ANSWER.
I CAN'T HIRE YOU NOW.
SIGH

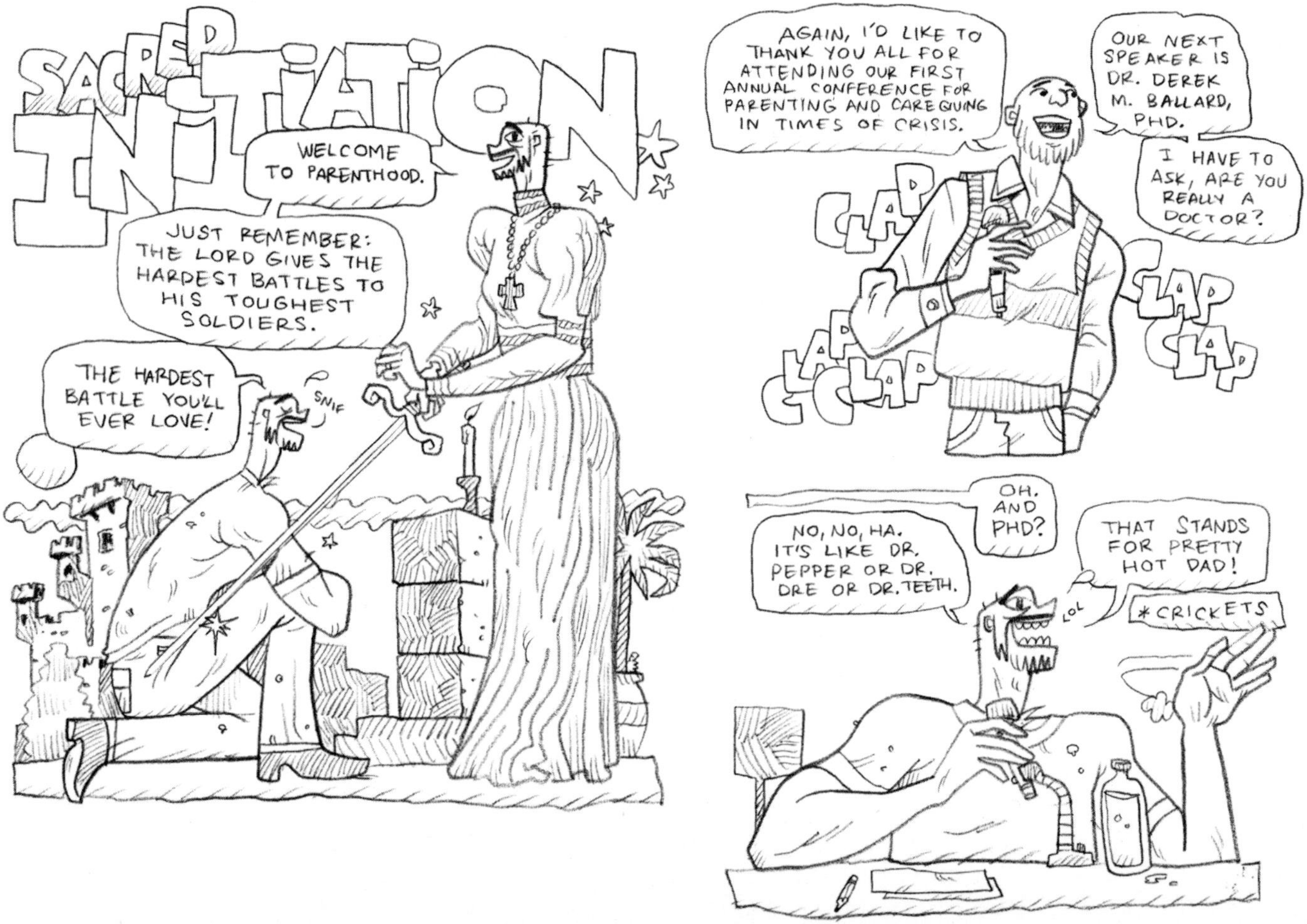
SACRED INITIATION
WELCOME TO PARENTHOOD.
JUST REMEMBER: THE LORD GIVES THE HARDEST BATTLES TO HIS TOUGHEST SOLDIERS.
THE HARDEST BATTLE YOU'LL EVER LOVE!
SNIF
AGAIN, I'D LIKE TO THANK YOU ALL FOR ATTENDING OUR FIRST ANNUAL CONFERENCE FOR PARENTING AND CAREGIVING IN TIMES OF CRISIS.
OUR NEXT SPEAKER IS DR. DEREK M. BALLARD, PHD.
CLAP CLAP CLAP CLAP CLAP CLAP
I HAVE TO ASK, ARE YOU REALLY A DOCTOR?
NO, NO, HA. IT'S LIKE DR. PEPPER OR DR. DRE OR DR. TEETH.
OH. AND PHD?
THAT STANDS FOR PRETTY HOT DAD!
LOL
*CRICKETS

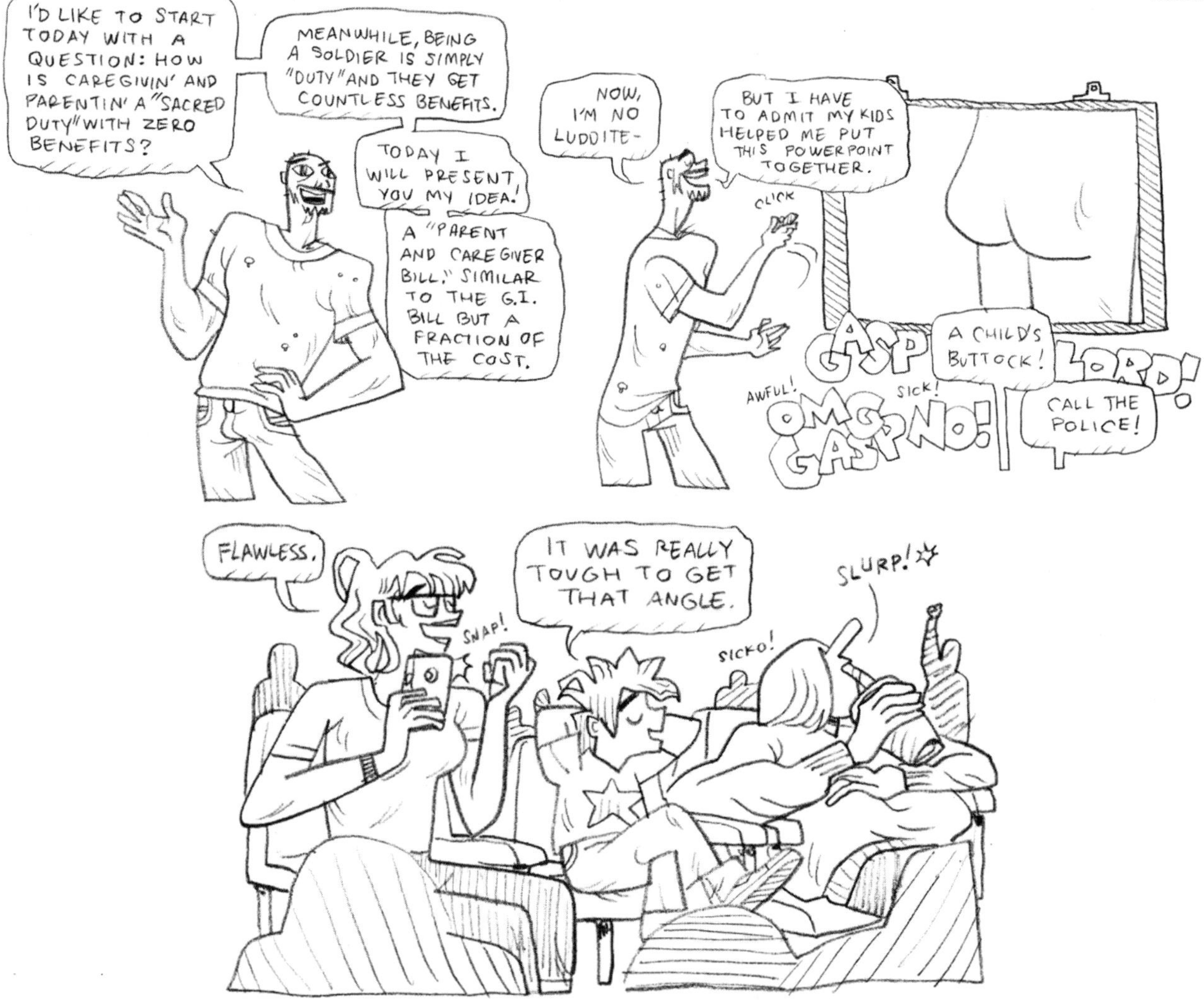
I'D LIKE TO START TODAY WITH A QUESTION: HOW IS CAREGIVIN' AND PARENTIN' A "SACRED DUTY" WITH ZERO BENEFITS?
MEANWHILE, BEING A SOLDIER IS SIMPLY "DUTY" AND THEY GET COUNTLESS BENEFITS.
TODAY I WILL PRESENT YOU MY IDEA!
A "PARENT AND CAREGIVER BILL," SIMILAR TO THE G.I. BILL BUT A FRACTION OF THE COST.
NOW, I'M NO LUDDITE-
BUT I HAVE TO ADMIT MY KIDS HELPED ME PUT THIS POWERPOINT TOGETHER.
CLICK
GASP
A CHILD'S BUTTOCK!
LORD!
AWFUL!
SICK!
OMG
GASP
NO!
CALL THE POLICE!
FLAWLESS.
SNAP!
IT WAS REALLY TOUGH TO GET THAT ANGLE.
SICKO!
SLURP!

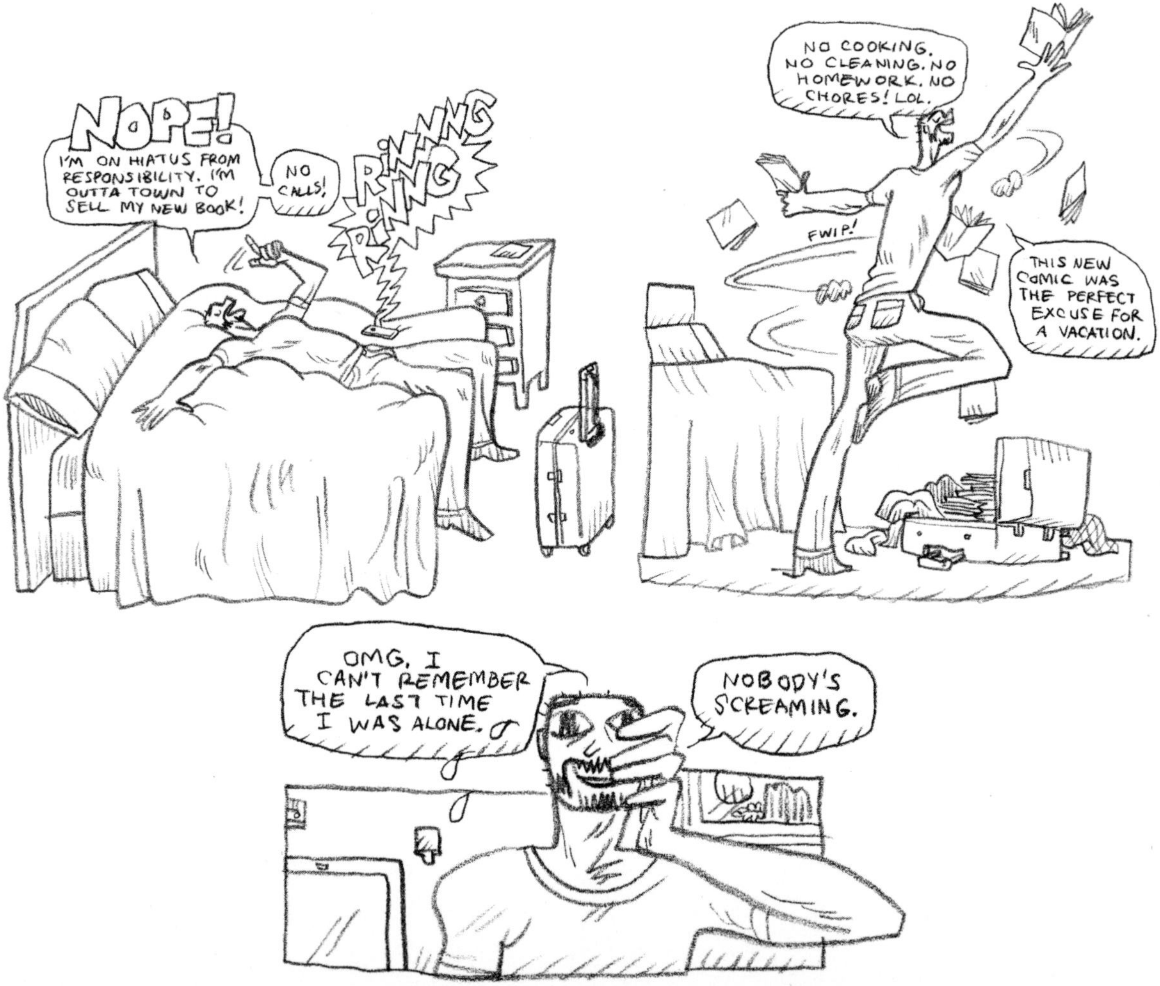
NOPE!
I'M ON HIATUS FROM RESPONSIBILITY. I'M OUTTA TOWN TO SELL MY NEW BOOK!
NO CALLS!
RINNNG RINNNG
RINNNG
NO COOKING. NO CLEANING. NO HOMEWORK. NO CHORES! LOL.
FWIP!
THIS NEW COMIC WAS THE PERFECT EXCUSE FOR A VACATION.
OMG. I CAN'T REMEMBER THE LAST TIME I WAS ALONE.
NOBODY'S SCREAMING.

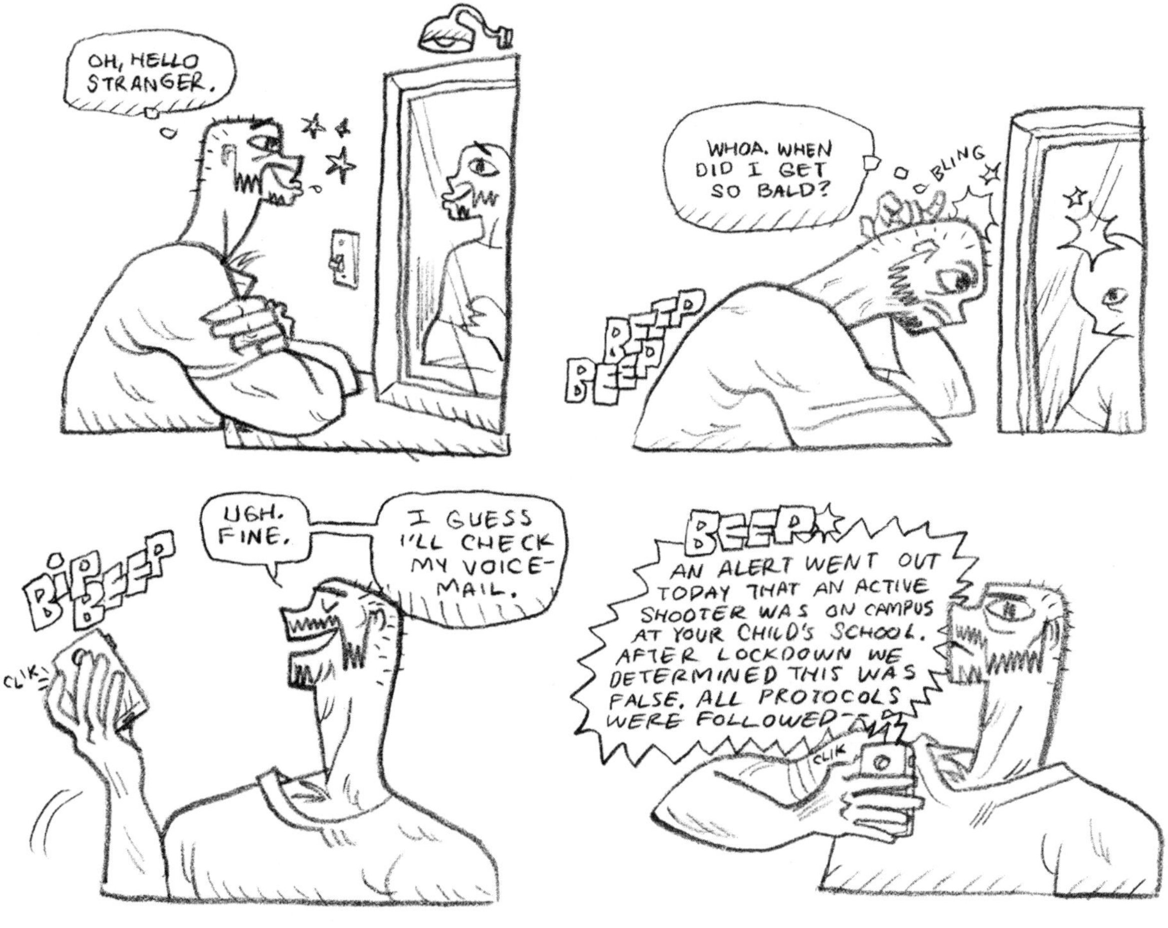
OH, HELLO STRANGER.
WHOA. WHEN DID I GET SO BALD?
BLING
BEEP
BEEP
BIP
BEEP
CLIK
UGH. FINE.
I GUESS I'LL CHECK MY VOICE-MAIL.
BEEP
AN ALERT WENT OUT TODAY THAT AN ACTIVE SHOOTER WAS ON CAMPUS AT YOUR CHILD'S SCHOOL. AFTER LOCKDOWN WE DETERMINED THIS WAS FALSE. ALL PROTOCOLS WERE FOLLOWED—
CLIK

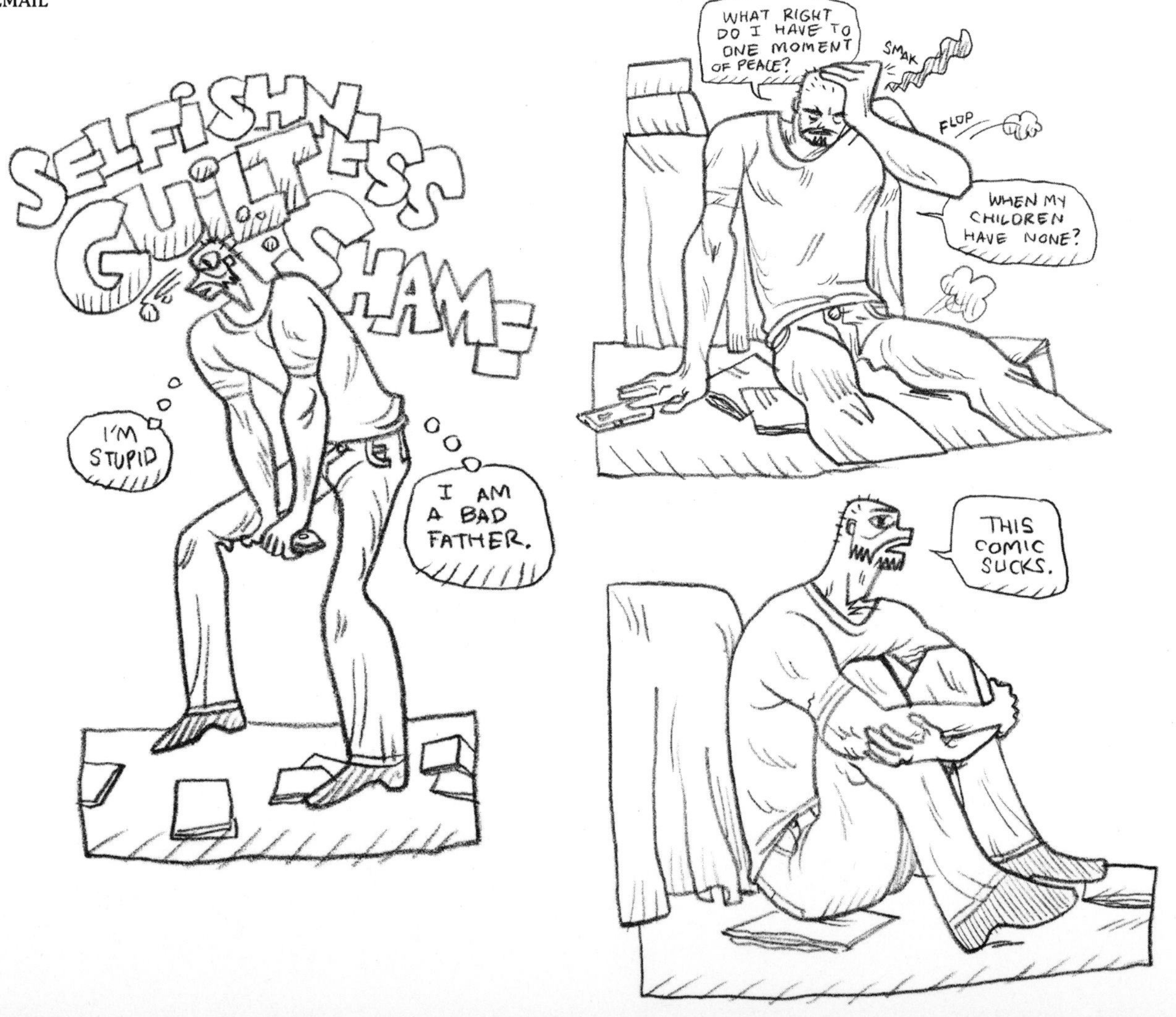
SELFISHNESS
GUILT
SHAME
I'M STUPID
I AM A BAD FATHER.
WHAT RIGHT DO I HAVE TO ONE MOMENT OF PEACE?
SMAK
FLOP
WHEN MY CHILDREN HAVE NONE?
THIS COMIC SUCKS.

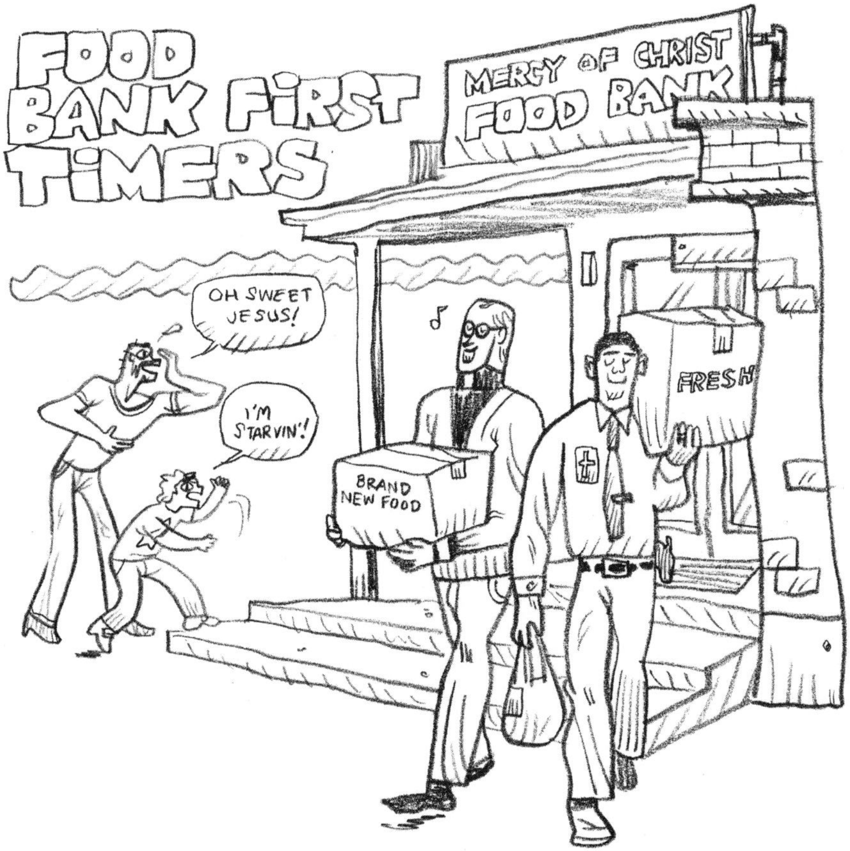
FOOD BANK FIRST TIMERS
MERCY OF CHRIST FOOD BANK
OH SWEET JESUS!
I'M STARVIN'!
BRAND NEW FOOD
FRESH

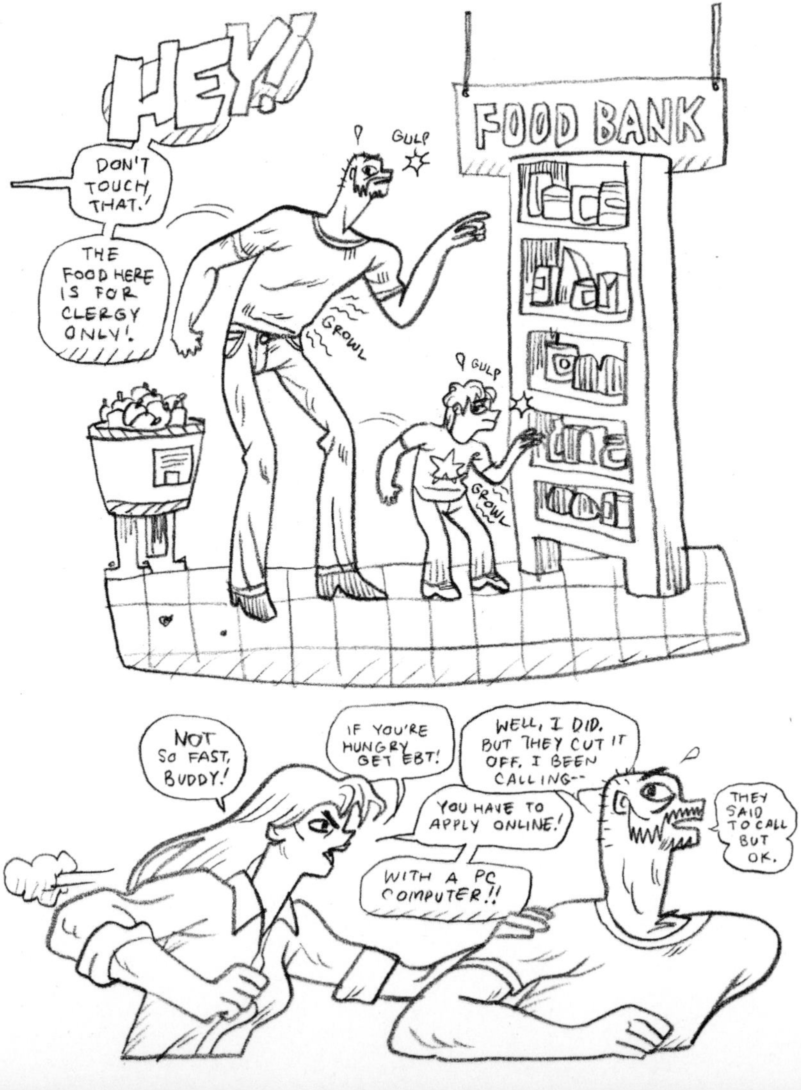
HEY!
DON'T TOUCH THAT.!
THE FOOD HERE IS FOR CLERGY ONLY!.
GULP
FOOD BANK
GROWL
GULP
GROWL
NOT SO FAST, BUDDY!
IF YOU'RE HUNGRY GET EBT!
WELL, I DID. BUT THEY CUT IT OFF. I BEEN CALLING--
YOU HAVE TO APPLY ONLINE!
WITH A PC COMPUTER!!
THEY SAID TO CALL BUT OK.

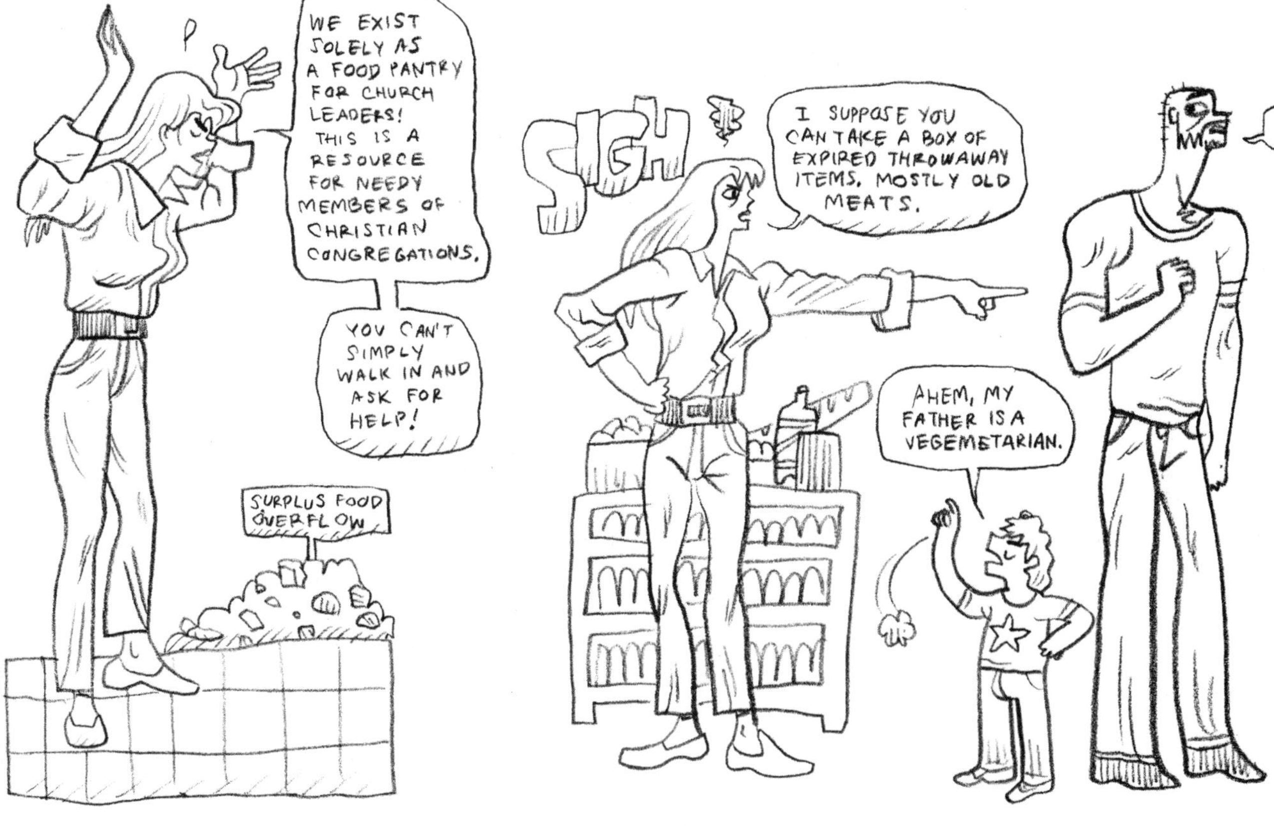
WE EXIST SOLELY AS A FOOD PANTRY FOR CHURCH LEADERS! THIS IS A RESOURCE FOR NEEDY MEMBERS OF CHRISTIAN CONGREGATIONS.
YOU CAN'T SIMPLY WALK IN AND ASK FOR HELP!
SURPLUS FOOD OVERFLOW
SIGH
I SUPPOSE YOU CAN TAKE A BOX OF EXPIRED THROWAWAY ITEMS, MOSTLY OLD MEATS.
OH.
AHEM, MY FATHER IS A VEGEMETARIAN.

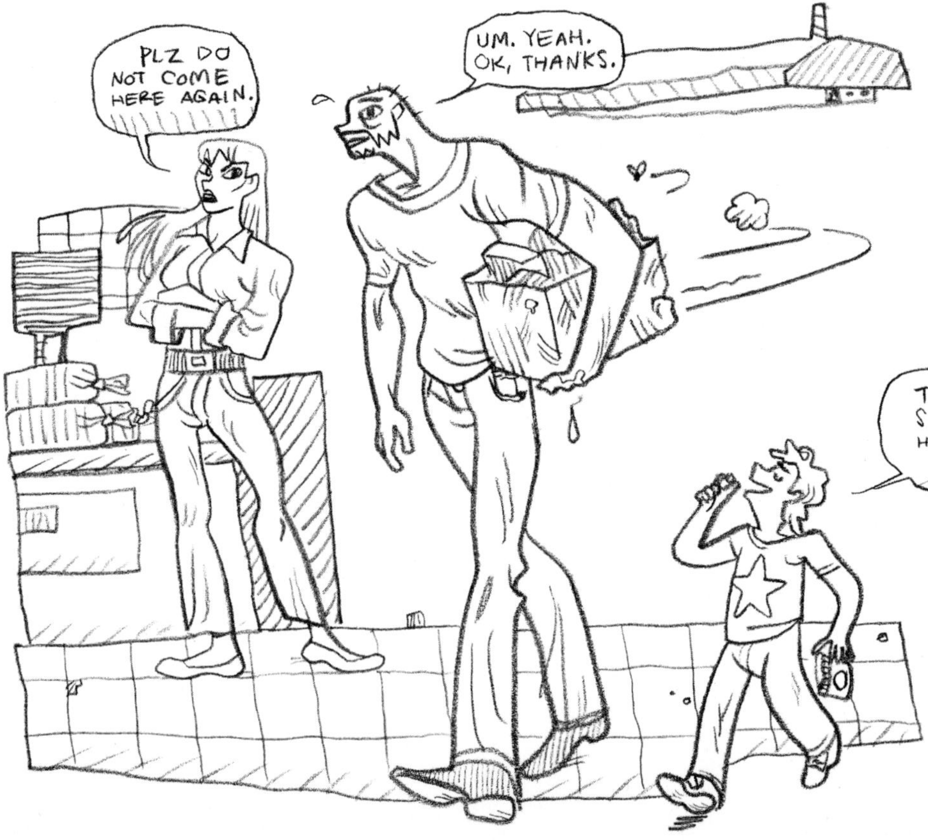
PLZ DO NOT COME HERE AGAIN.
UM. YEAH. OK, THANKS.
THESE FRUIT SNACKS ARE HARD LIKE GRAVEL!

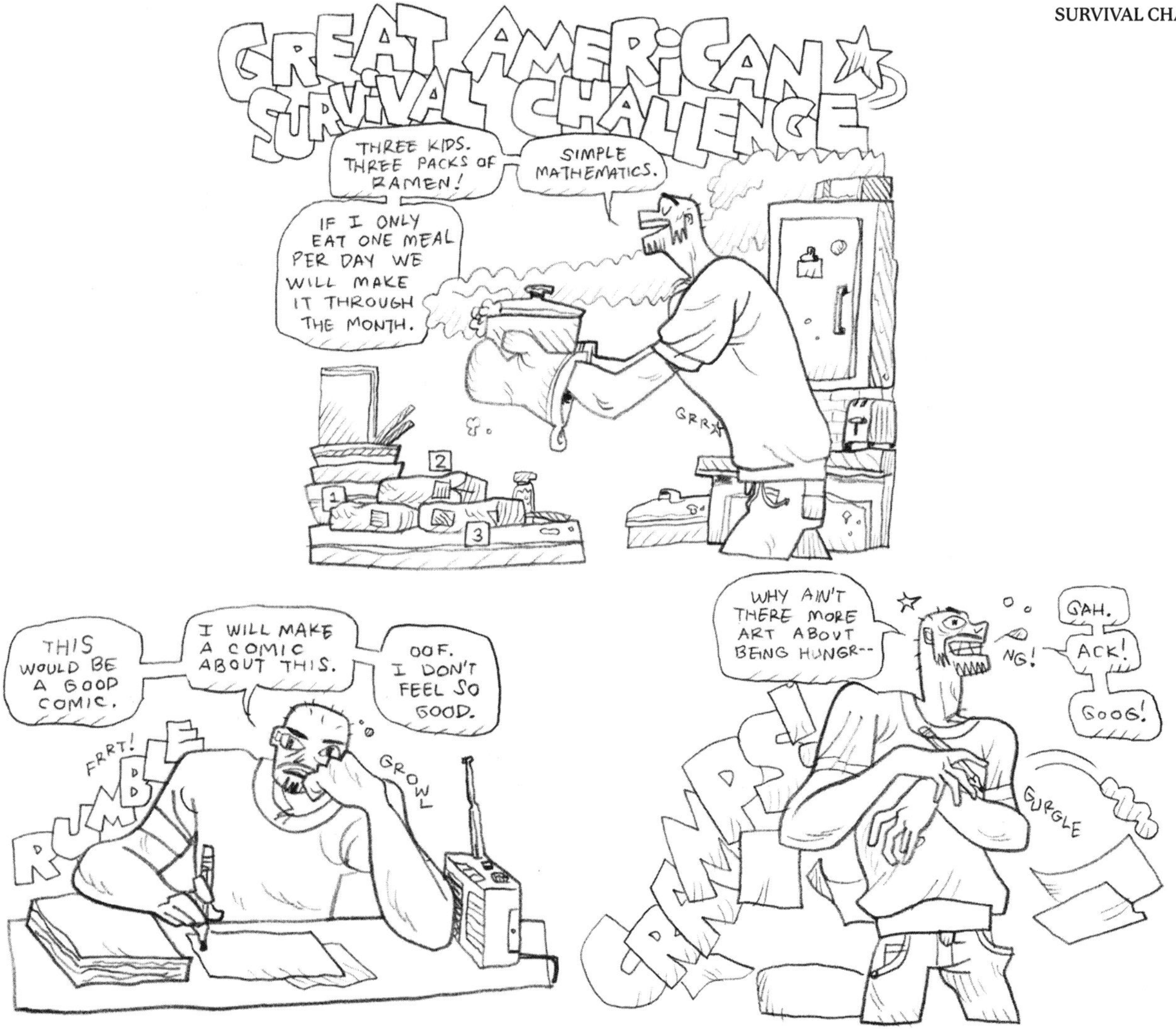
GREAT AMERICAN SURVIVAL CHALLENGE
THREE KIDS. THREE PACKS OF RAMEN!
SIMPLE MATHEMATICS.
IF I ONLY EAT ONE MEAL PER DAY WE WILL MAKE IT THROUGH THE MONTH.
1
2
3
GRR
THIS WOULD BE A GOOD COMIC.
I WILL MAKE A COMIC ABOUT THIS.
OOF. I DON'T FEEL SO GOOD.
FRRT!
RUMBLE
GROWL
WHY AIN'T THERE MORE ART ABOUT BEING HUNGR--
NG!
GAH.
ACK!
GOOG!
CRAMPS!
GURGLE

BARF! I DON'T THINK I CAN DRAW THROUGH THIS.
OH, I SEE WHY THERE'S NOT A LOTTA COMICS ABOUT BEIN' HUNGRY.
DUH, DEREK. LOL.
FRNT!
GUMBLE
MAYBE I HAVE SOME LOOSE CHANGE HERE?
SHAKE
I COULD BUY SOME-
GASP!
JACK POT!
AN OLD FRENCH FRY! MMM, LEATHERY.
CHEW
YOU LOSE TODAY, HUNGER!
VENI, VIDI, VICI.
HA
CLAP
HA
CLAP
HA

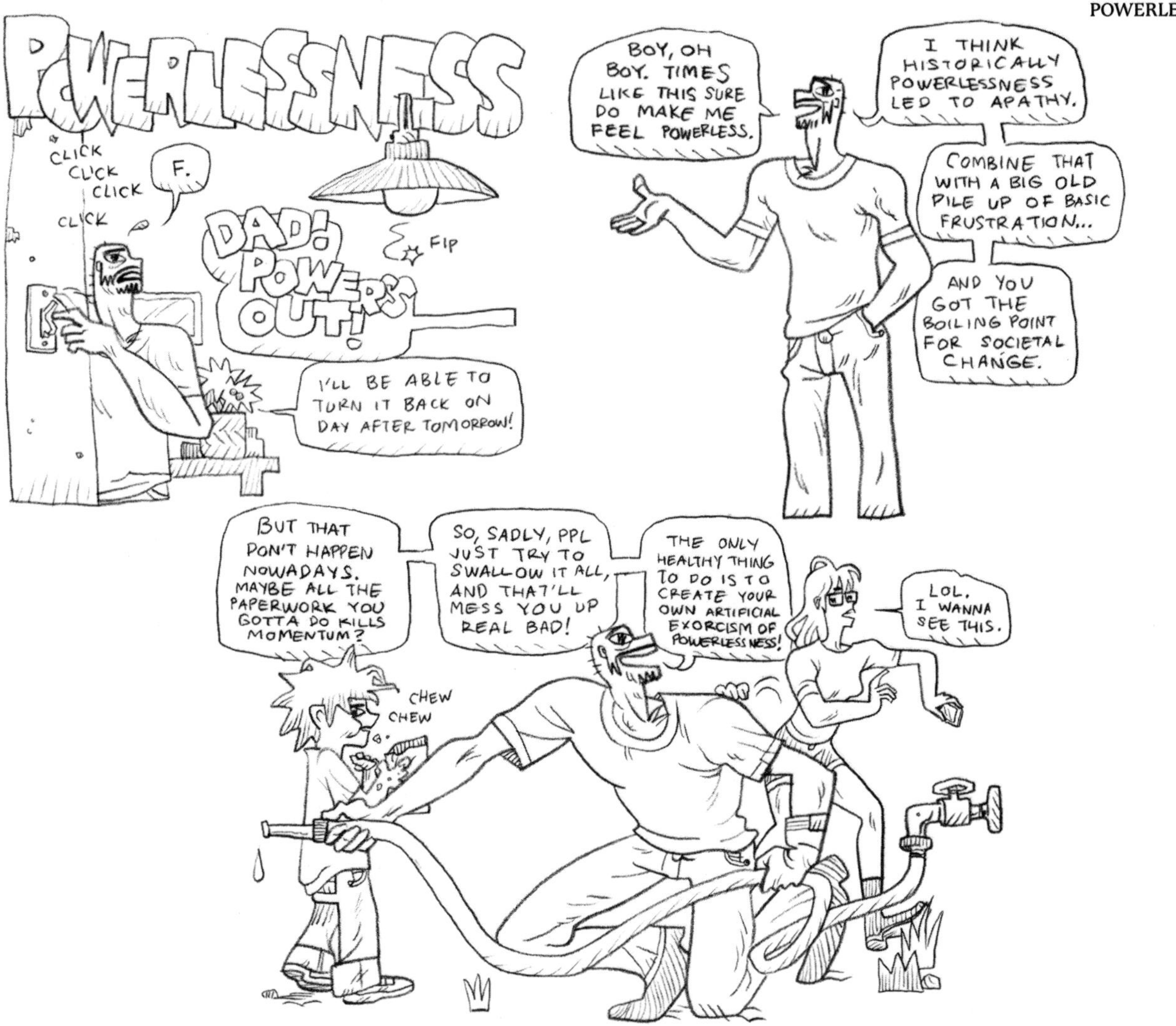
POWERLESSNESS
CLICK CLICK CLICK CLICK
F.
DAD! POWER'S OUT!
FIP
I'LL BE ABLE TO TURN IT BACK ON DAY AFTER TOMORROW!
BOY, OH BOY. TIMES LIKE THIS SURE DO MAKE ME FEEL POWERLESS.
I THINK HISTORICALLY POWERLESSNESS LED TO APATHY.
COMBINE THAT WITH A BIG OLD PILE UP OF BASIC FRUSTRATION...
AND YOU GOT THE BOILING POINT FOR SOCIETAL CHANGE.
BUT THAT DON'T HAPPEN NOWADAYS. MAYBE ALL THE PAPERWORK YOU GOTTA DO KILLS MOMENTUM?
SO, SADLY, PPL JUST TRY TO SWALLOW IT ALL, AND THAT'LL MESS YOU UP REAL BAD!
THE ONLY HEALTHY THING TO DO IS TO CREATE YOUR OWN ARTIFICIAL EXORCISM OF POWERLESSNESS!
LOL. I WANNA SEE THIS.
CHEW CHEW

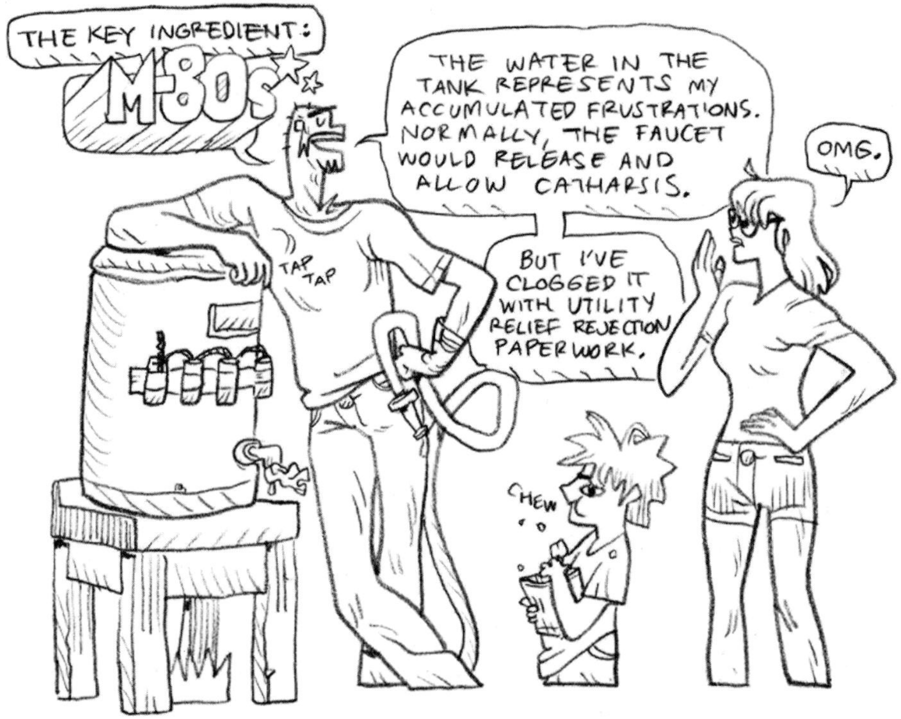
THE KEY INGREDIENT:
M-80s
THE WATER IN THE TANK REPRESENTS MY ACCUMULATED FRUSTRATIONS. NORMALLY, THE FAUCET WOULD RELEASE AND ALLOW CATHARSIS.
BUT I'VE CLOGGED IT WITH UTILITY RELIEF REJECTION PAPERWORK.
OMG.
TAP TAP
CHEW

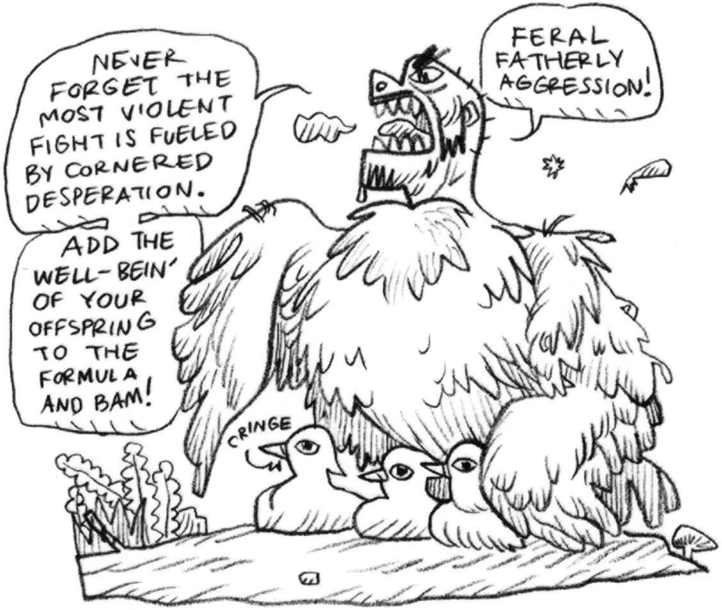
NEVER FORGET THE MOST VIOLENT FIGHT IS FUELED BY CORNERED DESPERATION.
ADD THE WELL-BEIN' OF YOUR OFFSPRING TO THE FORMULA AND BAM!
FERAL FATHERLY AGGRESSION!
CRINGE

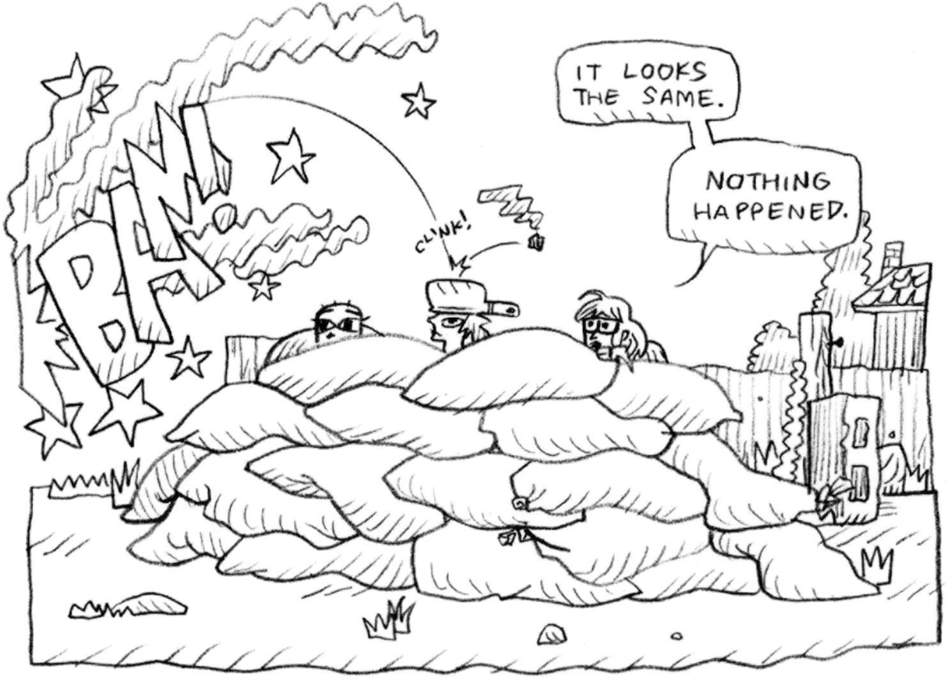
BAM!
CLINK!
IT LOOKS THE SAME.
NOTHING HAPPENED.

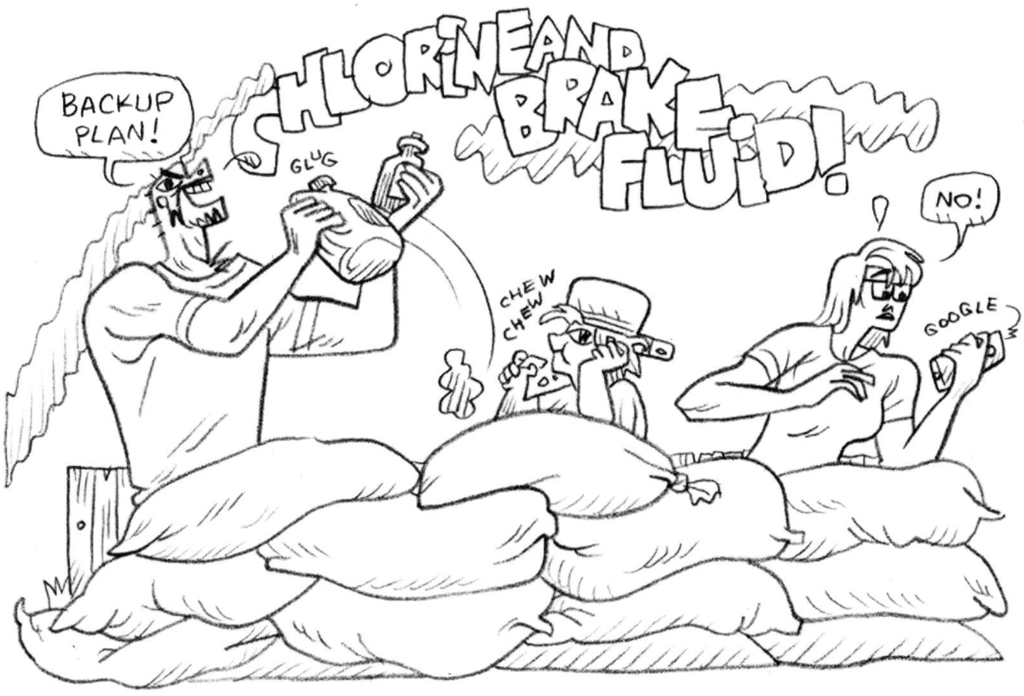
BACKUP PLAN!
GLUG
CHLORINE AND BRAKE FLUID!
NO!
CHEW CHEW
GOOGLE

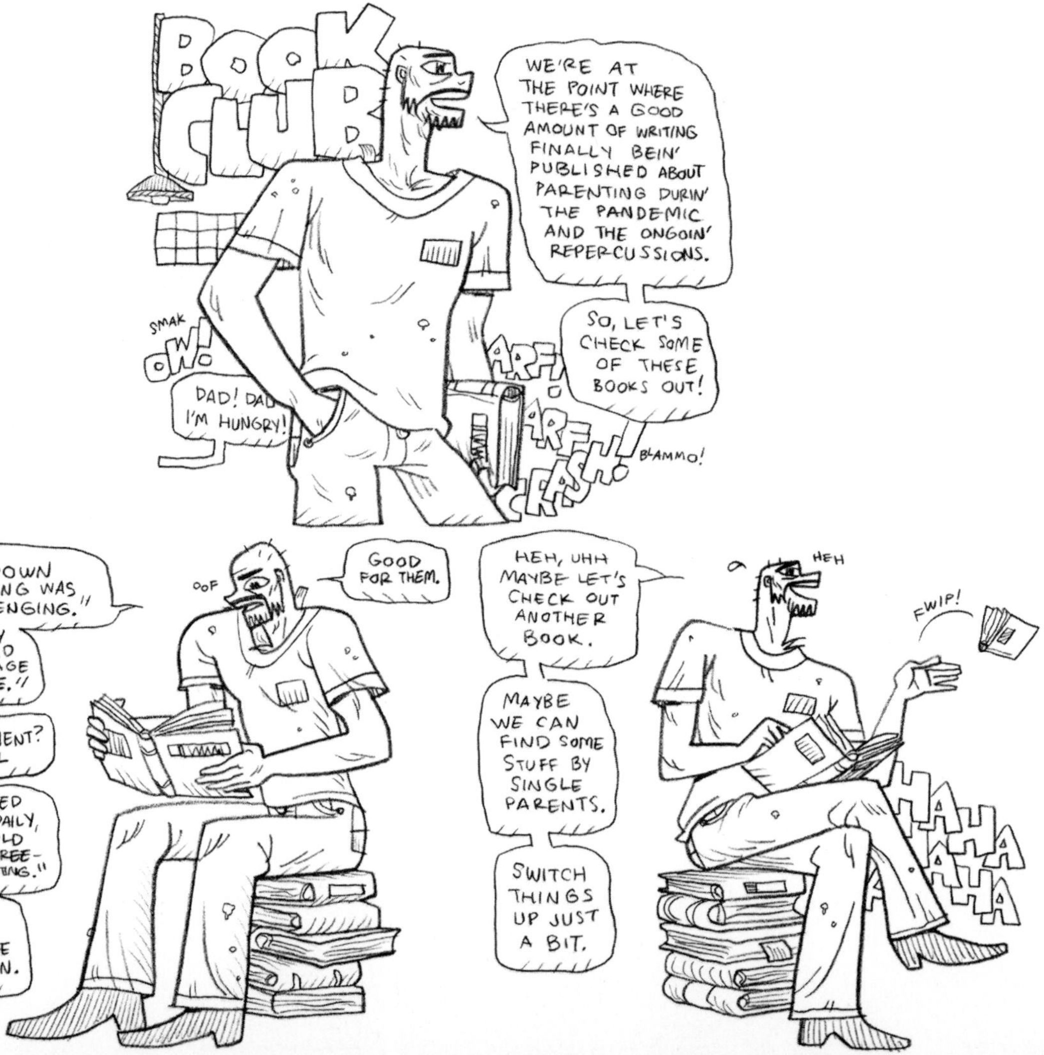
BOOK CLUB
WE'RE AT THE POINT WHERE THERE'S A GOOD AMOUNT OF WRITING FINALLY BEIN' PUBLISHED ABOUT PARENTING DURIN' THE PANDEMIC AND THE ONGOIN' REPERCUSSIONS.
SO, LET'S CHECK SOME OF THESE BOOKS OUT!
SMAK
OW!
DAD! DAD I'M HUNGRY!
BLAMMO!
CRASH!
"LOCKDOWN PARENTING WAS CHALLENGING."
OOF
GOOD FOR THEM.
"LUCKILY, MY PARENTS PAID OUR MORTGAGE IN SEATTLE."
UNEMPLOYMENT? OH, COOL
"WE ORDERED TAKEOUT DAILY, SO WE COULD CONTINUE FREE-LANCE WRITING."
THIS ACTUALLY SOUNDS LIKE A VACATION.
HEH, UHH MAYBE LET'S CHECK OUT ANOTHER BOOK.
HEH
MAYBE WE CAN FIND SOME STUFF BY SINGLE PARENTS.
SWITCH THINGS UP JUST A BIT.
FWIP!
HAHA HAHA HAHA

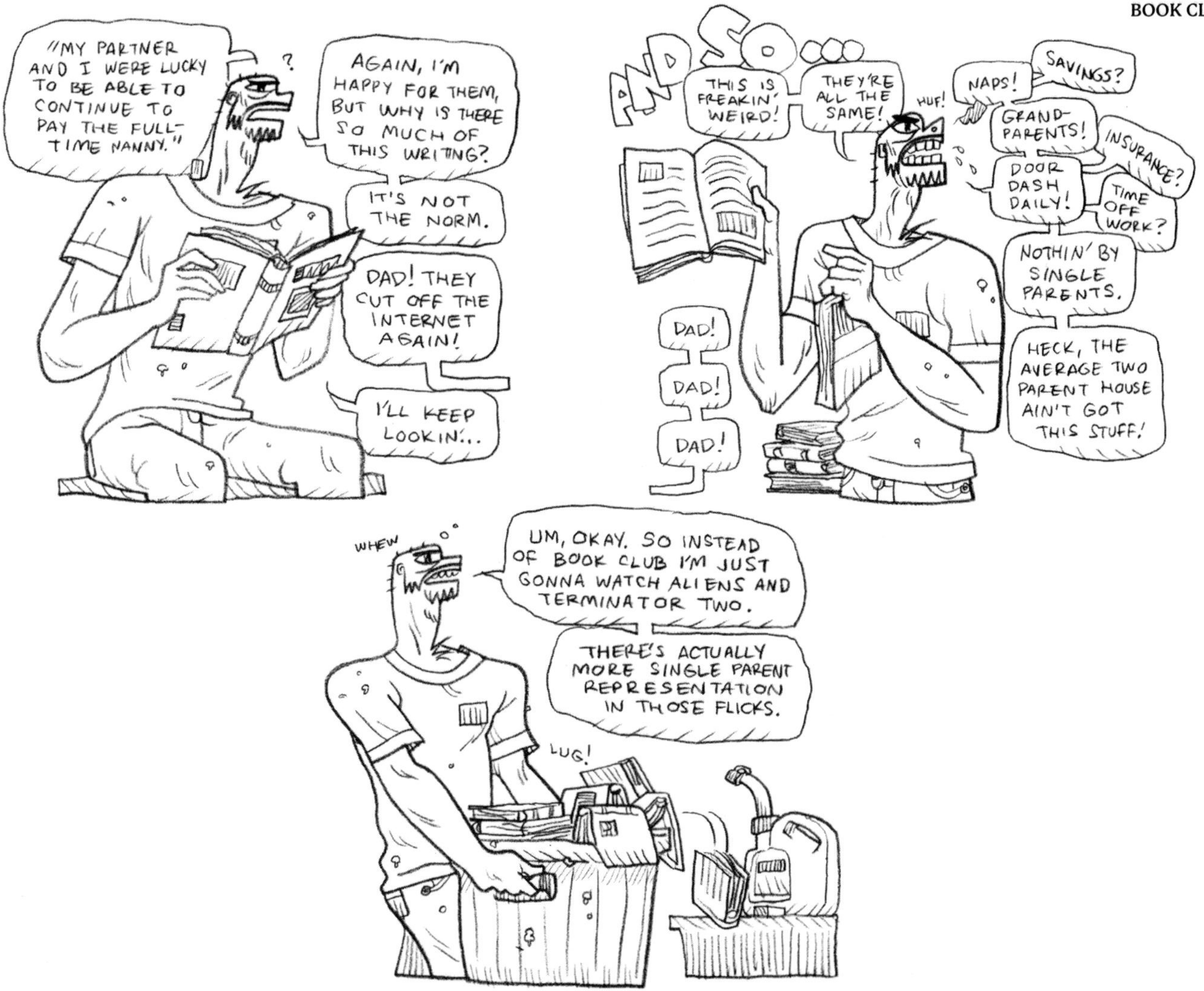
"MY PARTNER AND I WERE LUCKY TO BE ABLE TO CONTINUE TO PAY THE FULL-TIME NANNY."
?
AGAIN, I'M HAPPY FOR THEM, BUT WHY IS THERE SO MUCH OF THIS WRITING?
IT'S NOT THE NORM.
DAD! THEY CUT OFF THE INTERNET AGAIN!
I'LL KEEP LOOKIN'...
AND SO...
THIS IS FREAKIN' WEIRD!
THEY'RE ALL THE SAME!
HUF!
NAPS!
SAVINGS?
GRANDPARENTS!
INSURANCE?
DOOR DASH DAILY!
TIME OFF WORK?
NOTHIN' BY SINGLE PARENTS.
HECK, THE AVERAGE TWO PARENT HOUSE AIN'T GOT THIS STUFF!
DAD!
DAD!
DAD!
WHEW
UM, OKAY. SO INSTEAD OF BOOK CLUB I'M JUST GONNA WATCH ALIENS AND TERMINATOR TWO.
THERE'S ACTUALLY MORE SINGLE PARENT REPRESENTATION IN THOSE FLICKS.
LUG!

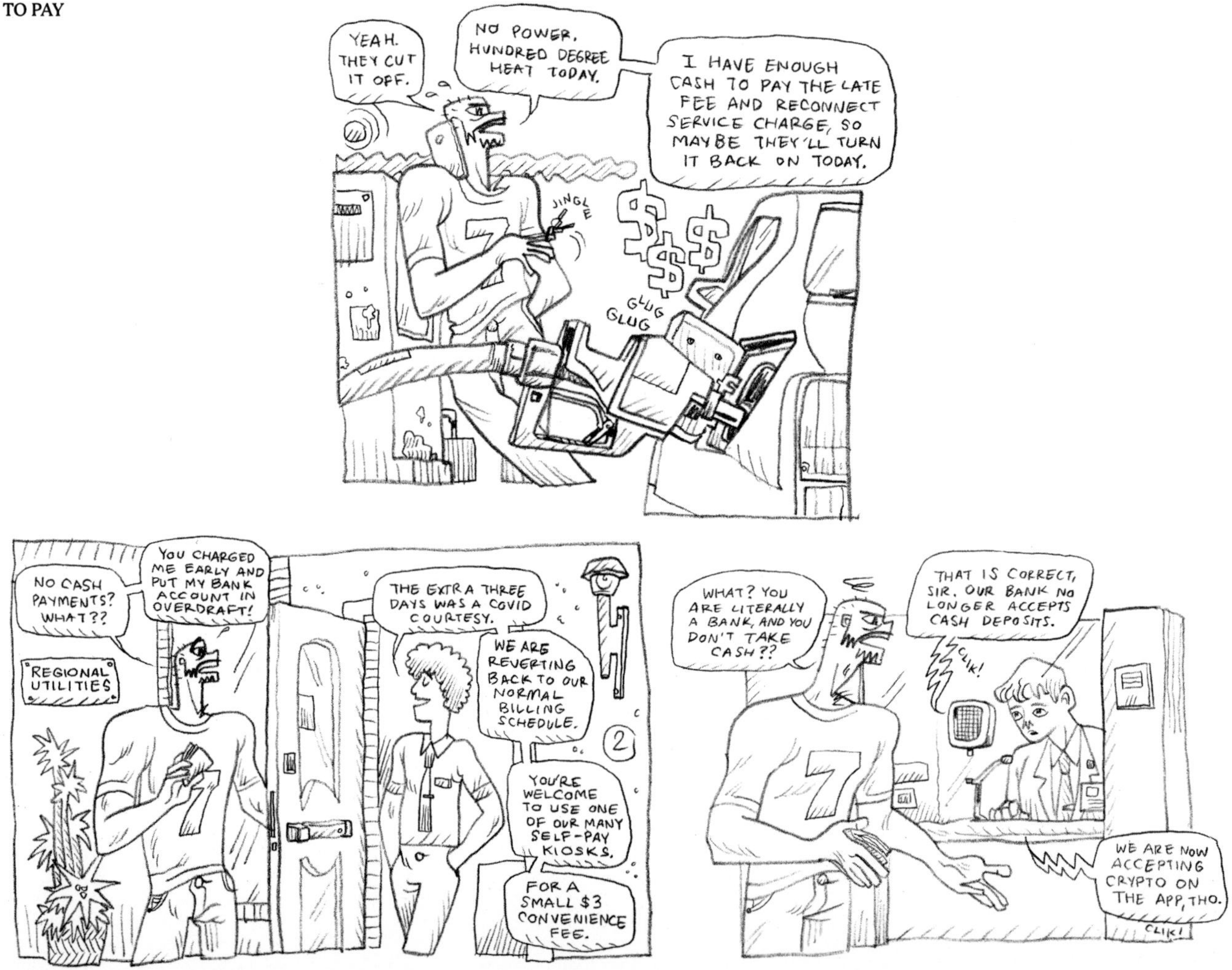
YEAH. THEY CUT IT OFF.
NO POWER. HUNDRED DEGREE HEAT TODAY.
I HAVE ENOUGH CASH TO PAY THE LATE FEE AND RECONNECT SERVICE CHARGE, SO MAYBE THEY'LL TURN IT BACK ON TODAY.
JINGLE
GLUG GLUG
NO CASH PAYMENTS? WHAT??
YOU CHARGED ME EARLY AND PUT MY BANK ACCOUNT IN OVERDRAFT!
REGIONAL UTILITIES
THE EXTRA THREE DAYS WAS A COVID COURTESY.
WE ARE REVERTING BACK TO OUR NORMAL BILLING SCHEDULE.
YOU'RE WELCOME TO USE ONE OF OUR MANY SELF-PAY KIOSKS.
FOR A SMALL $3 CONVENIENCE FEE.
WHAT? YOU ARE LITERALLY A BANK, AND YOU DON'T TAKE CASH??
THAT IS CORRECT, SIR. OUR BANK NO LONGER ACCEPTS CASH DEPOSITS.
CLIK!
WE ARE NOW ACCEPTING CRYPTO ON THE APP, THO.
CLIK!

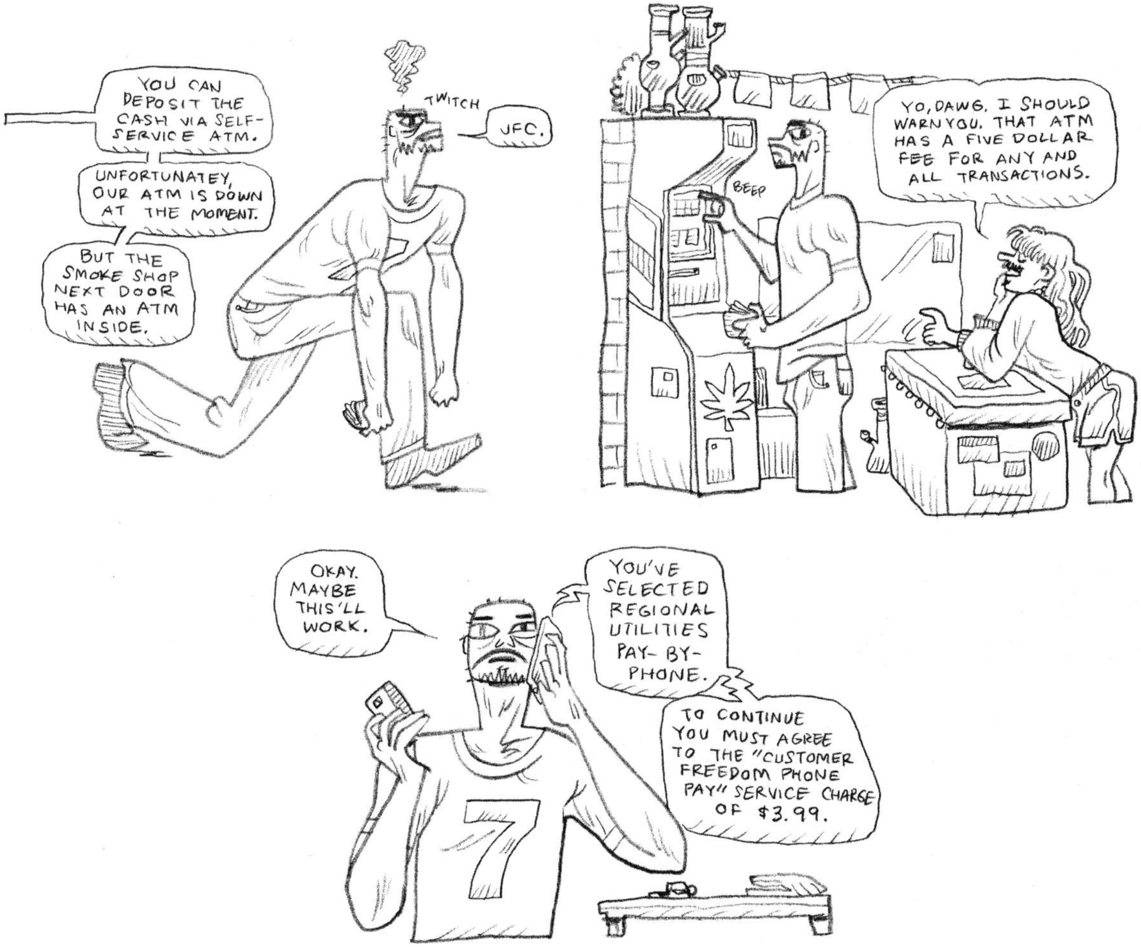
YOU CAN DEPOSIT THE CASH VIA SELF-SERVICE ATM.
UNFORTUNATEY, OUR ATM IS DOWN AT THE MOMENT.
BUT THE SMOKE SHOP NEXT DOOR HAS AN ATM INSIDE.
TWITCH
UFC.
BEEP
YO, DAWG. I SHOULD WARN YOU. THAT ATM HAS A FIVE DOLLAR FEE FOR ANY AND ALL TRANSACTIONS.
OKAY. MAYBE THIS'LL WORK.
YOU'VE SELECTED REGIONAL UTILITIES PAY-BY-PHONE.
TO CONTINUE YOU MUST AGREE TO THE "CUSTOMER FREEDOM PHONE PAY" SERVICE CHARGE OF $3.99.

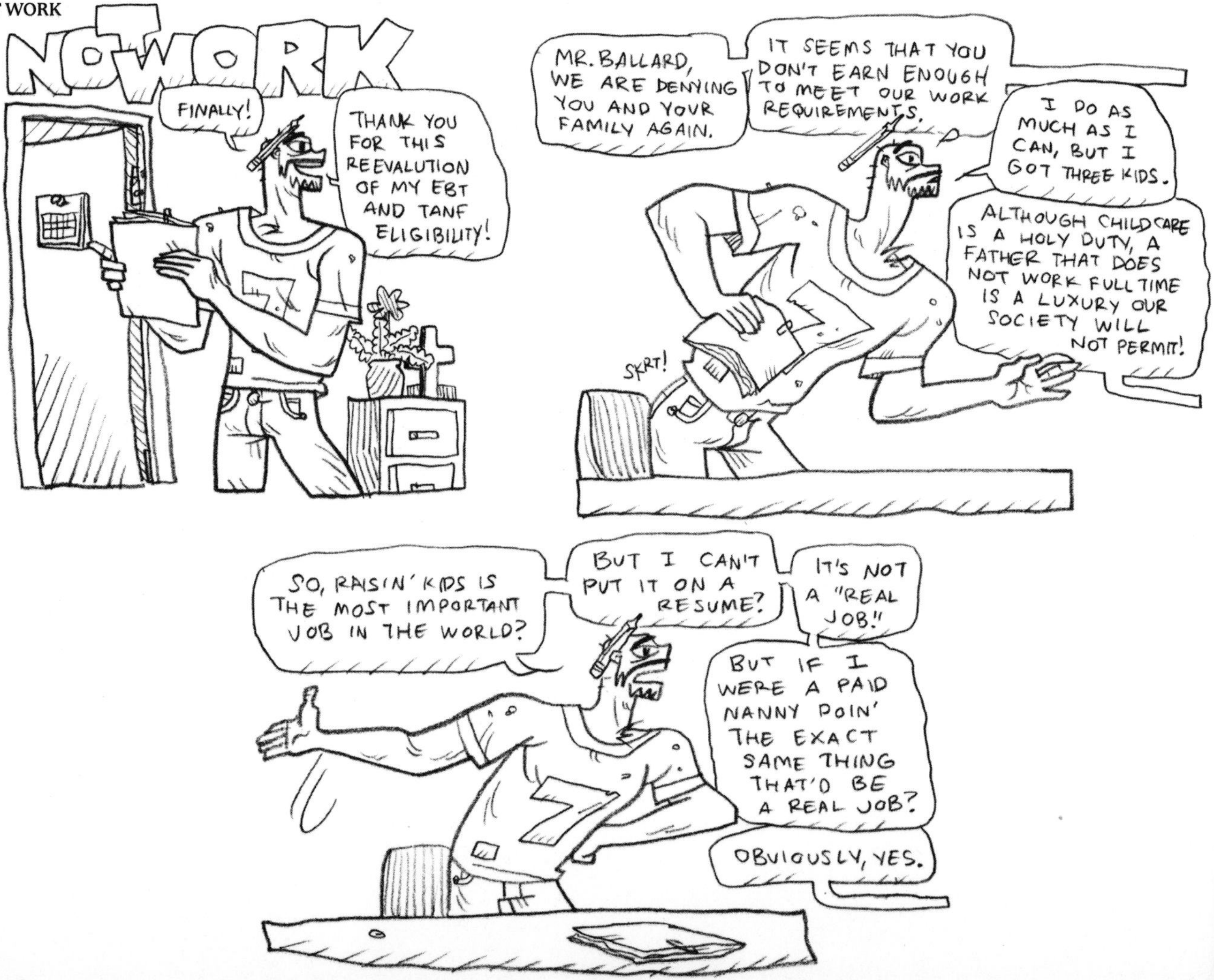
NOT WORK
FINALLY!
THANK YOU FOR THIS REEVALUTION OF MY EBT AND TANF ELIGIBILITY!
MR. BALLARD, WE ARE DENYING YOU AND YOUR FAMILY AGAIN.
IT SEEMS THAT YOU DON'T EARN ENOUGH TO MEET OUR WORK REQUIREMENTS.
I DO AS MUCH AS I CAN, BUT I GOT THREE KIDS.
ALTHOUGH CHILDCARE IS A HOLY DUTY, A FATHER THAT DOES NOT WORK FULLTIME IS A LUXURY OUR SOCIETY WILL NOT PERMIT!
SKRT!
SO, RAISIN' KIDS IS THE MOST IMPORTANT JOB IN THE WORLD?
BUT I CAN'T PUT IT ON A RESUME?
IT'S NOT A "REAL JOB!"
BUT IF I WERE A PAID NANNY DOIN' THE EXACT SAME THING THAT'D BE A REAL JOB?
OBVIOUSLY, YES.

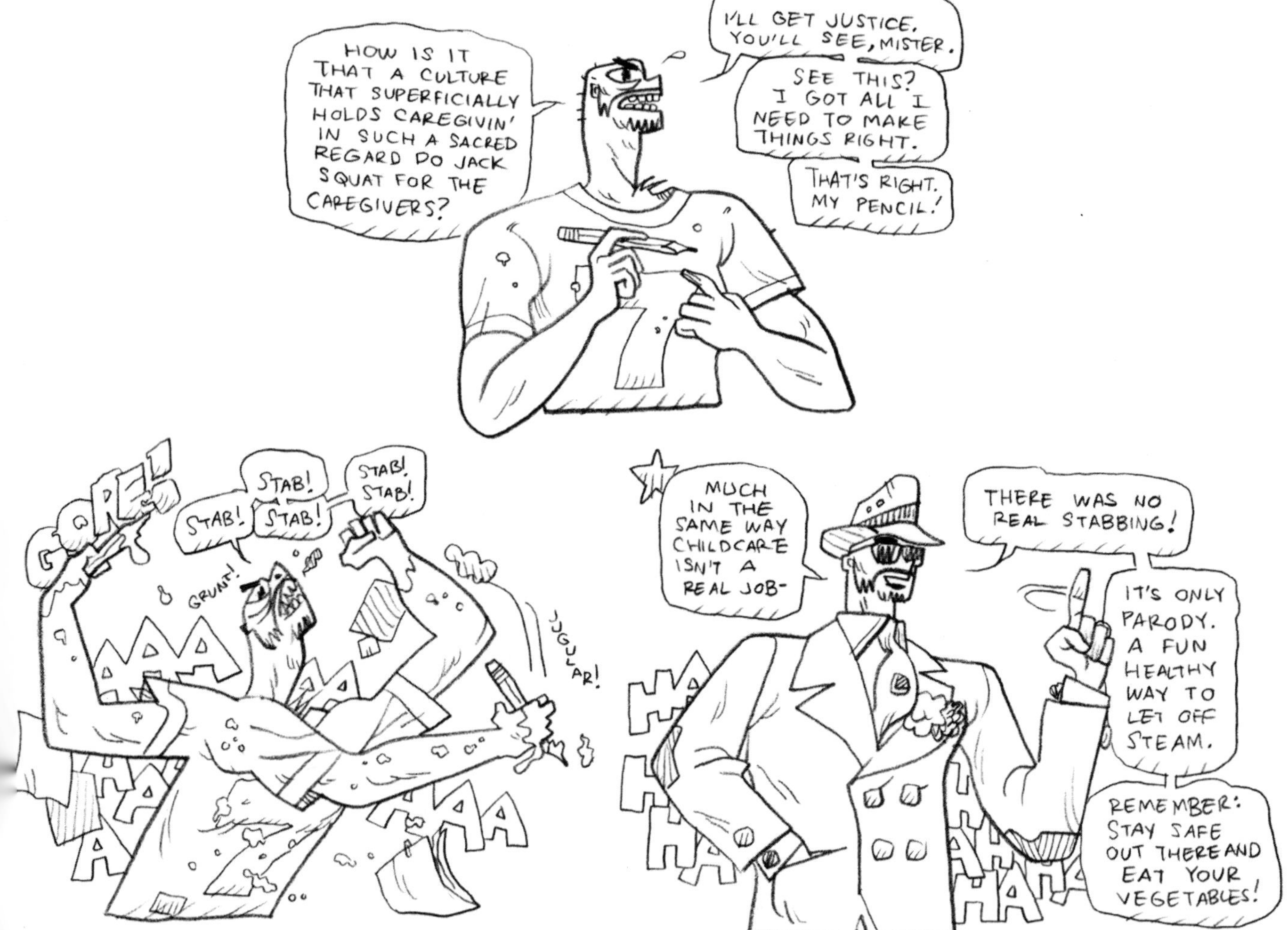
HOW IS IT THAT A CULTURE THAT SUPERFICIALLY HOLDS CAREGIVIN' IN SUCH A SACRED REGARD DO JACK SQUAT FOR THE CAREGIVERS?
I'LL GET JUSTICE. YOU'LL SEE, MISTER.
SEE THIS? I GOT ALL I NEED TO MAKE THINGS RIGHT.
THAT'S RIGHT. MY PENCIL!
GORE!
STAB!
STAB!
STAB!
STAB! STAB!
GRUNT!
JUGULAR!
MUCH IN THE SAME WAY CHILDCARE ISN'T A REAL JOB-
THERE WAS NO REAL STABBING!
IT'S ONLY PARODY. A FUN HEALTHY WAY TO LET OFF STEAM.
REMEMBER: STAY SAFE OUT THERE AND EAT YOUR VEGETABLES!

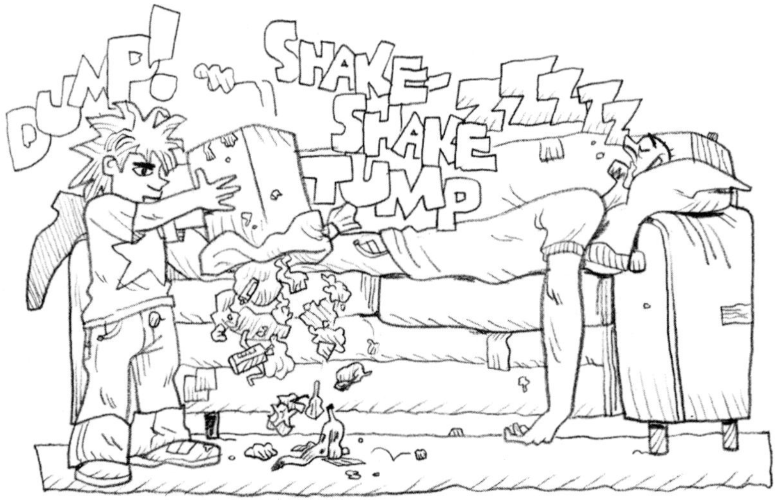
DUMP!
SHAKE-SHAKE
ZZZZZZ
TUMP

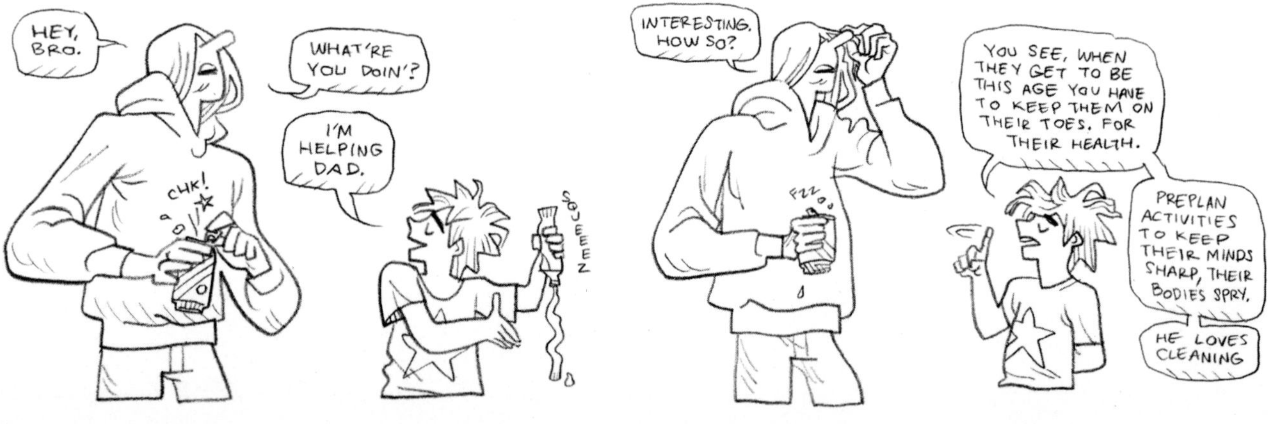
HEY, BRO.
WHAT'RE YOU DOIN'?
CHK!
I'M HELPING DAD.
SQUEEEZ
INTERESTING. HOW SO?
FZZ
YOU SEE, WHEN THEY GET TO BE THIS AGE YOU HAVE TO KEEP THEM ON THEIR TOES. FOR THEIR HEALTH.
PREPLAN ACTIVITIES TO KEEP THEIR MINDS SHARP, THEIR BODIES SPRY.
HE LOVES CLEANING

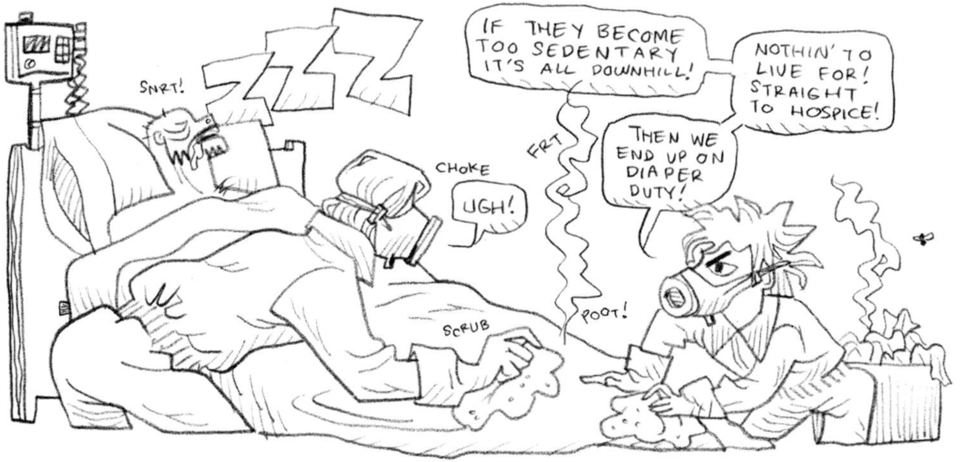
SNRT!
ZZZ
CHOKE
UGH!
SCRUB
IF THEY BECOME TOO SEDENTARY IT'S ALL DOWNHILL!
NOTHIN' TO LIVE FOR! STRAIGHT TO HOSPICE!
THEN WE END UP ON DIAPER DUTY!
FRT
POOT!

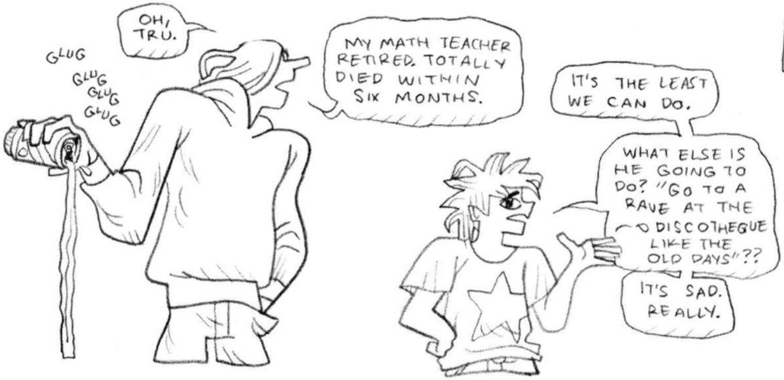
GLUG
GLUG
GLUG
GLUG
OH, TRU.
MY MATH TEACHER RETIRED. TOTALLY DIED WITHIN SIX MONTHS.
IT'S THE LEAST WE CAN DO.
WHAT ELSE IS HE GOING TO DO? "GO TO A RAVE AT THE DISCOTHEQUE LIKE THE OLD DAYS"??
IT'S SAD. REALLY.

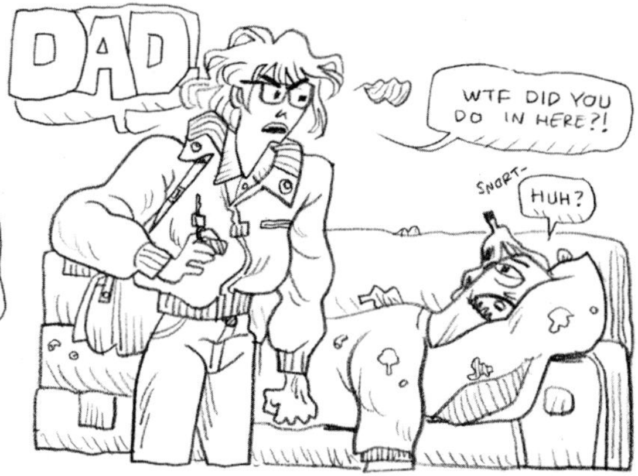
DAD
WTF DID YOU DO IN HERE?!
SNORT-
HUH?

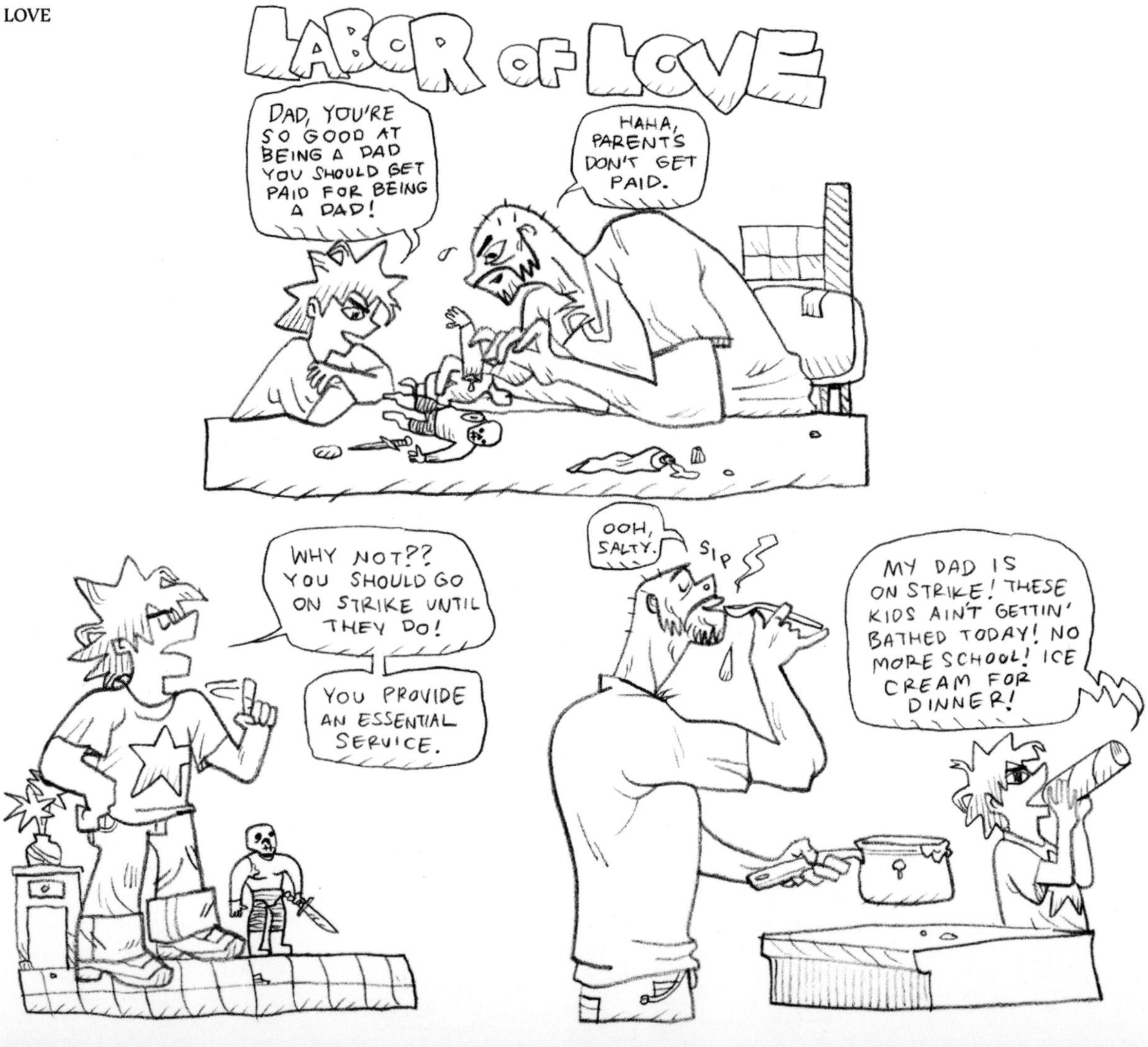
LABOR OF LOVE
DAD, YOU'RE SO GOOD AT BEING A DAD YOU SHOULD GET PAID FOR BEING A DAD!
HAHA, PARENTS DON'T GET PAID.
WHY NOT?? YOU SHOULD GO ON STRIKE UNTIL THEY DO!
YOU PROVIDE AN ESSENTIAL SERVICE.
OOH, SALTY.
SIP
MY DAD IS ON STRIKE! THESE KIDS AIN'T GETTIN' BATHED TODAY! NO MORE SCHOOL! ICE CREAM FOR DINNER!

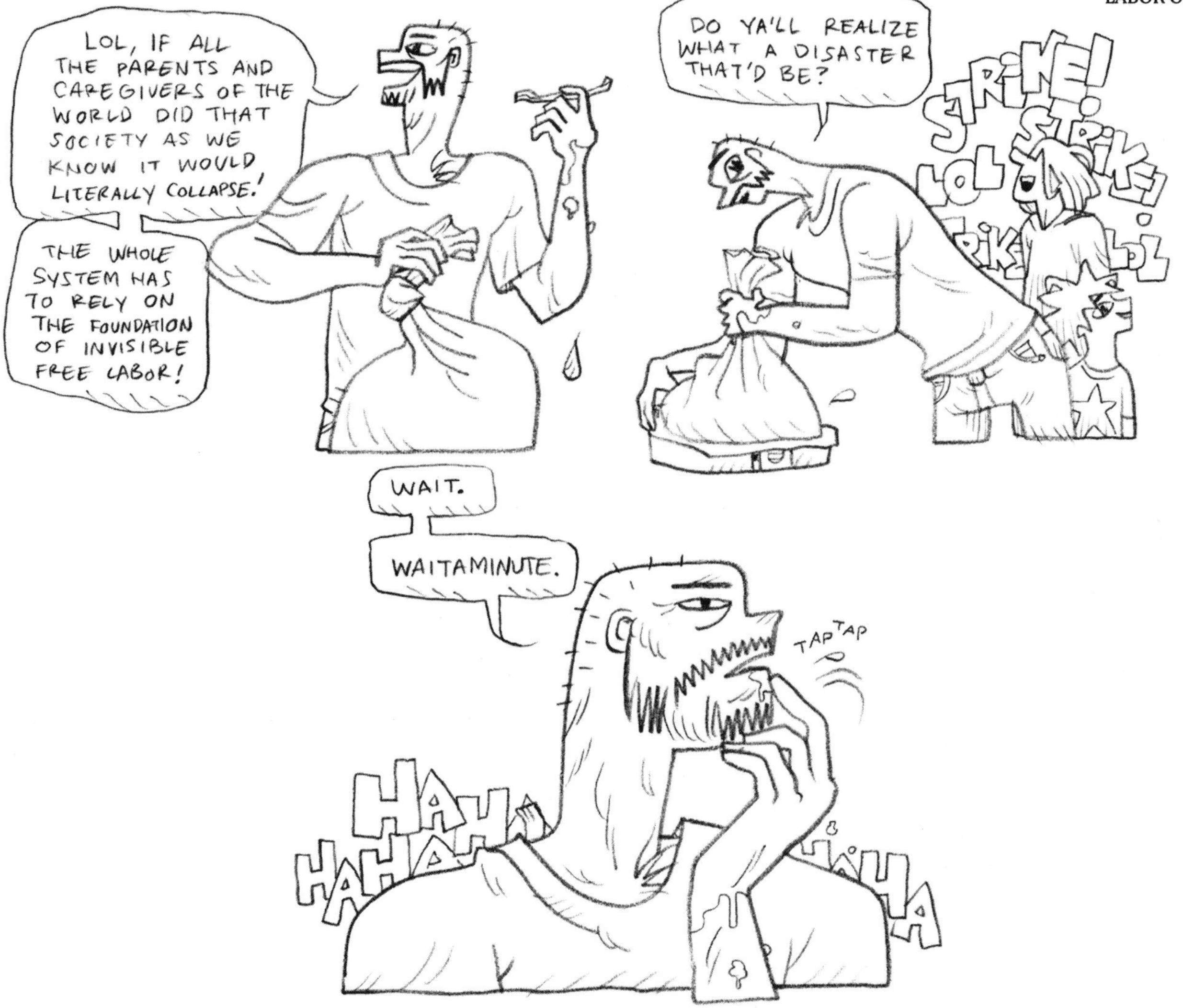
LOL, IF ALL THE PARENTS AND CAREGIVERS OF THE WORLD DID THAT SOCIETY AS WE KNOW IT WOULD LITERALLY COLLAPSE!
THE WHOLE SYSTEM HAS TO RELY ON THE FOUNDATION OF INVISIBLE FREE LABOR!
DO YA'LL REALIZE WHAT A DISASTER THAT'D BE?
STRIKE!
STRIKE!
LOL
LOL
WAIT.
WAITAMINUTE.
TAP TAP
HAHA
HAHA

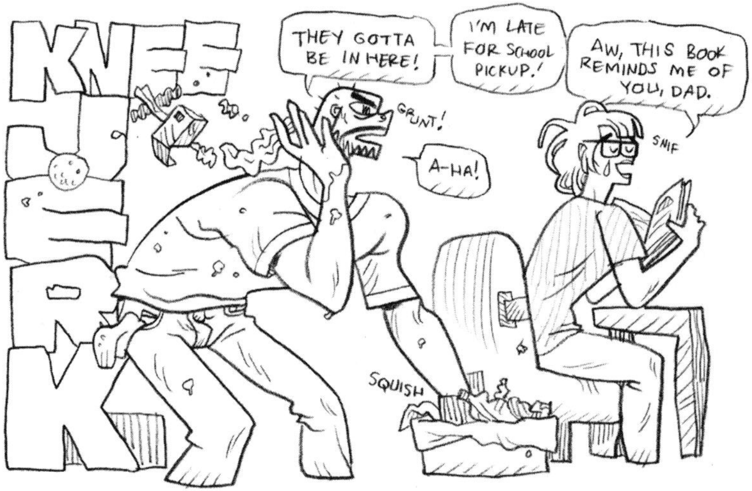
KNEEJERK
THEY GOTTA BE IN HERE!
I'M LATE FOR SCHOOL PICKUP!
GRUNT!
A-HA!
AW, THIS BOOK REMINDS ME OF YOU, DAD.
SNIF
SQUISH

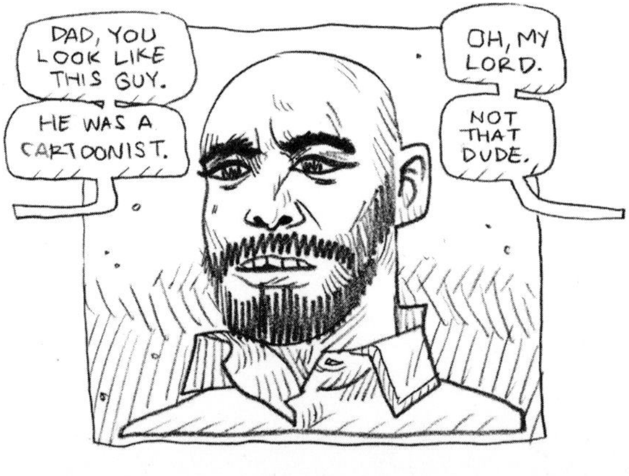
DAD, YOU LOOK LIKE THIS GUY.
HE WAS A CARTOONIST.
OH, MY LORD.
NOT THAT DUDE.

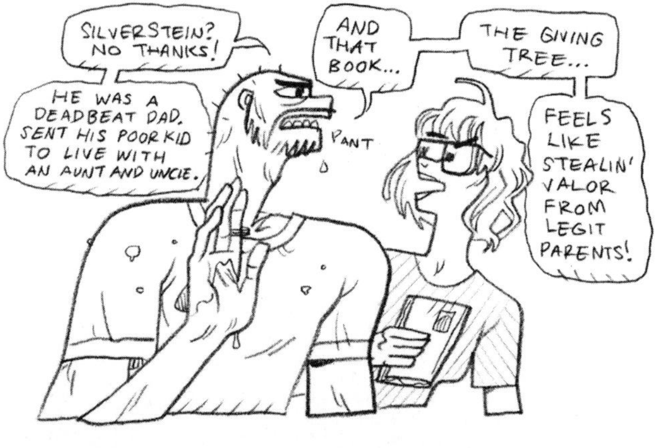
SILVERSTEIN? NO THANKS!
HE WAS A DEADBEAT DAD. SENT HIS POOR KID TO LIVE WITH AN AUNT AND UNCLE.
PANT
AND THAT BOOK...
THE GIVING TREE...
FEELS LIKE STEALIN' VALOR FROM LEGIT PARENTS!

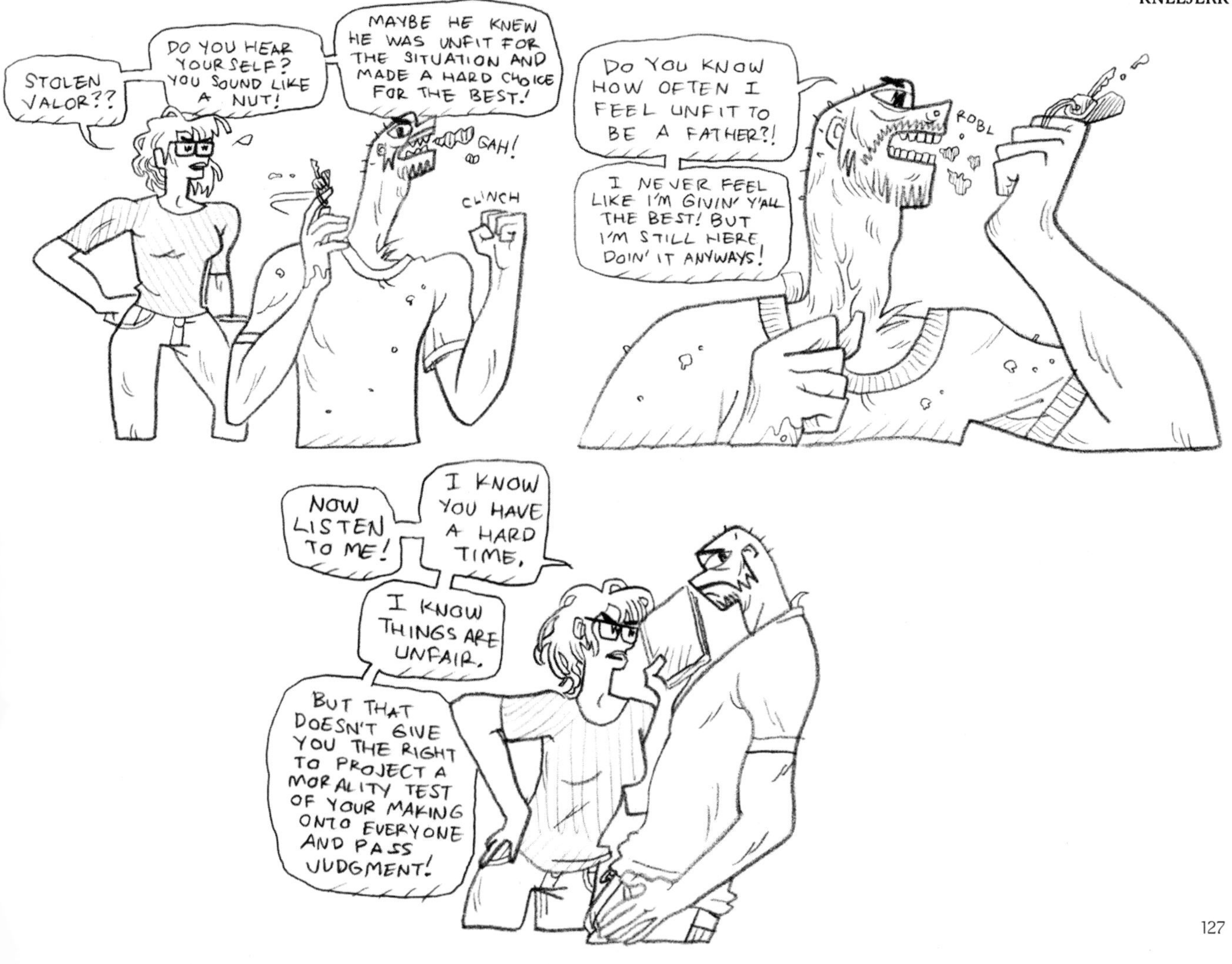
STOLEN VALOR??
DO YOU HEAR YOURSELF? YOU SOUND LIKE A NUT!
MAYBE HE KNEW HE WAS UNFIT FOR THE SITUATION AND MADE A HARD CHOICE FOR THE BEST!
GAH!
CLINCH
DO YOU KNOW HOW OFTEN I FEEL UNFIT TO BE A FATHER?!
I NEVER FEEL LIKE I'M GIVIN' Y'ALL THE BEST! BUT I'M STILL HERE DOIN' IT ANYWAYS!
ROBL
NOW LISTEN TO ME!
I KNOW YOU HAVE A HARD TIME.
I KNOW THINGS ARE UNFAIR.
BUT THAT DOESN'T GIVE YOU THE RIGHT TO PROJECT A MORALITY TEST OF YOUR MAKING ONTO EVERYONE AND PASS JUDGMENT!

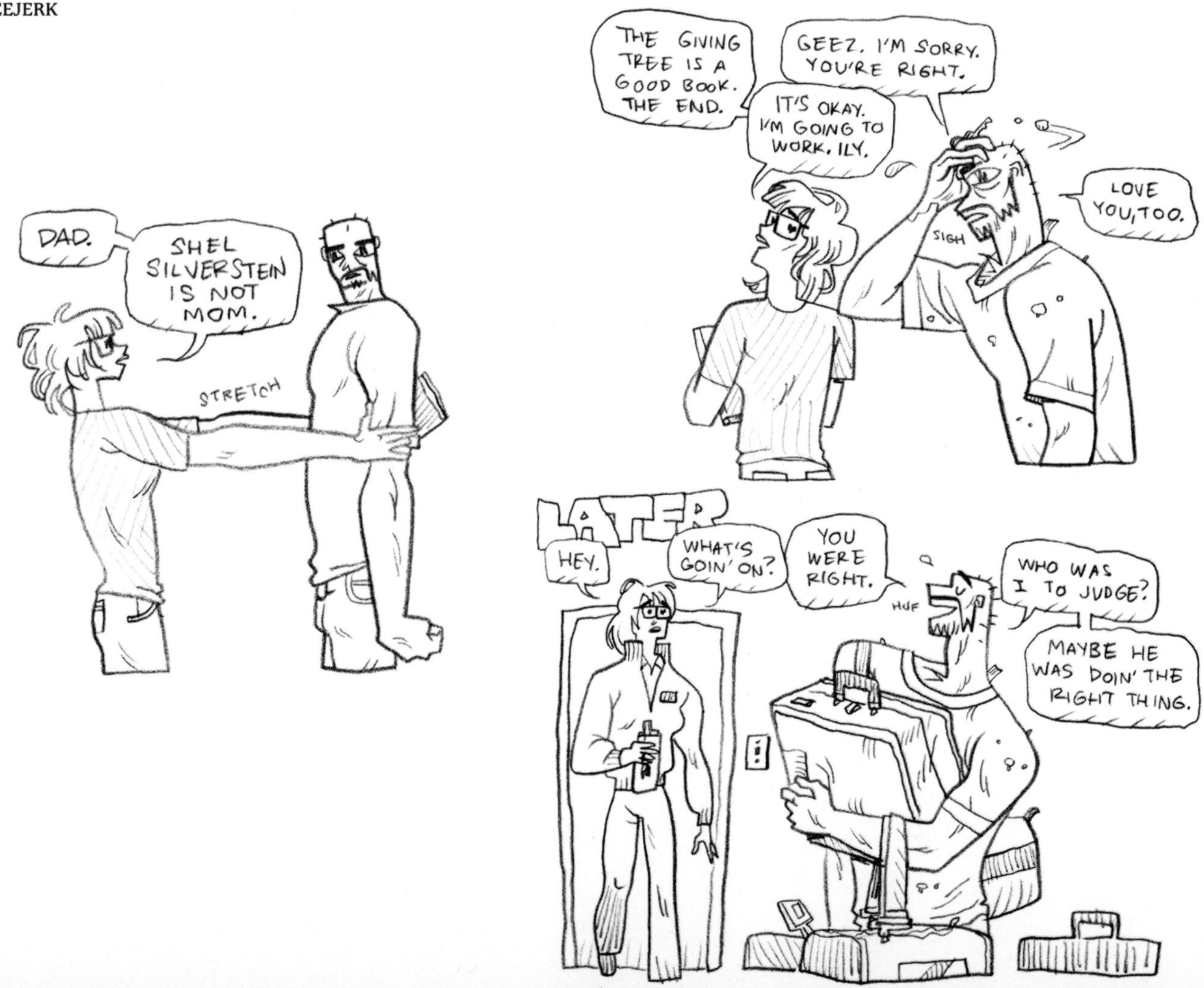
DAD.
SHEL SILVERSTEIN IS NOT MOM.
STRETCH
THE GIVING TREE IS A GOOD BOOK. THE END.
GEEZ, I'M SORRY. YOU'RE RIGHT.
IT'S OKAY. I'M GOING TO WORK. ILY.
SIGH
LOVE YOU, TOO.
LATER
HEY.
WHAT'S GOIN' ON?
YOU WERE RIGHT.
HUF
WHO WAS I TO JUDGE?
MAYBE HE WAS DOIN' THE RIGHT THING.

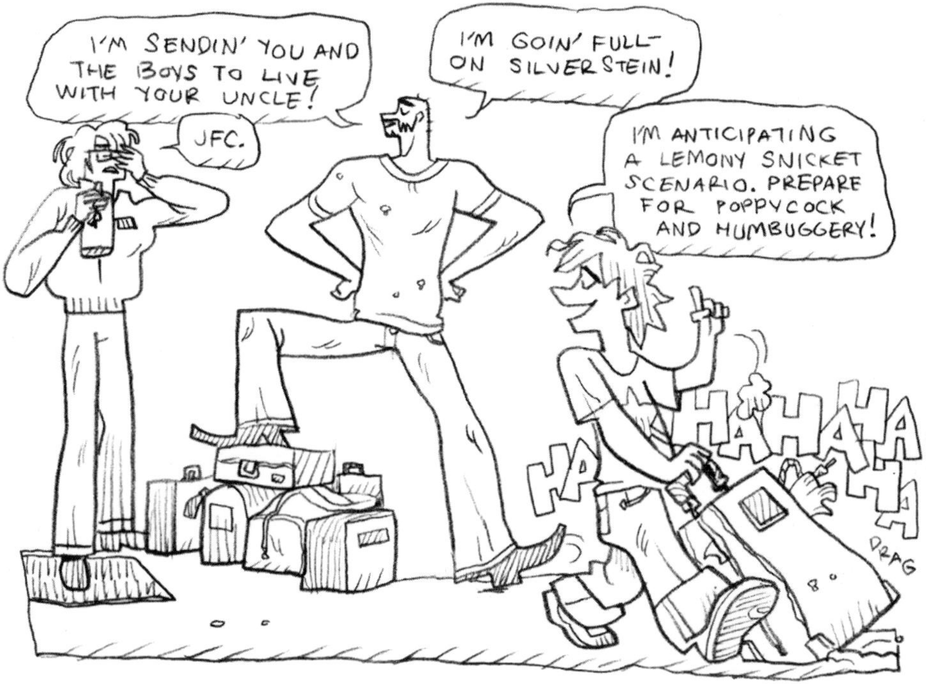
I'M SENDIN' YOU AND THE BOYS TO LIVE WITH YOUR UNCLE!
JFC.
I'M GOIN' FULL-ON SILVERSTEIN!
I'M ANTICIPATING A LEMONY SNICKET SCENARIO. PREPARE FOR POPPYCOCK AND HUMBUGGERY!
HAHAHAHAHA
HAHAHA
DRAG

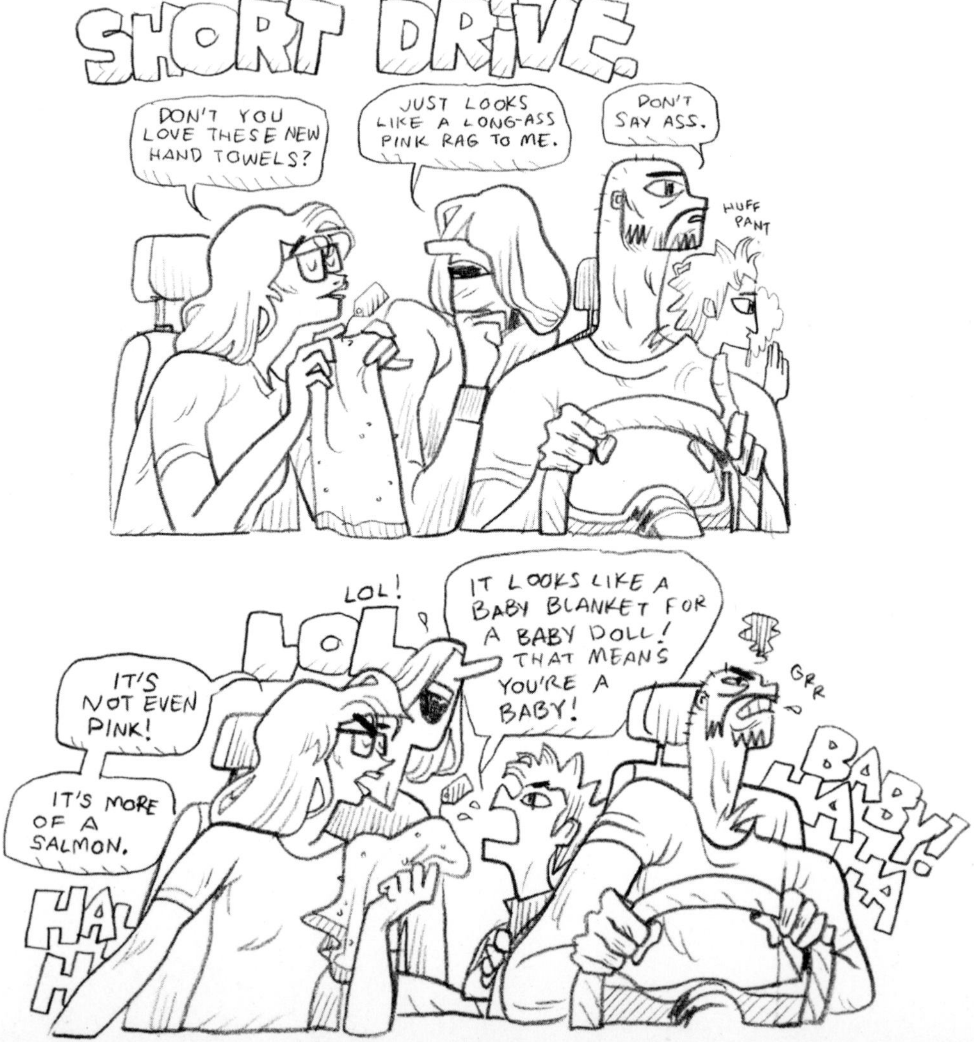
SHORT DRIVE.
DON'T YOU LOVE THESE NEW HAND TOWELS?
JUST LOOKS LIKE A LONG-ASS PINK RAG TO ME.
DON'T SAY ASS.
HUFF PANT
IT'S NOT EVEN PINK!
IT'S MORE OF A SALMON.
LOL!
LOL
IT LOOKS LIKE A BABY BLANKET FOR A BABY DOLL! THAT MEANS YOU'RE A BABY!
GRR
BABY!

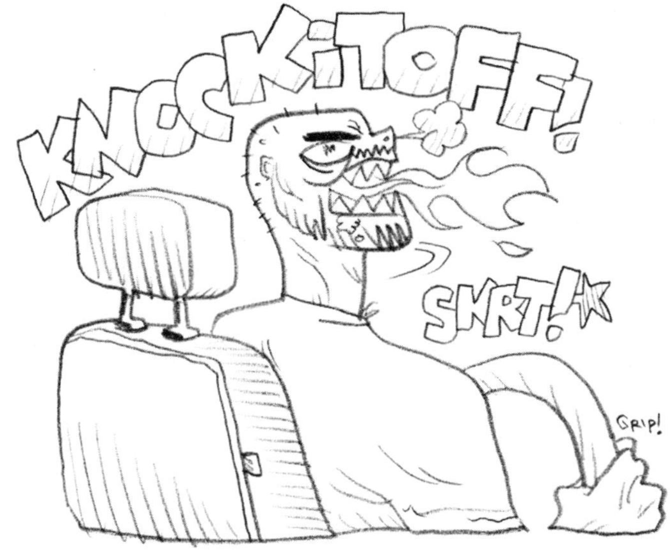
KNOCKITOFF!
SKRT!
GRIP!

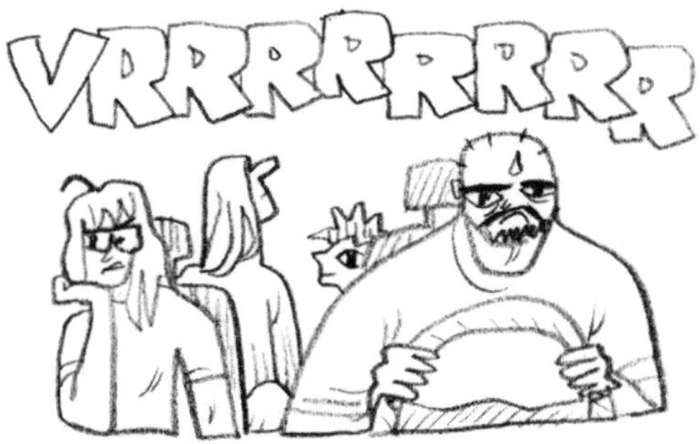
VRRRRRRRRR

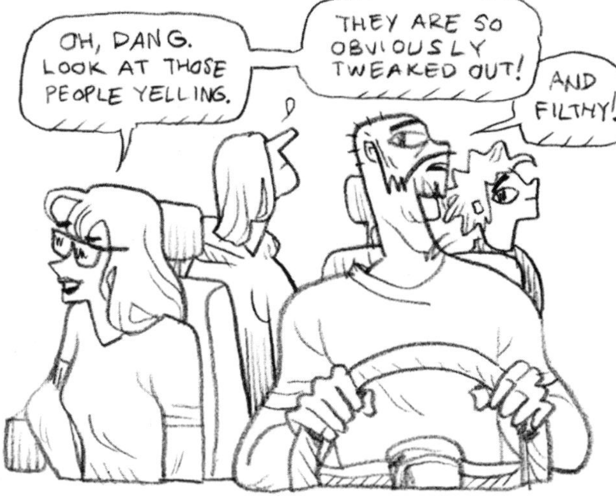
OH, DANG. LOOK AT THOSE PEOPLE YELLING.
THEY ARE SO OBVIOUSLY TWEAKED OUT!
AND FILTHY!

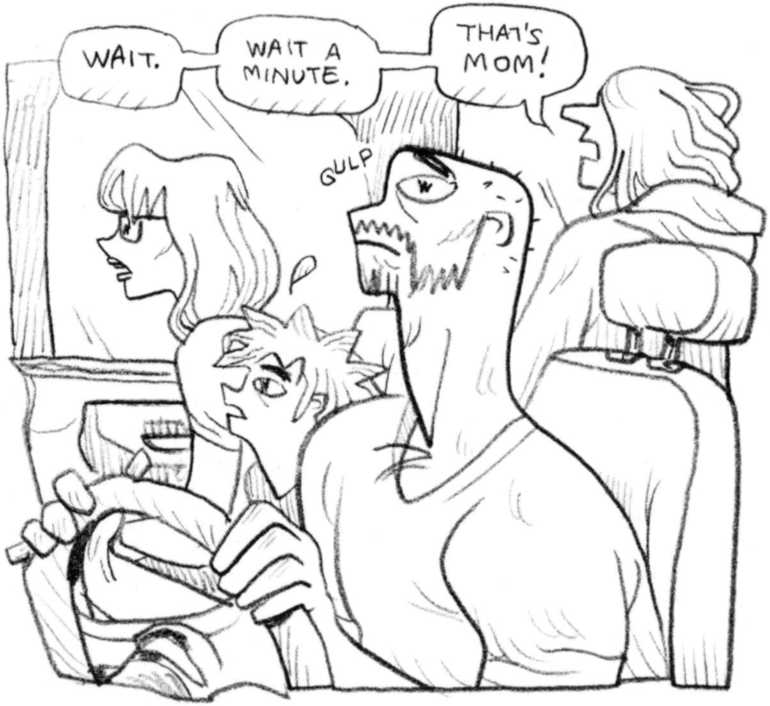
WAIT.
WAIT A MINUTE.
THAT'S MOM!
GULP

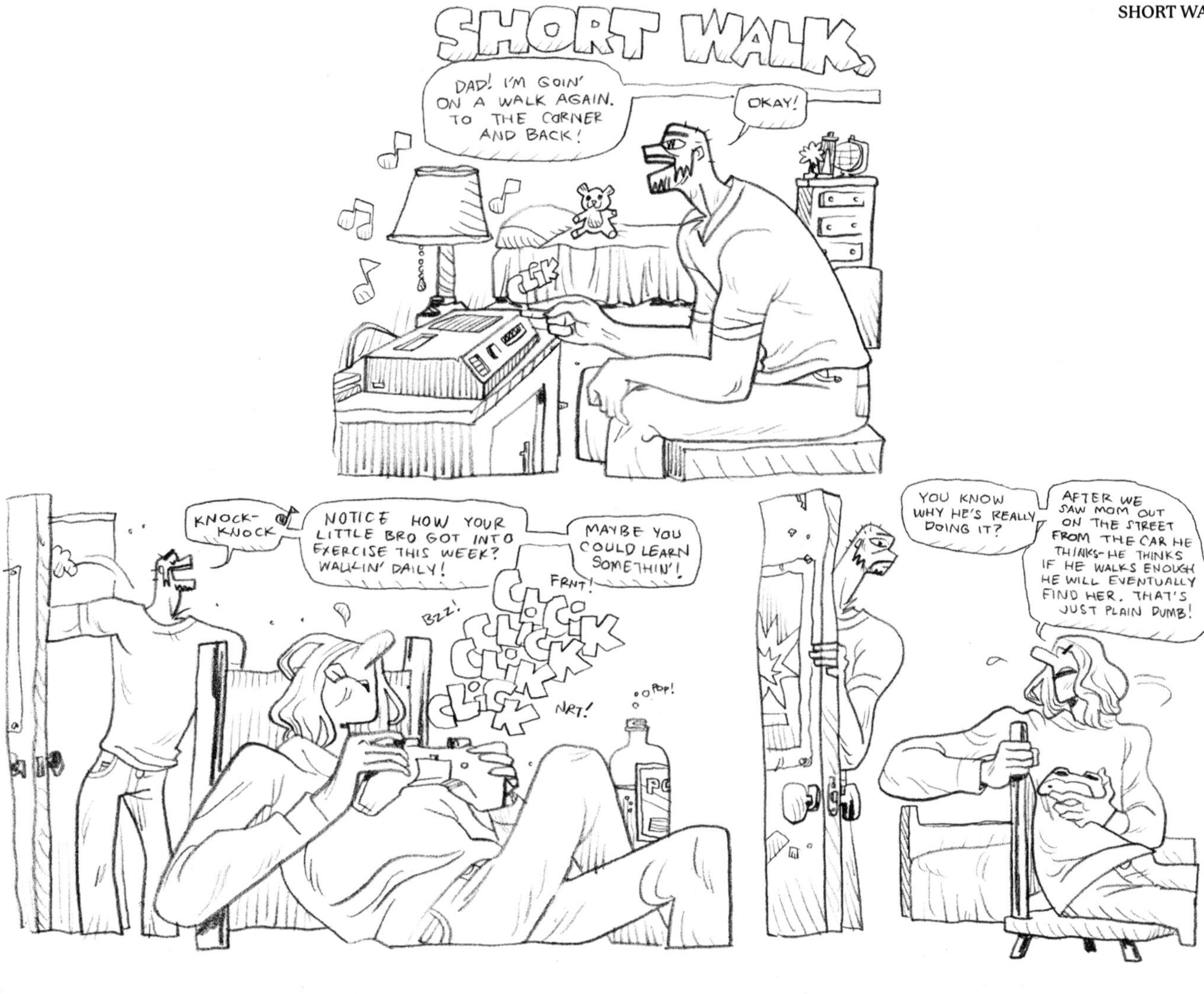
SHORT WALK,
DAD! I'M GOIN' ON A WALK AGAIN. TO THE CORNER AND BACK!
OKAY!
CLICK
KNOCK-KNOCK
NOTICE HOW YOUR LITTLE BRO GOT INTO EXERCISE THIS WEEK? WALKIN' DAILY!
MAYBE YOU COULD LEARN SOMETHIN'!
FRNT!
BZZ!
NRT!
POP!
YOU KNOW WHY HE'S REALLY DOING IT?
AFTER WE SAW MOM OUT ON THE STREET FROM THE CAR HE THINKS- HE THINKS IF HE WALKS ENOUGH HE WILL EVENTUALLY FIND HER. THAT'S JUST PLAIN DUMB!

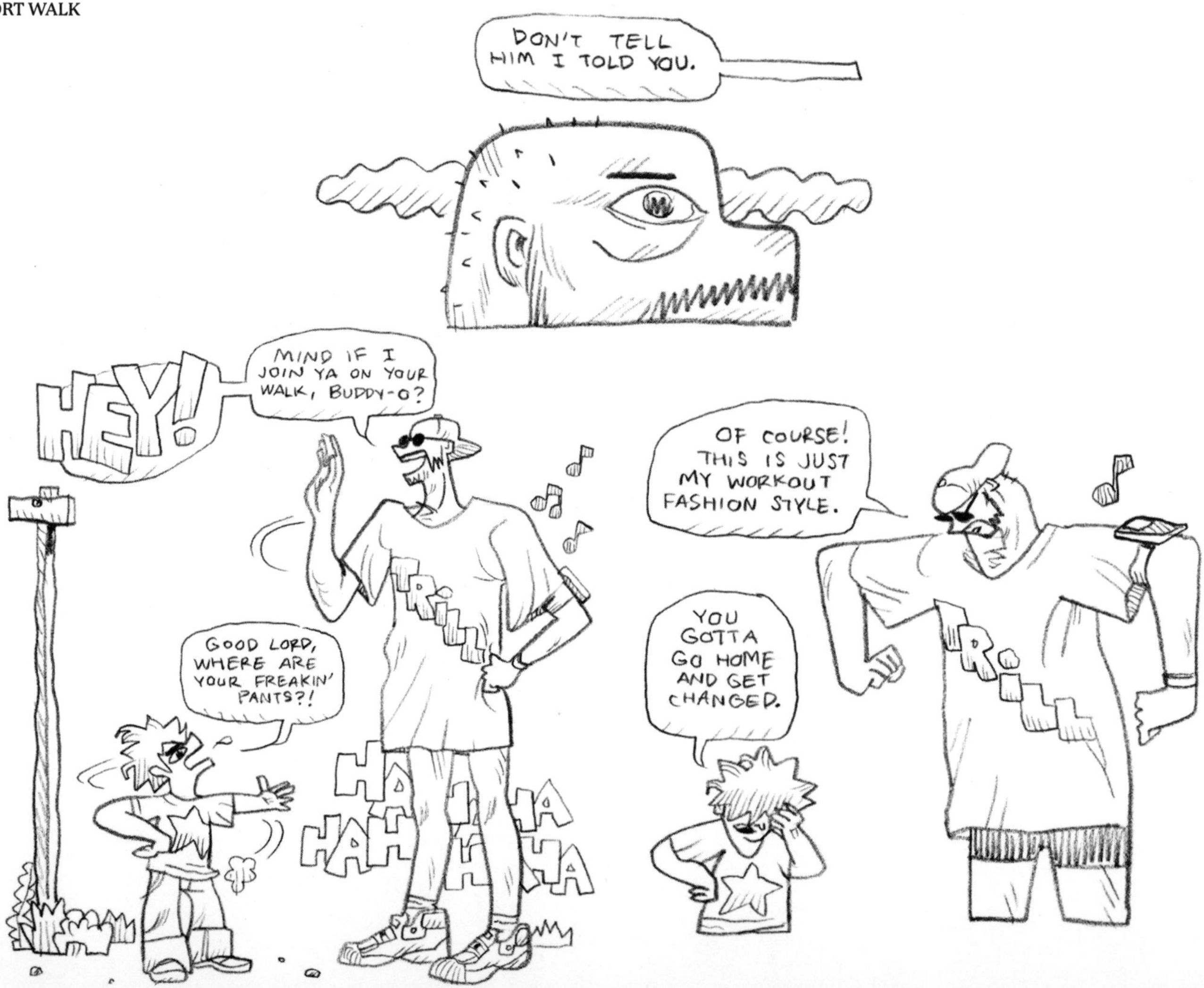
DON'T TELL HIM I TOLD YOU.
HEY!
MIND IF I JOIN YA ON YOUR WALK, BUDDY-O?
GOOD LORD, WHERE ARE YOUR FREAKIN' PANTS?!
HA HA HA HA HA HA HA HA
OF COURSE! THIS IS JUST MY WORKOUT FASHION STYLE.
YOU GOTTA GO HOME AND GET CHANGED.

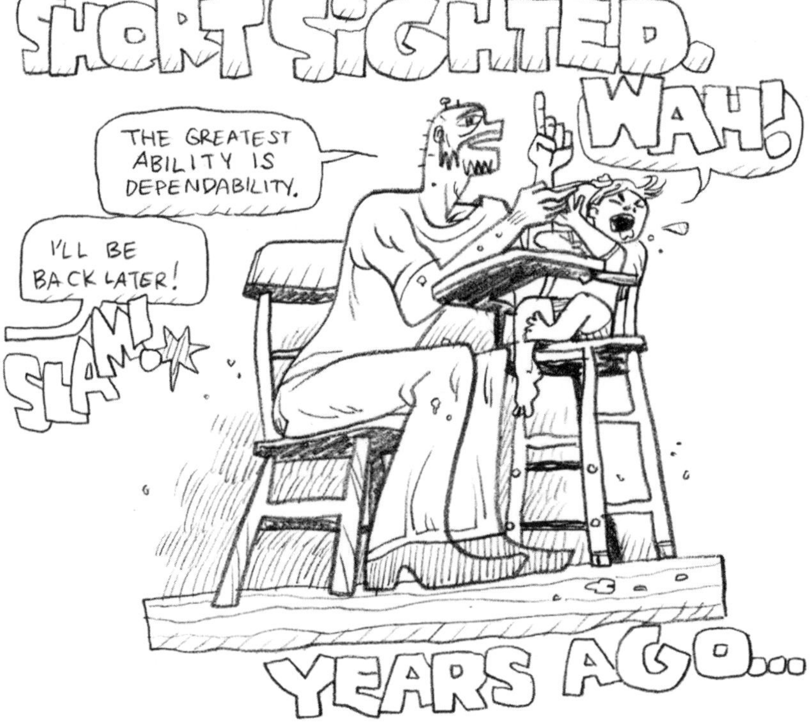
SHORTSIGHTED.
THE GREATEST ABILITY IS DEPENDABILITY.
WAH!
I'LL BE BACK LATER!
SLAM!
YEARS AGO...

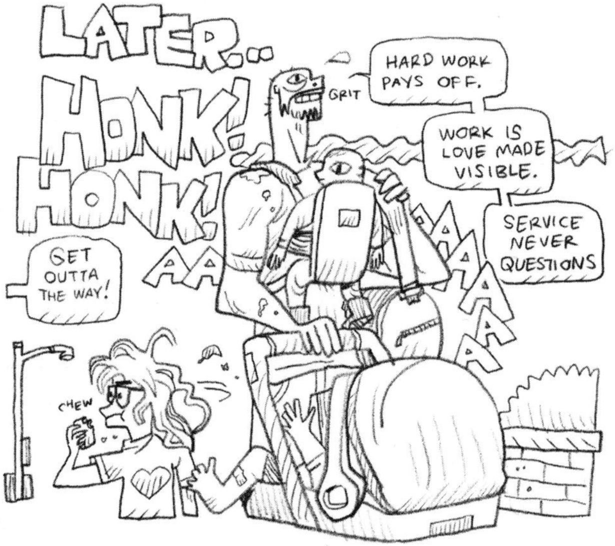
LATER...
HONK! HONK!
AAAAAAAAA
GRIT
HARD WORK PAYS OFF.
WORK IS LOVE MADE VISIBLE.
SERVICE NEVER QUESTIONS
GET OUTTA THE WAY!
CHEW

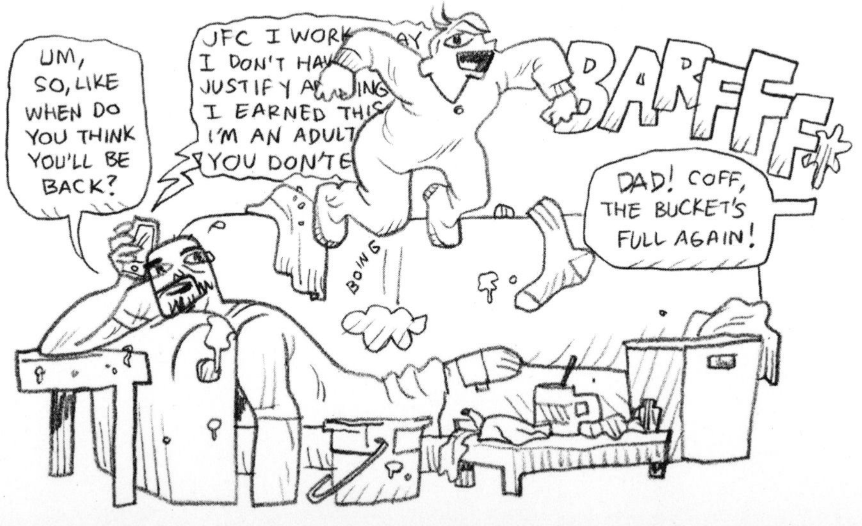
UM, SO, LIKE WHEN DO YOU THINK YOU'LL BE BACK?
JFC I WORK AY I DON'T HAV JUSTIFY A ING I EARNED THIS I'M AN ADULT YOU DON'TE
BARFFF
DAD! COFF, THE BUCKET'S FULL AGAIN!
BOING

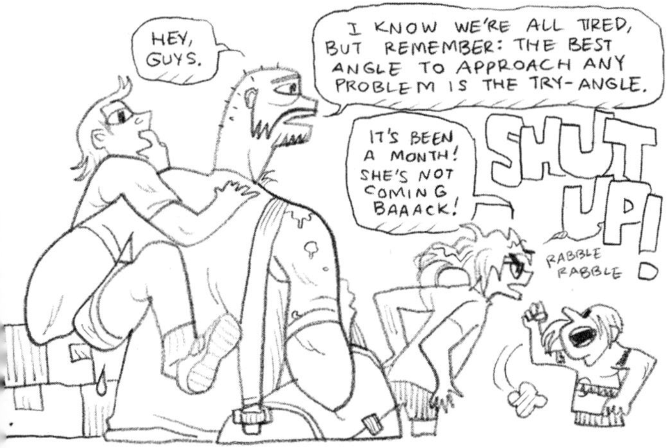
HEY, GUYS.
I KNOW WE'RE ALL TIRED, BUT REMEMBER: THE BEST ANGLE TO APPROACH ANY PROBLEM IS THE TRY-ANGLE.
IT'S BEEN A MONTH! SHE'S NOT COMING BAAACK!
SHUT UP!
RABBLE RABBLE

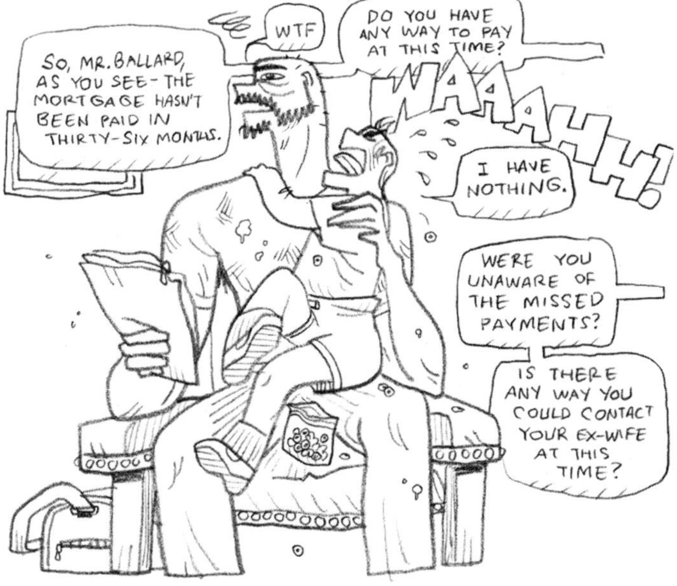
SO, MR. BALLARD, AS YOU SEE- THE MORTGAGE HASN'T BEEN PAID IN THIRTY-SIX MONTHS.
WTF
DO YOU HAVE ANY WAY TO PAY AT THIS TIME?
WAAAHH!
I HAVE NOTHING.
WERE YOU UNAWARE OF THE MISSED PAYMENTS?
IS THERE ANY WAY YOU COULD CONTACT YOUR EX-WIFE AT THIS TIME?

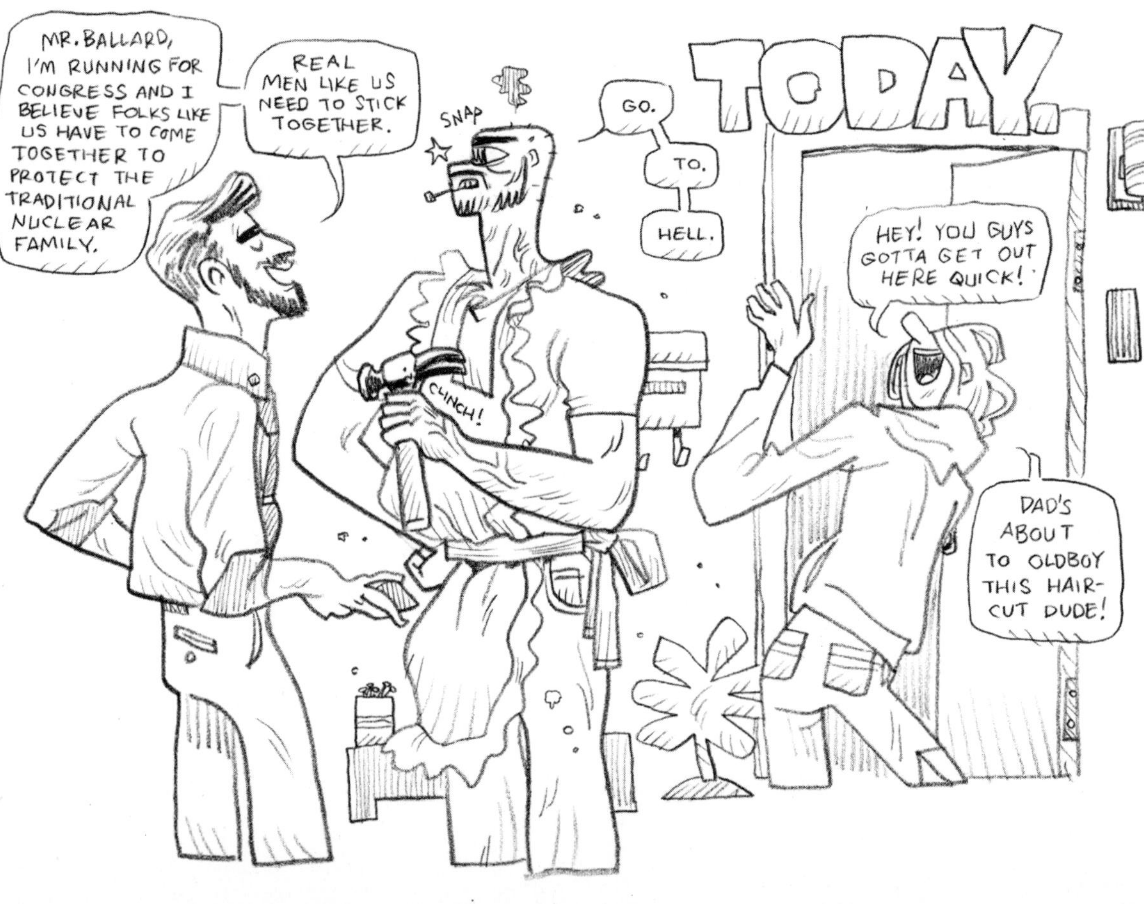
MR. BALLARD, I'M RUNNING FOR CONGRESS AND I BELIEVE FOLKS LIKE US HAVE TO COME TOGETHER TO PROTECT THE TRADITIONAL NUCLEAR FAMILY.
REAL MEN LIKE US NEED TO STICK TOGETHER.
SNAP
CLINCH!
GO.
TO.
HELL.
TODAY.
HEY! YOU GUYS GOTTA GET OUT HERE QUICK!
DAD'S ABOUT TO OLDBOY THIS HAIR-CUT DUDE!

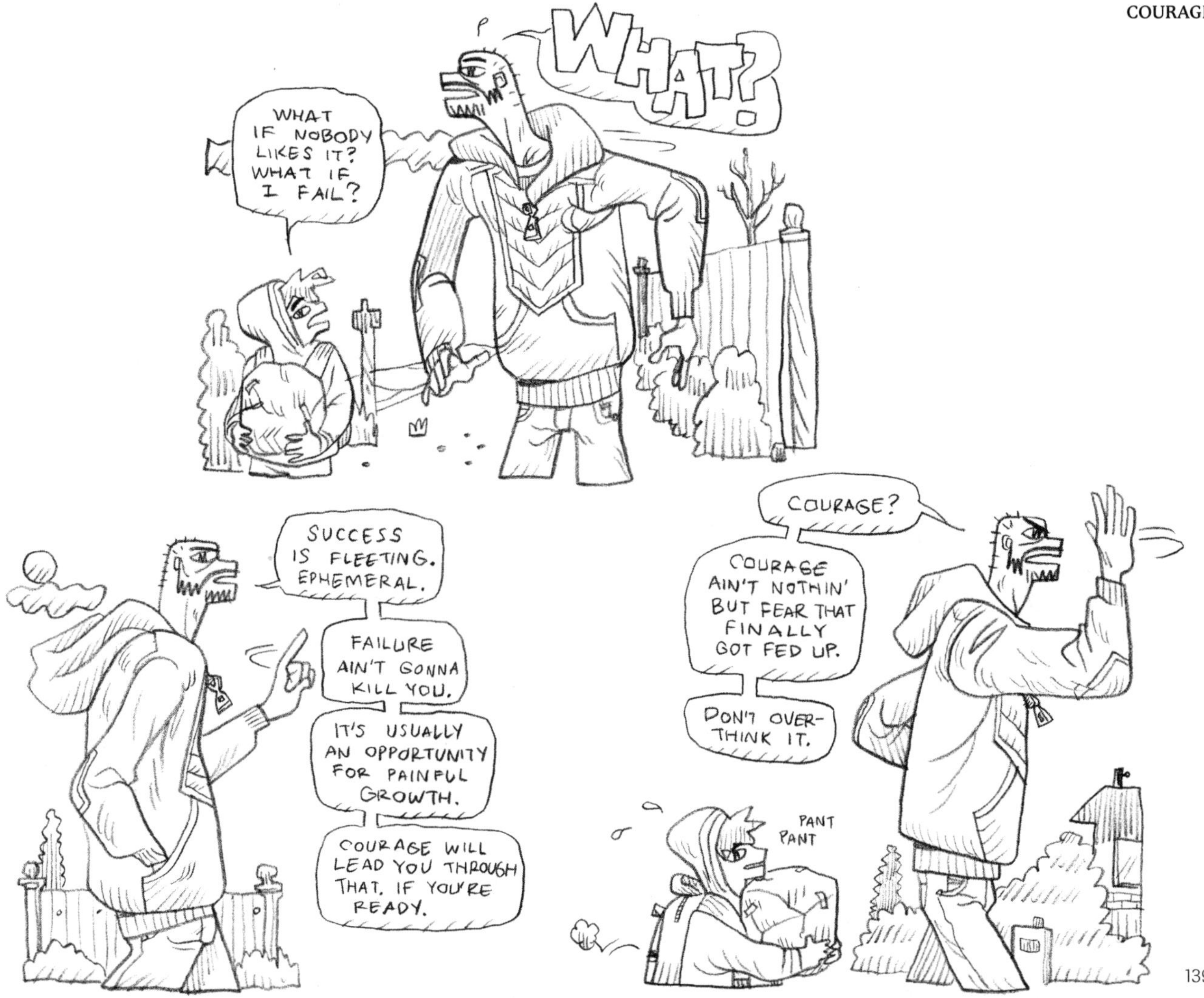
WHAT
WHAT IF NOBODY LIKES IT? WHAT IF I FAIL?
SUCCESS IS FLEETING. EPHEMERAL.
FAILURE AIN'T GONNA KILL YOU.
IT'S USUALLY AN OPPORTUNITY FOR PAINFUL GROWTH.
COURAGE WILL LEAD YOU THROUGH THAT, IF YOU'RE READY.
COURAGE?
COURAGE AIN'T NOTHIN' BUT FEAR THAT FINALLY GOT FED UP.
DON'T OVER-THINK IT.
PANT PANT

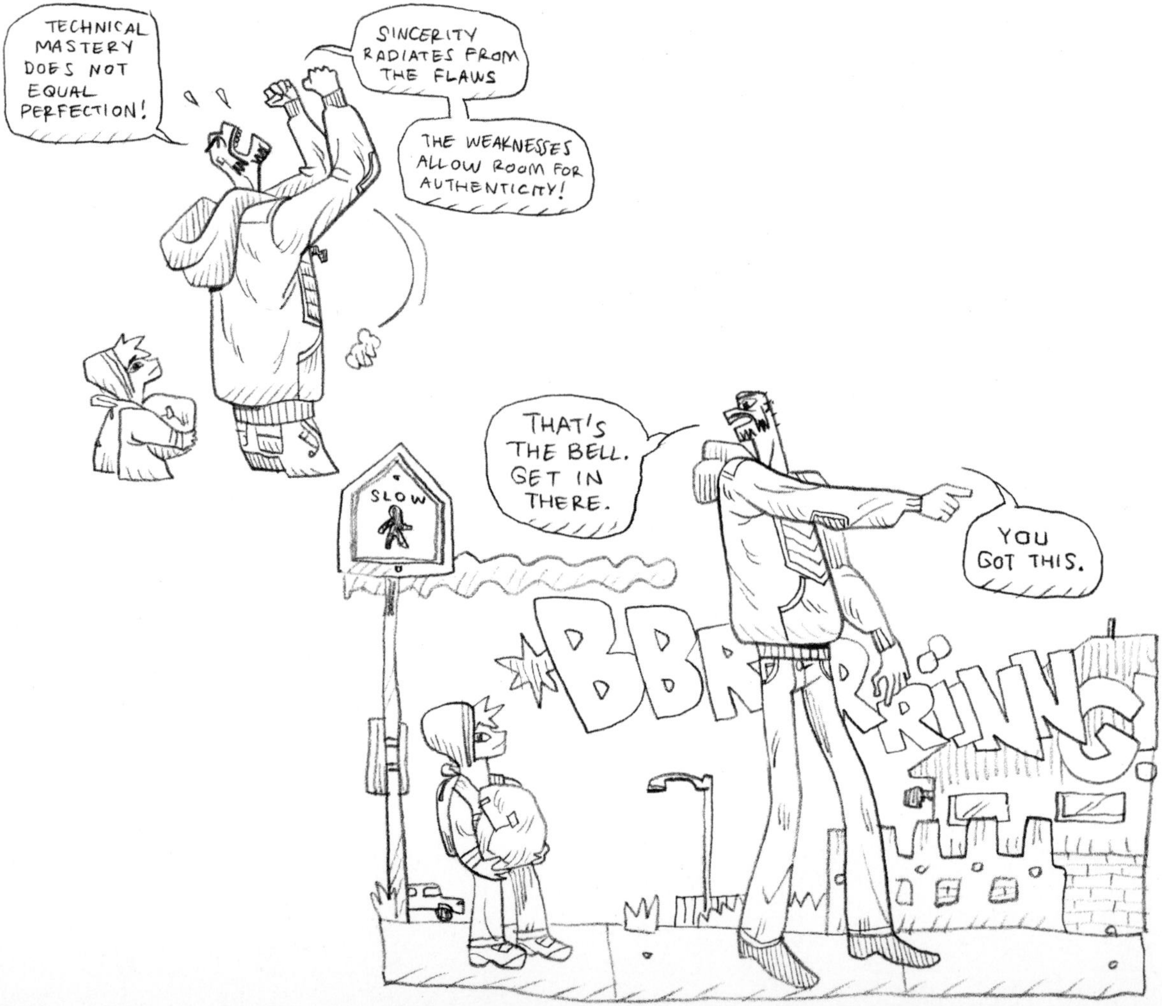
TECHNICAL MASTERY DOES NOT EQUAL PERFECTION!
SINCERITY RADIATES FROM THE FLAWS
THE WEAKNESSES ALLOW ROOM FOR AUTHENTICITY!
SLOW
THAT'S THE BELL. GET IN THERE.
YOU GOT THIS.
BBRRRIING!

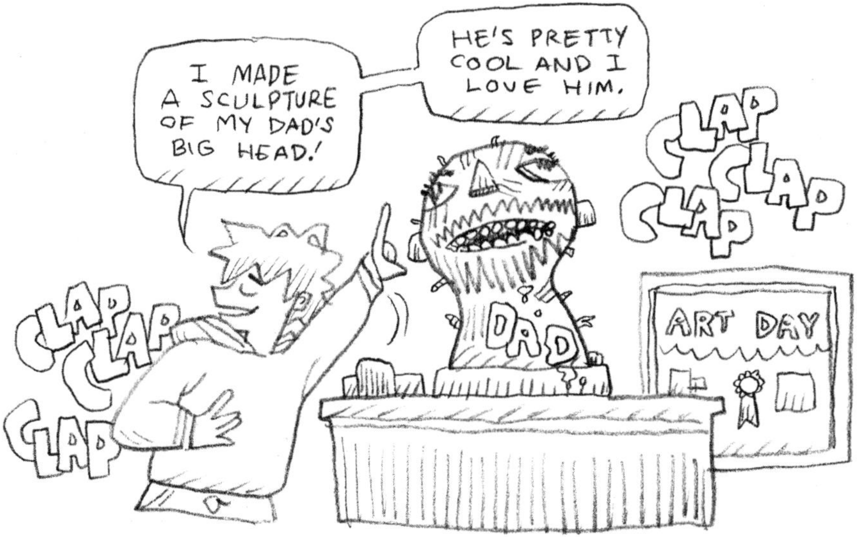
I MADE A SCULPTURE OF MY DAD'S BIG HEAD!
HE'S PRETTY COOL AND I LOVE HIM.
CLAP CLAP CLAP
CLAP CLAP CLAP
DAD
ART DAY

Derek M. Ballard is, first and foremost, a single parent of three kids in Gainesville, Florida.

Sometimes he's lucky and he gets to work on cartoons for Cartoon Network, Netflix, or HBO. Every now and then he's able to do some comics for The Nib. After he takes the kids to school and cooks dinner, he teaches some comics classes for The Sequential Artists Workshop.

But he's mainly just a plain old dad.